The Kaiser's U-boats in American Waters

by Gary Gentile

Bellerophon Bookworks

Copyright 2010 by Gary Gentile

All rights reserved. Except for the use of brief quotations embodied in critical articles and reviews, this book may not be reproduced in part or in whole, in any manner (including mechanical, electronic, photographic, and photocopy means), transmitted in any form, or recorded by any data storage and/or retrieval device, without express written permission from the author. Address all queries to:

Bellerophon Bookworks
P.O. Box 57137
Philadelphia, PA 19111

Additional copies of this book may be purchased from the same address by sending a check or money order in the amount of $25 U.S. for each copy (plus $4 postage per order, not per book, in the U.S. Inquire for shipping cost to foreign countries). Alternatively, copies may be purchased from the author's website, and paid by credit card:

http://www.ggentile.com

Picture Credits

Front cover photographs: the upper photo shows a lifeboat from the *Dwinsk* (courtesy of the National Archives); the middle photo shows the *Dorothy B. Barrett* after being shelled and set afire (from the author's collection); the bottom photo shows a World War One U-boat (courtesy of the National Archives).

International Standard Book Numbers (ISBN)
1-883056-40-3
978-1-883056-40-7

First Edition

Printed in the U.S.A.

CONTENTS

Undersea Raiders of the Great War	4
1916: First Merchant Cruise of the *Deutschland*	26
War Cruise of the *U-53*	41
Second Merchant Cruise of the *Deutschland*	56
1917 Liberty Bond Cruise of the *UC-5*	64
1918 War Cruise of the *U-151*	73
War Cruise of the *U-156*	130
War Cruise of the *U-140*	169
War Cruise of the *U-117*	193
War Cruise of the *U-155* (ex-*Deutschland*)	238
War Cruise of the *U-152*	262
Aborted War Cruise of the *U-139*	285
1919 Victory Bond Cruise of ex-German U-boats:	302
U-111, U-117, U-140	
UB-88, UB-148	
UC-97	
1921 Target Cruise	329
1992 Underwater Cruise	343
U-140, UB-148, U-117	
Appendices	351
1 - Attack Chronology	353
2 - U-boat Attacks (by Submarine)	357
plus Vessel and Victim Statistics	
3 - German/American Comparative Ranks	368
List of Illustrations	370
Vessel Index	374
Books by the author	380

UNDERSEA RAIDERS
OF THE
<u>GREAT WAR</u>

Not much has been written about the U-boat war off American shores during the First World War. It appears to be a subject that is forgotten by all but a few diehard historians and amateur history buffs. Most people do not even know that the German attacks of the Second World War were preceded by a similar rash of attacks in the previous World War, or that nearly one hundred vessels were sunk off the eastern seaboard in 1918.

It has often been said that those who forget history are bound to repeat it. When Germany made its second bid for world domination, its military leaders did not forget, but most Americans did. That was why the country was caught off guard in 1942, and was so unprepared for the U-boat attacks that commenced barely five weeks after the United States again declared war on Germany.

In 1918, the U.S. Navy knew that U-boat attacks were imminent. Yet the Navy was powerless to do much to prevent the eventual onslaught. This was not because the Navy had its collective head in the sand, but because the American government refused to dedicate funds to arm the Navy with the warships and personnel that were needed to defend coastal shipping. Forewarned does not necessarily mean forearmed. Ironically, this refusal to accept the reality of the situation was repeated a generation later.

In neither war was the U.S. Navy to blame. The blame must be placed on the U.S. Congressional leaders who held the Navy's purse strings, and on the people who elected their representatives in ignorance of the facts that the Navy tried to promote.

Most of the credit for defense against U-boats in

Undersea Raiders of the Great War 5

World War One must go to Great Britain. England had been fighting the German war machine since 1914. The British Admiralty established a U-boat tracking section that correlated data obtained from spies in Germany and France, from merchant marine skippers, from Royal Navy warship captains, and from survivors of U-boat attacks.

Many U-boats were tracked from the time they left the dock (courtesy of local spies). Their movements were tracked during their cruises (as sightings and attack positions were plotted).

These early U-boats were more like diving boats than true submarines. They acted primarily as surface raiders that could hide and escape submerged.

In 1916, Germany dispatched a merchant U-boat to Baltimore, Maryland – ostensibly to obtain a cargo of freight, but in reality to demonstrate that U-boats were capable of crossing the Atlantic Ocean to American shores. Veiled threats and intimidation soon turned to hostile activity when later that same year, Germany sent an armed U-boat to Newport, Rhode Island. After its departure, this U-boat made a show of force by sinking five Allied merchant vessels in international waters off Nantucket Island.

In April 1917, the U.S. Navy reported its first U-boat encounter in American waters since the declaration of war (on April 6): "At 3:30 A. M. on the 17th, an enemy submarine was sighted by the U.S.S. *Smith*, running apparently submerged. Submarine fired a torpedo at the U.S.S. *Smith*, which missed her by thirty yards. The wake of the torpedo was plainly seen crossing the bow. Submarine disappeared."

The location of the *Smith* at the time of the incident was given as "fifty-three miles northeast of Absecon Light, Atlantic City; fifty-five miles southeast of Sandy Hook, thirty-nine miles south of Fire Island Inlet, on the Long Island coast, and 155 miles west of the Nantucket Shoals Light vessel."

In shipping circles it was suggested, "The lookout on the *Smith* had perhaps mistaken a large fish for a torpedo in the uncertain light of the early morning."

Secretary of the Navy Josephus Daniels stated, "We are acting on the theory that this information is correct, and have everything at work along the coast."

Galvanized to action, the Navy dispatched destroyers, submarine chasers, and other units of the naval coast patrol to comb the seas for the enemy submarine. No U-boats were sighted – not for more than a year – and no corroboration was received from British intelligence sources that a U-boat had departed Germany for America.

No subsequent sightings were made. Nonetheless, the incident served to put the U.S. Navy on alert that a U-boat war was coming.

In the meantime, the Navy dispatched Admiral William Sims to England so he could ascertain the facts about the naval war with Germany, and send advice to the Navy about U-boat operations. Admiral Sims telegraphed memoranda regularly throughout the war. Thus the U.S. Navy was well informed when U-boats were deployed to the American eastern seaboard – even though it did not have the wherewithal to interdict them.

Consider this cablegram that was marked Very Secret, and sent on October 4, 1917: "Following message received by Admiralty from Copenhagen dated October 3 quote U.S. Consul General has for sometime been collecting evidence that Germany intends to send submarine to attack the American Coast based at first on North and South Atlantic ports. Submarines expected to sail early this month and evidence points to Newport News, Pensacola and Mobile as objectives. There is absolute evidence that Scandinavian mechanics have enlisted to serve in depot ships and it was reported that the Swedish S.S. *Ellen* was to leave Kiel second October with supplies. She is reported to be armed and to have Germans on board unquote Director Intelligence Division Admiralty expresses scepticism [sic] and has no reliable evidence to corroborate. Subject considered worth further investigation."

In the event, this particular intelligence was proven

Undersea Raiders of the Great War

false with regard to U-boat departures for America at that particular time. But it demonstrates the range of the intelligence gathering service that was made available to Sims, and the kind of detailed dialogue that he initiated.

Throughout the remainder of the war, Admiral Sims and his staff continued to advise the U.S. Navy on U-boat movements, projected tracks, and estimated times of arrival in American waters. For administrative purposes, the U.S. Navy arbitrarily defined "American waters" as that part of the Atlantic Ocean that lay west of 40° west longitude; east of that meridian constituted European waters.

The tragic aftermath of U-boat incursion in American waters is the subject matter of the book in hand.

My initial introduction to the U-boat wars came through scuba diving. People dive for many reasons: to observe the color and beauty of living coral reefs, to spear fish, to catch lobsters, to collect shellfish, to take photographs, and to explore sunken shipwrecks. When I started wreck-diving off the New Jersey coast, most of the wrecks that I explored were U-boat casualties from both world wars.

By now I have dived on fifty-two wrecks that were sunk by U-boat action during World War Two, and fifteen wrecks that were sunk during World War One. I have also dived on ten U-boats.

Wreck-diving and my sense of history led me to learn about the wrecks that I was exploring under water. First I read books about shipwrecks, then I conducted primary research in archives and museums, then I wrote books about shipwrecks – thirty-six of them at last count.

The initial book that I read about the first German U-boat campaign was entitled, appropriately enough, *When the U-boats Came to America*, by William Bell Clark. It was published in 1929 and has been out of print ever since. I was so impressed by the clarity of detail that I concluded that there was no reason for anyone to ever write another account. Clark had done an admirable job of capturing the flavor and the incidents of the first German U-boat campaign against American shores.

I read other books about shipwrecks, but after a while I became dissatisfied with secondary sources. Some shipwrecks accounts were meager, some were contradictory, and some were just plain wrong. This dissatisfaction inspired me to conduct primary research at the National Archives in Washington, DC: that cornucopia of official documentation.

Over the years, I have uncovered a wealth of shipwreck information – largely from the National Archives but from other primary sources as well. In relation to the present volume, I soon learned that Clark's accounts were deficient and suffered from paucity of detail. I did not know this when I had nothing to compare to his book, but once I embarked on the trail of primary research, Clark's shortfalls became all too obvious.

After Clark's death, some of his papers were donated to the Historical Society of Pennsylvania, in my hometown of Philadelphia. When I accessed his World War One files, I quickly realized that he had *not* done a poor job of reporting the U-boat war. He had done as good a job as possible in light of the information that was available to him at the time he wrote the book.

The basis and primary source for *When the U-boats Came to America* was *German Submarine Activities on the Atlantic Coast of the United States and Canada*, Publication No. 1, published by the Government Printing Office in 1920. This was the official version of the U-boat war, complete with photographs, statistics, and foldout charts. The book is not without errors. Later editions add four pages of errata totaling more than seventy mistakes (although most of the mistakes were misspellings or typographical errors). Too, some of the information regarding U-boat movements was speculative.

Clark added information from newspaper accounts

Undersea Raiders of the Great War

to create a book that was more readable than its formally written predecessor. Yet here, too, he was somewhat hampered. Consider this notice that appeared in the *New York Maritime Register* on September 4, 1918: "Publications of particulars of casualties will be temporarily omitted from this list at the urgent request of the U.S. Navy Department. Such particulars may be had by our subscribers by written application to our office."

The *New York Maritime Register* was a weekly maritime newspaper. In addition to shipping news, vessel movements, and advertisements, it published a casualty list. The Navy ordered suspension of the list because enemy agents could read it like everyone else, and collect information pertaining to vessel losses and locations.

What Clark did *not* do was to access the primary documents from which Publication No. 1 was distilled: official reports, warship deck logs, interrogation of survivors, and so on. Indeed, this kind of primary documentation was not available for public consumption because of the terms of government confidentiality, which prevented the release of such information for thirty years. In essence, Clark was forced to write a book with his pen tied behind his back. This makes his accomplishment all the more exemplary.

Furthermore, Clark did not have access to Admiral Sims' advices. All this information is now available for public consumption.

A handful of other books covered the U-boat war, but none had the scope and stylistic clarity of *When the U-boats came to America*.

In 1973, Richard A. von Doenhoff and Harry E. Rilley compiled another official World War One U-boat history for government publication. The manuscript was entitled *U-boat Operations in the Western Atlantic During World War I*. Von Doenhoff and Rilley were civilian historians who were employed by the Naval Historical Center, the offices of which were located at the Washington Navy Yard in Washington, DC. Von Doenhoff and Rilley were given the task by Vice Admiral Edwin Hooper, then Director of Naval History.

The manuscript was pieced together with snippets that were photocopied from Publication No. 1, plus official statements from survivors and U-boat deck logs, to which von Doenhoff and Rilley added connecting narrative. The manuscript reached the paste-up stage, but was then shelved and stored away in five blue boxes in the back room of the Naval Historical Center.

Throughout the years, I have copied sections of the manuscript that related to shipwrecks that I was exploring at the time, or that I was searching for off the U.S. eastern seaboard. I was never able to photocopy the manuscript in its entirety because of a limitation that the NHC imposed on the number of pages that a researcher could photocopy: fifty pages per year. Because I was doing research in bulk, I couldn't afford to spend my meager allotment all at once. There were other documents that I needed to photocopy, especially when I started to write books about shipwrecks and nautical history.

I first met von Doenhoff in the late 1970's, by which time he had gone to work as an archivist at the National Archives. We discussed the manuscript at length. He told me that Vice Admiral Hooper wanted the completed book to show how U.S. citizens had been traumatized by U-boat activity so close to American shores. However, the facts belied the admiral's pet theme. Even a casual perusal of contemporary newspaper accounts demonstrated the contrary. If anything, the people were galvanized to action against the arrogant invading Huns.

Neither von Doenhoff nor Rilley backed down from their position. Frustrated by his misconceptions, the admiral refused to permit the publication of the manuscript. And so it has languished on a shelf ever since, practically forgotten.

There is another curious twist to the saga of this mothballed manuscript. As I noted above, I have peri-

Undersea Raiders of the Great War

odically accessed the manuscript throughout the 1970's and 1980's. In those days, Bernard Cavalcante was the head archivist of the NHC, and Mike Walker was the primary research assistant in charge of locating documents for researchers. To these two historians I owe a great debt of gratitude.

In the mid 1990's, after the departure of Cavalcante and Walker, the character of the NHC began to change. What I didn't know at the time was that the new guard did just that: they guarded public documents instead of producing them at the request of researchers. If they did not like you or what you stood for, they withheld public documents. Highest on the list of people they did not like were wreck-divers, and highest on the list of wreck-divers was my name.

Bill Dudley headed the new restrictive regime, with Kathy Lloyd acting as his sergeant at arms. These two civilians and three of their henchmen controlled access to public documents with an iron fist. They became witch-hunters whose goal was to persecute wreck-divers, and to prevent them from having access to documents that were held by the Navy in the public trust.

This handful of self-appointed watchdogs kept a wealth of information from me when I was working on the companion piece to the present volume, *The Fuhrer's U-boats in American Waters*, and by extension kept that information from my readers. I learned this in October 2000, when a new research assistant who was assigned to help me that day, told me that Kathy Lloyd had ordered him specifically to withhold certain documents from me.

The research assistant – an ex-Navy officer – was incensed by her attitude because he believed that the public should have access to public documents, as Congress had ruled. But she stood over him and prevented him from producing certain documents for me.

In December 2006, in preparation for the book in hand, I made a regular appearance at the NHC and asked to see the von Doenhoff and Rilley manuscript. At first they told me that they had no record of any such manuscript. When I insisted that I had accessed it periodically for a quarter of a century, and described the boxes in which it was stored, they changed their tune and said that they no longer had it. Lloyd told me personally that the manuscript had been transferred out of the holdings of the Operational Archives to the Navy Library downstairs. Yet the library did not have it, and Lloyd was unable to produce a transfer slip.

After my return home, I wrote a letter of complaint to the director of the Naval Historical Center, Admiral Paul Tobin, outlining the deceit that I had received at the hands of his minions. I also informed him about the situation that occurred in October 2000. He defended Lloyd's actions with justifications, but acknowledged that the NHC did in fact possess the manuscript, and stated that it would be made available to me on my next research trip.

By that time I no longer needed it, because I had already photocopied thousands of pages of primary documents at the National Archives, all pertaining to the subject matter of the present volume. The National Archives has no limitation on the number of pages that a researcher may photocopy.

Never let it be said that research is easy. It is made more difficult, sometimes even impossible, by selfish and self-appointed guardians who place obstacles in the way of honest researchers who seek only truth – and often find obstructionism.

As noted above, at the National Archives I photocopied a wealth of information pursuant to World War One U-boat casualties. I was able to do this because the 30-year ban on the release of information relating to World War One had been lifted as a result of the requisite passage of time. This meant that I had access to documents to which Clark did not have access.

Furthermore, it appears that I delved into numerous file boxes that no one else had *ever* looked into before. Nearly all the World War One documents that I accessed were stamped "Confidential" or "Secret."

Undersea Raiders of the Great War

Although these classifications had long since expired by government fiat, the National Archives maintained a policy of not letting photocopies of such documents leave the building without being stamped with a declassification notice. Once the notice was stamped on a document, subsequent researchers were not required to have the document stamped again.

Practically none of the documents that I photocopied in the preparation of this book had a prior declassification stamp. I nearly ran myself ragged having staff members stamp declassification notices on documents before I was permitted to photocopy them.

What this implies is that I was the first researcher to see or make use of these documents. That is why I believe that much of the information in the following pages has never been published before.

(Note: the stamping policy has recently been changed because someone in authority realized that stamping an original document violated standard archival practice. Primary documents are not allowed to be altered in any way. Nowadays, staff members provide the researcher with a declassification sticker that is dated and initialed, and that the researcher must place on the glass of the photocopy machine when he photocopies the document. This way the declassification notice appears only on the photocopy and not on the original document.)

I must mention something else that von Doenhoff told me during the course of conversation. He said that of all the documents that have ever been generated, less than 3% have been saved. Barry Zerby, von Doenhoff's successor at the National Archives, told me years later that he thought that von Doenhoff was being generous. Zerby thought that less than 2% have been saved. Present day archivists concur with Zerby's estimate.

Today practically every government document is saved. But the farther back you go in history, the more meager is the documentation that has been preserved, or that has survived archival purges that were performed years ago in order to make space available for documents that contemporary archivists determined arbitrarily were more valuable or relevant.

I found far less material extant about the Kaiser's U-boat war than I did about the Fuhrer's U-boat war. Of the material that I found, more of it related to vessels than to the people who survived their sinking: wood and steel instead of flesh and bone.

The Office of Naval Intelligence created the vast majority of documentation that pertained to U-boat casualties. It was ONI's responsibility to interrogate survivors. The primary interest of ONI concerned U-boat movements and descriptions, not human victims. Interrogators focused more on a survivor's description of the U-boat that attacked his vessel than on how the survivor was rescued.

Time and again the archival record of a particular casualty contained reams of detailed questions and answers about a U-boat's dimensions, size and placement of armament, wireless apparatus, paint scheme, rust, and – if the survivor was taken inside the pressure hull – the interior layout. Survivors were questioned about conversations they had with German officers and crewmen, about what information they divulged, how long they had been at sea, and so on. ONI also wanted particulars on how the target vessel was sunk.

This does not imply that survivors were not questioned about their means of rescue. It implies that ONI saved more descriptions of U-boats than descriptions of survival and rescue – the latter being the focal point of the book in hand. All too often the existing archival records make no mention at all about the suffering of the survivors: how they abandoned ship, how many were killed in the attack, who picked them up, and so on. Those reports were apparently discarded in favor of military intelligence that centered on how best to prosecute the war.

ONI's measure of importance was different from mine. Such are the vagaries of historical documenta-

Undersea Raiders of the Great War

tion, and the frustrations of an historian. This is the reason why certain incidents are told in greater detail than others; and why certain incidents are tossed off in only a paragraph.

After the Allies invaded Berlin and ended World War Two, the British dispatched a staff of technicians to microfilm German military records, in order to compile a two-sided history of the war. As part of this process the Brits microfilmed all the U-boat deck logs that they found in German military archives – and not just deck logs from World War Two, but some deck logs from World War One.

These deck logs were unavailable to Clark. As far as I know, *The Kaiser's U-boats in American Waters* is the first published book to take advantage of this German source of primary documentation. Log entries compliment the information that is available from American sources, and add a perspective that is not possible without them.

Unterseeboot is a German word that translates literally as "undersea boat." From the very beginning of Germany's acquisition of vessels that could submerge beneath the surface of the sea, the Imperial German Navy adopted a naming convention in which each submarine was assigned a number that followed the letter U. Thus *U-1* was the first unterseeboot to be commissioned in the German Navy.

Winston Churchill, England's most famous statesman and the First Sea Lord during World War One, made the following distinction (with intentional irony): "Enemy submarines are to be called 'U-boats.' The term 'submarine' is to be reserved for Allied underwater vessels. U-boats are those dastardly villains who sink our ships, while submarines are those gallant and noble craft which sink theirs."

In light of this distinction, it is technically redundant to refer to an enemy submarine as a German U-boat. All U-boats are inherently German, but not everyone knows this, so the phrase appears often in literature for purposes of clarity.

During World War One, Germany distinguished among three types of U-boats. In addition to the suffix U there were the suffixes UB and UC.

U followed by a number designated a class of U-boat whose tonnage was greater than 800 tons surface displacement, whose radius of action exceeded 3,000 miles, and that was fitted with torpedo tubes and deck guns. This U-boat was intended for long-range cruises.

UB followed by a number designated a class whose tonnage fell between 300 and 700 tons, whose radius of action was less than 3,000 miles, and that was fitted with torpedo tubes and deck guns. This U-boat was intended for coastal defense.

UC followed by a number designated a class whose primary function was to deploy mines. Small mine-laying U-boats did not have torpedo tubes or deck guns. Large mine-laying U-boats might have torpedo tubes in addition to mine-laying tubes, and one deck gun (generally of smaller caliber than the guns carried by a U class).

When Germany started the war, its naval fleet possessed only a couple dozen U-boats. Average construction time from keel laying to commissioning was two years. Most of these U-boats were small enough that they could be placed on railroad flatbed cars and transported in sections to the coast of choice. After arrival, the sections could be assembled and launched in a couple of weeks.

Production increased rapidly as soon as hostilities commenced. The Germania Yard in Kiel and the Weser Yard in Bremen started turning out small U-boats with assembly-line rapidity. Later, the Blohm and Voss Yard near Hamburg was employed to build U-boats.

The greatest defect of these transportable U-boats was their single-screw and single-engine means of propulsion. A mechanical breakdown of any kind left the U-boat helpless and without motive power.

Larger models hit the planning boards. The next

Undersea Raiders of the Great War

generation of U-boat was fitted with two independent driving systems, each providing power to a separate propeller. This design offered greater speed and range. The twin propulsion design also provided a backup in case of failure of one of the propulsion systems.

Each propulsion system consisted of a diesel engine for motive power on the surface, and an electric motor and battery accumulators for motive power under water. Diesel engines could not be used when the submarine was submerged because they required great quantities of atmospheric oxygen to burn fuel. Batteries were recharged from generators when the submarine's hatches were open to the air.

Larger hulls enabled the use of larger deck guns. But these larger hulls could not be transported overland by rail.

Manufacturing efficiency increased quickly to the point at which U-boats could be constructed in less than a year.

Unlike muggings and knife fights, war is conducted in accordance with humanitarian guidelines – an oxymoron if there ever was one. Various treaties, such as the Geneva Convention that was first formulated in Switzerland in 1864, established rules for the treatment of prisoners of war, the sick, and the wounded. Most occidental nations have ratified the original Geneva Convention and its subsequent articles and protocols that, for example, outlawed certain forms of warfare that were deemed too horrible to employ.

Another international law to which most so-called civilized nations subscribed concerned the destruction of merchant vessels by belligerents. For example, "Vessels belonging to the enemy state, and notably warships, may be attacked, captured, or destroyed by a belligerent man-of-war anywhere on the high seas or in the territorial waters of the contending belligerents, at any time and without notice. But enemy merchantmen are not to be subjected to such summary and drastic treatment.

"There are several reasons for such differentiation. In the first place enemy merchantmen are not combatants. International law and practice have long recognized a line of demarcation between combatants and non-combatants, both in war on land and in war on sea. In the case of the former we have now the Hague Regulations; and in the case of the latter we have, on the one hand, the Declaration of Paris, 1856, which abolished privateering; and, on the other, the more detailed provisions of the seventh Hague Convention.

"Secondly, an enemy merchant ship may actually belong to a class of vessels exempted from capture and destruction by special conventions and usage. [For example, hospital ships and coastal fishing vessels (including the crews, boats, equipment, and cargoes of fresh fish).]

"Thirdly, enemy merchantmen may have neutral persons and neutral cargoes on board; for neutral passengers are not debarred from sailing in the merchant ships of a belligerent, neutral crews are not prohibited from taking service therein, and neutral merchants are not forbidden to continue their commercial intercourse with the belligerents and to ship their goods in the merchant ships belonging to any of the belligerents.

"Indeed, the Declaration of Paris expressly provides that neutral goods, with the exception of contraband of war, are not liable to capture under the enemy flag.

"From these considerations it follows that the commander of a belligerent warship may not dispense with the practice of visit and search in regard to suspected or enemy merchantmen. It is his duty, before resorting to forcible measures, to ascertain the true character of the vessel, the nationality of the passengers and crew on board, and the nature and destination of the cargo. . . . It is sufficient to emphasize that the belligerent is obliged to visit an enemy merchantman, and that he has no right to destroy her in any case without examining her or making a reasonable attempt to examine her."

What all this boils down to is that, while warships

Undersea Raiders of the Great War

and armed merchantmen were open game and always in season, a belligerent was not permitted to destroy merchant vessels without warning, but must ascribe to "prize rules."

The Rules of Prize Warfare were outlined in the Hague Conventions of 1899 and 1907, to which most European nations adhered. According to these rules, a belligerent was not allowed to sink passenger vessels under any circumstances – this because the rules of engagement proscribed the killing of civilians; only military personnel were allowed to be killed.

The Rules also prohibited endangering the lives of crews of merchant vessels by sinking their ships unannounced. A warship was first supposed to stop a merchant vessel by firing a shot across the bow. The merchant vessel was then supposed to heave to, and show her papers to an officer of the warship. If the vessel was registered to a neutral nation, the warship was supposed to let her proceed without further molestation. If the vessel was registered to a nation with which the belligerent was at war, then the vessel could be sunk.

But, the crews of merchant vessels could not be harmed, nor could they be placed in a position in which they might come to harm. They could be taken aboard the attacking warship, then transported to a neutral port for disembarkation. Or they could be placed in lifeboats within reach of land, but only if weather conditions were mild enough to offer a reasonable opportunity for survival. They could not be set adrift in the middle of the ocean with little or no hope of making land.

These gentlemanly rules of conduct were generally inappropriate for submersible warships. Submarines were too small to support large numbers of detainees. The primary means of a submarine's escape was to proceed under water at slow speed.

The problem with this legal model is that every country has its own views and contentions with which other countries may disagree.

The nature of submarine warfare militated against destruction after prior warning and evacuation. A surfaced submarine was a sitting duck for faster and better-armed surface warships. For that reason, Germany instituted what came to be known as "unrestricted submarine warfare." This meant that it was legal in accordance with convenient German conventions to torpedo merchant vessels without warning, so that the U-boat did not give away its location to enemy warships in the vicinity.

Germany relaxed its policy of unrestricted submarine warfare on occasion – such as after the turmoil that was created by the sinking of the *Lusitania*, which resulted in the deaths of 1,198 passengers and crew, of which 123 fatalities were American passengers – but always found that U-boats were either ineffective or were put in danger by having to announce their presence.

U-boats were more like underwater snipers or roving guerrillas than full-fledged warships.

Ultimately, Germany concluded that the only way in which it could beat its implacable foes was by sinking as many merchant vessels as possible, because those vessels transported food and supplies to the beleaguered British Isles.

There are two misconceptions about World War One that many Americans continue to hold.

The first belief is that the sinking of the *Lusitania* was responsible for bringing the United States into the war. On the contrary, despite reams of outspoken rhetoric that were spoken and published after the *U-20* torpedoed the *Lusitania* (on May 7, 1915), the United States did not declare war against the Central Powers (Germany, Austria-Hungary, Bulgaria, and Turkey) until nearly two years later (April 6, 1917).

Wars are not started on the spur of the moment. They are the result of years, sometimes decades, of unarmed conflict between nations that disagree on boundary lines or political ideology.

Unrest has existed in Europe ever since mankind first inhabited the territory. Wars have been fought

Undersea Raiders of the Great War

there on a continuous basis. Allies have changed sides like the flipping of an electrical switch. People in power have wasted the lives of their fellow countrymen and women in their endless games of intrigue and personal aggrandizement. War is as much a part of the continent as gravity.

On June 28, 1914, ongoing discontent among neighboring nations was brought to a head by the assassination of Archduke Franz Ferdinand. This event incited the local populace, and resulted in a rash of diplomatic contrivances that were putatively designed to address long-term grievances, but which in reality created excuses for invasion in order to extend national influence and enlarge boundary lines.

Austria-Hungary declared war on Serbia on July 28, 1914. Alliances were quickly formed, the sides being chosen to the greatest advantage of each participating country, and the Great War commenced.

The president of the United States was Woodrow Wilson. He was an adherent of isolationism. According to this philosophy, the fighting "over there" was someone else's war in which the U.S. should not get involved. He won the 1916 presidential election on the campaign promise to keep the United States out of the European war.

Wilson did not ignore or overlook the excesses of the Central Powers. He addressed them by seeking "strict accountability" in the form of apologies and reparations. Germany made apologies – again and again and again; it did not make reparations. In any case, no placation or monetary compensation could bring back a human life. Wilson's noble cause was unsupportable in light of overseas atrocities.

The second misconception is that the U.S. government and American citizens adopted a stance against the Central Powers from the very onset of the war. Nothing could be farther from the truth. There was a great deal of pro-German sentiment during the beginning stages of military engagement. Many people and their representatives initially sided with Germany – not so much because they supported the German cause, but because they did *not* support the cause of Germany's enemies.

A great deal of anti-British sentiment resulted from England's deployment of mines in European shipping lanes. While the placement of these mines was intended to prevent food, supplies, and war materiel from reaching Germany, it had the unfortunate side effect of curbing international commerce. Because mines cannot distinguish between friend and foe, they constitute a form of unrestricted warfare.

Most U.S. companies that traded with Germany prior to the commencement of hostilities, continued to trade with Germany afterward. These companies did not want to lose their profitable business. Many companies traded with countries on both sides of the conflict. Business proceeded not just as usual; it was booming because of increased needs for product.

What was of prime important to Americans – the government in particular – was freedom of the seas. Americans were infuriated by British minefields because they violated this time-honored freedom.

Americans today must remember that the first war ever instigated by the fledgling United States was fought because North African countries supported piracy, the capture of U.S. merchant vessels, and the enslavement of passengers and crews. The Barbary Wars were fought in the Mediterranean Sea. This was where U.S. marines landed "on the shores of Tripoli."

A century later, Americans were still rankled by any scheme that took away their freedom of the seas. Minefields adversely affected international commerce because they were responsible for the loss of American vessels, cargoes, and lives. So it was that initially the British were perceived as the bad guys, and by extension the Allies (alias Entente Powers).

The tide turned slowly against Germany. It can perhaps be said to have started when Germany introduced chlorine gas as an offensive measure against enemy soldiers. The use of poison gas was in direct contraven-

Undersea Raiders of the Great War 23

tion to the Hague Conventions. The problem with outlawing poison gas was the same as outlawing the ownership of guns today: only outlaws have them.

Once Pandora's box was opened, the British quickly followed suit. Then France joined the fracas by introducing a gas that was more virulent than chlorine, called phosgene.

Germany countered British mine-laying tactics by laying mines in the English Channel. Worse, Germany restricted American trade with England by declaring a Danger Zone around the British Isles, inside of which *all* vessels were liable to be sunk regardless of nationality or neutrality.

And so the war escalated . . .

Germany sank twenty American vessels before President Wilson asked Congress for a declaration of war. The first was the four-masted ship *William P. Frye*, which was sunk by the auxiliary cruiser *Prinz Eitel Friedrich* on January 28, 1915. Next was the freighter *Evelyn*, which struck a German mine on February 19, 1915 while, ironically, transporting a cargo of cotton to Germany. The first American vessel to be torpedoed by a U-boat (*U-30*) was the tanker *Gulflight*, on March 1, 1915. Historians often overlook this latter incident because of the torpedoing of the *Lusitania* six days later.

On January 31, 1917, Germany announced the resumption of unrestricted submarine warfare. This was the major factor that convinced the U.S. government to enter the war against the Central Powers. In rapid order Germany then sank ten American vessels (which are included in the count of twenty that is noted above). The last straw had been placed.

It is somewhat ironic that by the time Germany got around to sending U-boats to American waters – fully a year after the American declaration of war, and more than six months after Admiral Sims's initial warning – U-boats were already losing the battle against merchant shipping.

The job of the U-boat arm was to sink more "bottoms" (as merchant vessels were called) than the enemy could build. This was easily accomplished in the beginning of the war, when the Allies were unprepared to deal with the methods of submerged attack. As the war progressed, the British introduced the convoy system, merchant vessels were armed and were manned by naval gun crews, escort vessels were outfitted with depth charges, patrol boats were constructed with assembly-line regularity, and the construction of bottoms was increased dramatically so that it more than compensated for losses.

Consider these statistics that the United States Shipping Board compiled in September 1918: in August 1917 there were 61 shipyards in the U.S.; a year later there were 203. The number of launching ways increased from 235 to 1,020. The number of shipyard employees increased from under 50,000 to 386,000. U.S. shipyards constructed four times as many vessels in the twelve-month period than in any other twelve-month period in American history.

"The American merchant marine is today expanding more rapidly than any other in the world. In August of this year the United States took rank as the leading shipbuilding nation in the world. It now has more shipyards, more shipways, more shipworkers, more ships under construction, and is building more ships every month than any other country, not excepting the United Kingdom, hitherto easily the first shipbuilding power. Prior to the war the United States stood a poor third among the shipbuilding nations.

"Since August, 1917, more seagoing tonnage has been launched from American shipyards than was ever launched before, in a similar period anywhere. The total, as of September 1, 1918, 574 vessels, of 3,017,238 dead-weight tons, is nearly four times all the seagoing tonnage (of over 1,500 dead-weight tons) built in the United States in any four pre-war years. The total launchings since the first of this year, 482 vessels, of 2,392,692 dead-weight tons, are more than eight times

Undersea Raiders of the Great War

the seagoing tonnage (of over 1,500 dead-weight tons) produced in this country than in any pre-war year."

While it is true that Germany increased the construction of U-boats after the onset of hostilities, and succeeded in building more than two hundred before the end of the war, it is also true that Allied antisubmarine warfare techniques became more effective in sinking U-boats, or in keeping them submerged while convoys and merchant vessels escaped. U-boats were gradually put on the defensive.

The industrial might of the United States produced more bottoms than U-boats could sink. Once the pendulum swung the other way, it never swung back. Germany's last-ditch measure against American coastal shipping in 1918 came too late to avert the inevitable.

In effect, the American U-boat campaign was the last gasp of the Kaiser's bid to dominate the world.

A German mine that washed ashore on Fire Island, New York. The horns that trigger the explosive charge are to the left. (Courtesy of the Naval Photographic Center.)

FIRST MERCHANT CRUISE
OF THE
DEUTSCHLAND

In 1915, the German government commenced the construction of a pair of cargo-carrying submarines: the *Deutschland* and the *Bremen*. Deutsche Ozean Reederei was a dummy company that was created to pose as the owner of these submersible freighters. Although individuals were named as investors who fronted the money for the purchase, the Kaiser's government backed their investments.

The company that built the merchant U-boats was the famous manufacturer of arms and munitions that was familiarly known as Krupps.

Because the submarines were registered as merchant vessels instead of warships, international law permitted them to visit neutral countries for extended times without fear of internment. By contrast, a commissioned warship was permitted to remain in the harbor of a neutral country for no longer than twenty-four hours before it was forced to depart, or else suffer internment for the duration of hostilities between belligerent nations.

The merchant submarines carried no armament: neither torpedoes, nor mines, nor deck guns. Nor were they fitted with torpedo tubes or mine tubes.

The *Deutschland* was duly registered in the United States by the Bureau of Navigation under the Department of Commerce. According to the Certificate of Admeasurement, the *Deutschland* grossed 2,241 tons. (Gross tonnage is not a measure of actual weight, but a calculation based upon interior volume.) The length of the hull measured 64.88 meters (212.86 feet); the breadth measured 9.07 meters (29.75 feet); the depth of hold measured 6.2 meters (20.34 feet).

First Merchant Cruise of the *Deutschland*

According to a contemporary description, "The interior cylindrical hull is divided by four transverse bulkheads into five separate water-tight compartments. Compartment No. 1, at the bow, contains the anchor cables and electric winches for handling the anchor; also general ship stores, and a certain amount of cargo. Compartment No. 2 is given up entirely to cargo. Compartment No. 3, which is considerably larger than any of the others, contains the living quarters of the officers and crew. At the after end of this compartment, and communicating with it, is the conning tower. Compartment No. 4 is given up entirely to cargo. Compartment No. 5 contains the propelling machinery, consisting of two heavy oil engines and two electric motors. The storage batteries are carried in the bottom of the boat, below the living compartment. For purposes of communication, a gangway, 2 feet 6 inches wide by 6 feet high, is built through each cargo compartment, thus rendering it possible for the crew to pass entirely from one end of the boat to the other."

Surrounding the interior cylinder was an outer hull, or skin. This outer hull was designed to provide a hydrodynamic shape that could cleave through water better than the blunt-nosed cylinder. Fuel tanks, ballast tanks, pumps, piping, and miscellaneous machinery occupied the space between the inner and outer hulls.

The diesel engines could be used for propulsion only on the surface, because they consumed huge quantities of oxygen. They were also used to recharge the batteries. The electric motors were used for propulsion when the submarine was submerged.

The person who was assigned to command the *Deutschland* was Paul Koenig. He was a respected ocean liner captain who worked for North German Lloyd. His most recent merchant command was the *Schleswig*. With the onset of war and the cessation of German transatlantic passenger service, Koenig became an officer in the Imperial German Navy. He was an excellent choice for command of the *Deutschland* because he had a great deal of experience in navigating around American ports. He also spoke fluent English.

In Koenig's own words, "The idea for building submarine cargo boats for long distance is to me an idea growing out of the resolve of the German people to nullify the blockade of the German and American coasts, as well as the complete cutting-off of our legitimate imports."

In other words, the submarines were designed to transport goods through the British blockade by running submerged when it was necessary to avoid confrontation.

Koenig was given special training in U-boats while the *Deutschland* was under construction. By June 1916, both he and his submarine were ready for sea trials. His crew was selected from seasoned veterans serving in the U-boat flotilla. The men turned in their military uniforms for civilian clothing.

The *Deutschland* departed from the Germania Shipyard in Bremen on June 13. Its first stop was Heligoland, an island off the coast of Germany. For the next week and a half the *Deutschland* underwent various trials at sea: to exercise the crewmen at their jobs, to become familiar with the vessel's maneuvering characteristics, to practice submerging, to test the hull's watertight integrity at depth, and so on. The well-honed crew worked out the final kinks in the complicated systems that operated the submarine. Shore-side mechanics made adjustments and last minute modifications.

On June 23, with its holds loaded, crewmembers slipped the mooring lines off the dock for the final time, and the *Deutschland* commenced its maiden voyage. Its destination was Newport News, Virginia. It carried a cargo of medicine and dyestuffs that weighed 791 tons, and was worth some $6 million.

The twin diesel engines propelled the hull on the surface at the respectable speed of 12 to 13 knots. Under water, working off batteries and electric motors, the vessel could proceed at just about 7 knots.

Because of its squat shape and fat sides, the Ger-

First Merchant Cruise of the *Deutschland*

man submariners referred to their boat as a "bath-tub."

The *Deutschland* shaped a course through the North Sea that would take the submarine north of Scotland. The passage was not without moments of interest. The *Deutschland* scared off one merchant vessel because the U-boat looked like, well, a U-boat. Koenig and his twenty-eight crewmembers laughed hardily as the zigzagging merchantman raced for the horizon.

They did not laugh so hardily when they encountered a British destroyer. In severely rough seas, Koenig gave the order for an emergency dive. Men slid off their feet as the deck tilted sharply downward by the head. The U-boat descended out of control. It came a sudden shock that knocked everyone to the deck. The submarine had crashed into the seabed, and hung at an angle of 36 degrees.

Koenig: "Our stern was still oscillating up and down like a mighty pendulum. . . . According to the chart we should have some 31 meters depth at this spot, but the steep slant of the long vessel must have caused the stern to go raking above the surface for a considerable distance. This would furnish a splendid target for an enemy destroyer. As long as the engines still ran, the following must also have occurred: Every time the hollow of a wave raced over us, the propellers raced in empty air part of the time, and no doubt increased our powers of attraction by flinging up fountains of water and whirls of foam. Klees had at once recognized this by the racing of the motors, and his presence of mind had at least obviated the more immediate peril."

Klees switched the engine-signal to stop. Engine room personnel shut down the electric motors.

Luck was with them, for the destroyer had failed to notice the presence of the submarine. But the bow was still stuck in the mud. Water was shifted from the forward ballast tanks to the after tanks. Koenig: "Thus by balancing and trimming with the tanks we finally managed to get the bows clear of the bottom. We now began to rise, but were at once obliged to offset the inclination to oscillate caused by the full aft-tanks. After a time the center of gravity was again restored and I once more had the *Deutschland* well in hand."

Although the low profile usually enabled the submarine to evade enemy vessels without having to submerge, some ninety miles of the North Sea passage was conducted under water, mostly at periscope depth. Once in the open Atlantic, proceeding at full speed on the surface, Koenig began to get the feel of the lumbering tublike freighter.

The submarine responded ponderously to the steering rudders, and proved to be difficult to handle because of its large volume. Maintaining trim under water was a constant battle. On the surface, the hull rolled so excessively in rough seas that the men had to brace themselves. Koenig: "In addition, some of the crew were suffering from seasickness, for the short jerky motions of the ship were dreadful."

The cramped spaces of the interior were uncomfortable. Condensation and dampness were chronic problems. After only three days at sea, the men had to air out their moist belongings.

Koenig: "The whole deck was full of mattresses, blankets, clothes and boots. The underwear was fastened to the wires of the hand-rail and fluttered merrily in the wind as upon a wash-line. The men lay about between and sunned themselves like lizards. In order to increase the fan ventilation of the quarters below by good draughts of natural air, wind catchers were put up around all the manholes or trap-doors. The curved, greenish body of the *Deutschland* rigged out with these things took on the appearance of some fantastic prehistoric fish-monster. We must have presented a remarkable spectacle!"

The first few days were fraught with foul weather. After the storms abated, "The boring part of our trip has now arrived. The boat keeps on her course always twisting a little, now and then we evade a steamer. Days go by without our seeing anything whatsoever. The gramophones play and everybody is in excellent spirits."

First Merchant Cruise of the *Deutschland*

Taking sextant sightings from the conning tower was an ordeal. Koenig: "Jammed in an oval steel tank of about the size of a lady's small trunk, you cling for dear life to a small flap-seat, press one shoulder against the parapet and try to hold the sextant upright with a convulsive grip – until the image of the sun appears directly on the artificial horizon. You are then obliged to shield the instrument quickly behind the protecting wall and to scuttle down the ladder into the central [control room], just as you had previously scuttled up – hugging the instruments and charts against your breast and bracing yourself with back and knees. You then wedge yourself once more through the turret manhole, your eye kept peeled for every breaker, and get to work with compass and parallel ruler.

"Your chart-table is your knee, and you have the consciousness of having made your entire calculations in a cowering attitude."

The close confines of the interior were unendurable even in calm seas. Koenig: "Fresh air no longer entered. In the engine-room two 6-cylinder combustion motors kept hammering away in a maddening two-four time. They hurled the power of their explosions into the whirling crank-shafts. The red-hot breath of the consumed gases went crashing out through the exhausts, but the glow of these incessant firings remained in the cylinders and communicated itself to the entire oil-dripping environment of steel. A choking cloud of heat and oily vapor streamed from the engines and spread itself like a leaden pressure through the entire ship."

In the Gulf Stream, during the heat of the day, the interior temperature rose as high as 127 degrees Fahrenheit. Koenig: "The watch off duty, naked to the skin, groaned and writhed in their bunks. It was no longer possible to think of sleep. And when one of the men fell into a dull stupor, then he would be aroused by the sweat which ran incessantly over his forehead and into his eyes, and would awake to new torment.

"It was almost like a blessed deliverance when the eight hours of rest were over, and a new watch was called to the central or the engine-room.

"But there the real martyrdom began. Clad only in an undershirt and drawers, the men stood at their posts, a cloth wound about their foreheads to keep the running sweat from streaming into their eyes. Their blood hammered and raced in their temples. Every vein boiled as with fever. It was only by the exertion of the most tremendous will-power that it was possible to force the dripping human body to perform its mechanical duty and to remain upright during the four hours of the watch."

Koenig decided to approach the American coast at night, partially submerged. The lookouts spotted the beacon lights of Cape Charles and Cape Henry. These lights guarded the entrance to the Chesapeake Bay. Koenig was familiar with these lights, for he had passed between them often during his days as a merchant marine skipper.

Koenig: "We now began to pass the bobbing lantern-buoys of the channel. I recognized the well-known howling of a whistling buoy with which I was familiar from my former trips, and so the sense of hearing also contributed to the feeling that land was close at hand.

"After we had passed the whistling buoy we emerged [surfaced] completely. We now saw the lights of various passenger steamers. The steamers, however, did not observe us, as we still proceeded with blinded lights until we ran close off Cape Henry and had reached the American three-mile limit.

"This was on the 8th of July, at half-past eleven at night."

Koenig expected to be met by a tugboat of the North German Lloyd line. The *Thomas J. Timmins* had been patrolling the capes for a week and a half in anticipation of the U-boat's arrival. They had missed each other in the dark.

"Once within the American neutrality zone, we set our lights, and made our way quietly into the entrance between the two capes until we made out the red and white top-lights of the pilot steamer.

First Merchant Cruise of the *Deutschland*

"We stopped and burned the customary blue fire. Hereupon the pilot boat at once directed its searchlight upon us, and as it was unable to see the outlines of a steamer, it approached us very carefully."

After some communication via megaphone, the pilot boarded the *Deutschland*, and said, "I'll be damned, here she is!"

Koenig: "Then he shook our hands again and again out of sheer honest heartiness, and gave vent to his genuine delight in being the first American to greet the *U-Deutschland*, in the land of liberty." This was an odd statement for Koenig to make, in light of Germany's ongoing war to take liberty away from the lands that it wished to subjugate.

Upon questioning, the pilot informed Koenig that the tugboat should be in the vicinity. The *Deutschland* found her after a two-hour search. The tugboat skipper informed Koenig of a change in destination. He was to proceed to Baltimore, Maryland. The pilot departed. The tugboat escorted the *Deutschland* upstream along the Chesapeake Bay. The distance from the mouth of the bay to Baltimore was approximately 175 miles.

The U-boat flew the German flag. Koenig: "Thus in the gray of the morning, we entered the Bay. Our

This postcard picture shows the tublike shape of the *Deutschland* and its tiny conning tower. The tug is the *Thomas J. Timmins*. The inset photo is Captain Paul Koenig.

course gradually became a triumphal procession. All the neutral steamers that we passed, American and others, saluted us with three blasts of their sirens and steam whistles. Only an English steamer swept by us in a poisonous silence, the while we let the black-white-red banner stream proudly in the wind. . . .

"The farther we moved up the bay, the madder grew the noise. We were delighted beyond measure with this for we could plainly perceive in this uproar the sympathies which the Americans cherished for us and our voyage. . . .

"The rumors of our arrival must have spread with miraculous rapidity, for to our great astonishment boats full of reporters and film operators began to meet us while we were still many miles from Baltimore. . . .

"At eleven o'clock at night we stopped at the Baltimore Quarantine Station, and our anchor rattled for the first time into American waters.

"*U-Deutschland* had arrived." The passage had taken sixteen days.

The following morning, the physician of the Quarantine Station arrived to take the submarine's certificate of health. Koenig: "Then we weighed anchor, and under the guidance of the *Timmins*, we proceeded to our anchorage at Locust Point, where we were to discharge our cargo."

The *Deutschland* berthed with its starboard side against a wooden pier "which was built out into the stream, and under cover of a large shed, in which the goods we were to carry back were already stored." The pier was owned by the Eastern Forwarding Company, another dummy company that was owned and operated by the German government.

"This region was so little frequented that communication between the pier and the nearest good street had first to be established. The entire place toward the land side was cut off by a large ditch and barbed wire entanglements.

"In the [Patapsco] river the *Deutschland* was protected on one side by the pier and the North German

First Merchant Cruise of the *Deutschland*

The bow of the *Deutschland* protrudes beyond the hull of a lighter. The *Neckar* is in the background. The warehouse is on the pier. Note the onlookers in the foreground, and the log barricade in the water. (Courtesy of the National Archives.)

Lloyd steamer *Neckar*. The *Neckar* had lain in Baltimore since the outbreak of war. It was now to serve as our home. From here we could always keep an eye on the *Deutschland*."

Chains of floating logs and nets protected the submarine from marine traffic, while small steamers and lighters pressed against the submarine's port side and stern. The *Deutschland* lay snug like a babe in arms. A detail of special police guarded the entry to the pier. Curious onlookers clambered around the docks and peered through the fence, but were disallowed access.

As a public relations maneuver, Koenig took his men outside the compound and posed for press photographers and film companies.

Koenig: "My first trip to the city resembled a triumphal procession. The auto was obliged to halt every moment, and I was congratulated upon all sides, and everybody wished to shake my hand. I grew to be a sort of obstruction to traffic during those first days in Baltimore. Thus I slowly made my way to the agency of the North German Lloyd. This was surrounded by dense masses of people. . . . The following days were to become one continual festival for us."

In one officious ceremony, Christine Langenhan presented Captain Koenig with a silver loving cup for the first submarine to cross the Atlantic.

While the public was enamored by the German achievement, officialdom was less enthusiastic. The American government was cautious; the British government was openly suspicious.

Koenig: "A government commission of three American naval officers came down from Washington on July 12th. They were to make a most detailed inspection of the *Deutschland*. Since we had absolutely no armament of any nature, and no provisions for mounting any on board, we were able to show these gentlemen everything with absolute confidence.

"After an examination of three hours, which covered every nook and corner of the boat, and which cost the participants much perspiration in crawling about the hot and glowing steel hull, the Commission confirmed the purely mercantile character of the *U-Deutschland*. These gentlemen were full of intense admiration for the genius shown in the construction of the entire boat, and were particularly impressed by the staggering fact of the complicated nature of the entire mechanism."

After passing muster, the partying resumed. German-Americans in Baltimore organized a festival in honor of the submariners. The crewmen were toasted "again and again."

Koenig: "On July 20th, the *Deutschland* received a visit from Count Bernstorff, the German Ambassador, who had come to Baltimore with several gentlemen from the summer seat of the Embassy. We showed them our faithful boat, whose inspection amidst the process of loading cargo and in a terrific heat was scarcely an unalloyed pleasure.

"On the evening of the same day, an official dinner was given by the Mayor of Baltimore in honor of the presence of the German Ambassador. This had been preceded by a small lunch in the select precincts of the

First Merchant Cruise of the *Deutschland*

Germania clubhouse. The dinner given by the Mayor, was of an exclusively political nature, and was attended only by politicians and official personages. There was a long series of excellent courses and of drinks, and, according to American custom, the close of the dinner and the appearance of innumerable new drinks were the occasion for a number of speeches. In these the arrival of the *Deutschland* in America, the significance of this event to the city of Baltimore and for friendly German-American relations were duly celebrated. . . .

"This was a very pretty symbol of friendship and understanding between the two peoples, both of whose interests are bound up in the freedom of the seas."

Again, it is ironic to say the least that Koenig remarked about freedom of the seas while at that very moment his country was endeavoring to dominate the peoples of neighboring nations – people who struggled to maintain freedom of the land as well as freedom of the seas.

Koenig also made remarks that emphasized his ingrained conviction of German superiority, and that presaged the belief in Arian supremacy that the succeeding generation embraced: "The entire work upon the boat and on the freight pier was carried out by negroes, whose slight degree of education and weak powers of observation were in this case a special recommendation."

Meanwhile, instead of great derricks, steel windlasses, and hydraulic cranes, wooden hoists were erected over the "ordinary hatches of the U-boat" to offload sacks and chests of cargo. After the freight compartments were emptied, the job of refilling them commenced.

The return cargo consisted of approximately 400 tons of nickel, 90 tons of tin, 400 tons of crude rubber, and half a ton of jute. These commodities were valued at about $1.5 million. Proper stowage was critically important because uneven distribution of such a large weight could disturb the submarine's equilibrium, particularly during a crash dive. Every sack of nickel and rubber, and every pig of tin, was carefully weighed and stowed.

Rumors abounded that the tin was actually gold that was plated to look like tin; that the gold had been smuggled from the *Kronprinzessim Cecile*, which was interned in Boston; that the gold was worth $4 million. These rumors were never substantiated. Perhaps British intelligence started the rumors in order to create trouble.

Two railroad tank cars delivered diesel fuel to top off the *Deutschland's* bunkers. Koenig professed that refueling was not necessary, nor even a precaution. The U-boat could return to Germany without taking on additional fuel. He refueled because American diesel fuel was less expensive and better refined than the diesel fuel in Germany. Perhaps it was also more readily available.

The submarine conducted trial dives at the dock; these were underwater stability tests. Koenig: "There was just enough depth at our anchorage for us to carry this out. For this trial dive all the men were ordered to their stations. The submersion tanks were slowly opened and the boat was filled with just enough water to cause it to float with the hatch of the turret appearing above the surface.

"In this position, the body of the boat was made to oscillate by ballasting the two trimming-tanks in different ways. This permitted us to judge whether the burdens in the boat had been properly distributed." They were.

Koenig now faced a quandary. In London, the July 18th issue of the *Morning Post* published a warning that was issued by the British government: "The *Deutschland*, in consequence of its character as a submarine, is to be regarded as a war vessel and is to be treated as such. The warships of the Allies will, therefore, seek every opportunity to waylay the vessel beyond the American three-mile limit and will sink it without warning."

First Merchant Cruise of the *Deutschland*

Although the cargo was stowed to his satisfaction, Koenig bided his time. He delayed departure until August 1. To the cheers and waves of hundreds of spectators, the *Deutschland* floated high on the rising tide in mid-afternoon, and commenced the return passage to Germany. The *Thomas J. Timmins* accompanied the *Deutschland* downstream.

Koenig proceeded slowly. Half way down the bay he stopped to conduct another submersion test at a place where the chart indicted a depth of 30 meters [100 feet]. The descent struck fear into every submariner's heart, for the U-boat descended past the charted depth without touching bottom. Not until the manometers registered 50 meters did the hull come to rest gently on the mud. Koenig: "There could be only one explanation; we must have sunk into a hole which had not been marked upon the chart."

Next, the compass needle commenced a slow spin, boxing the compass as if it had gone crazy. This was disconcerting to say the least.

Koenig gave the order to activate the exhaust pumps in order to eject the water in the ballast tanks. The pumps whirred, but the U-boat did not rise. The compass needle steadied, and the manometer registered deeper water. The pumps continued to whir. The needle indicated 49 meters. Suddenly, the needle jumped to 20 meters, then returned to 49 meters, then back to 20 meters, then to 120 meters!

The redoubtable Klees had a brainstorm. He yanked a lever that released a rush of compressed air. This instantly brought the manometer needle back to 49 meters, at which point it steadied. Koenig and Klees reasoned that a plug of mud had "stopped up the opening of the manometer from without" and "was instantly blown away with a whiff of compressed air."

After an anxious hour and a half on the bottom, the submarine slowly began to rise. The *Deutschland* surfaced about two miles away from the *Thomas J. Timmins*, whose crewmembers were only slightly less anxious than the Germans.

40   First Merchant Cruise of the *Deutschland*

Koenig concluded that the rotating peregrinations of the compass needle were due to a strange current that spun the boat in a circle at the bottom of the hole.

With the tugboat alongside to watch for approaching vessels, Koenig made another test dive and return to periscope depth. This dive was accomplished successfully.

The *Deutschland* reached the mouth of the bay at dusk. Anxiety mounted again when the searchlight beams of nearby fishing vessels stabbed at Koenig's eyes. He submerged, drove forward for half an hour, rose to obtain his bearings from the lighthouses on the capes, then proceeded through the darkness at periscope depth.

Beyond the three-mile territorial limit, British patrol boats created a blockade and swung their searchlight beams to and fro. The *Deutschland* evaded them without being spotted. Koenig surfaced at midnight, switched on the diesel engines, and proceeded eastward at full speed.

Koenig: "*We had broken through!*"

The return passage was relatively uneventful. The *Deutschland* proceeded by way of the English Channel. The U-boat had no difficulty in evading British patrol boats. After stopping at Heligoland, the *Deutschland* continued on to the German mainland.

Koenig: "Our journey up the Weser [River] shaped itself to a triumphal progress beyond all comparison. Behind the hundreds of thousands who had come to cheer us from the banks of the river stood invisible millions of the German people, all imbued with the same emotion. . . .

"After overcoming a distance of some 8,450 nautical miles, of which not more than 190 were covered under water, the first of all merchant submarines had come back to its native port. The *U-Deutschland's* voyage to America was over."

WAR CRUISE
OF THE
U-53

After Koenig returned to Germany at the end of August, editors compiled a book about his U-boat experiences: *Voyage of the Deutschland*. The text was assembled from Koenig's deck log and reminiscences, plus naval documents and newspaper articles. Work on the book proceeded at breakneck speed. The German edition was ready for publication by the end of September.

Paul Koenig's byline was printed on the cover as the author, but the book was actually ghostwritten by Ernst Bischof.

Immediately upon the return of the *Deutschland*, sister ship *Bremen* departed for Baltimore with a valuable cargo of pharmaceuticals. It was never seen again.

For years there were persistent rumors that the British had either sunk or captured the second merchant U-boat. Some people claim to have seen it secreted in a number of backwater harbors. None of these rumors was ever corroborated, and no British documents exist which lend credence to its sinking or capture. There was also speculation that the *Bremen* struck a mine in the North Sea; but no debris was ever found.

Best-case scenario is that the *Bremen* suffered an uncontrolled descent like the one in which the *Deutschland* slammed into the seabed, but in deeper water that exceeded the submarine's crush depth.

While American citizens rejoiced over the *Deutschland's* technological feat, Naval Intelligence held misgivings about the underlying portent of the U-boat's ability to travel undetected and to cross the Atlantic Ocean without refueling. As noted in the previous chapter, although the *Deutschland* took on diesel fuel in Baltimore, this was more of an expedience than a necessity. The submarine could have completed the return passage without refueling.

The message was clear: if a merchant submarine could accomplish such a clandestine voyage, then so could a submersible warship.

The next U-boat that Germany dispatched to the United States was the *U-53*. Under the command of Kapitanleutnant Hans Rose, it departed from Wilhelmshaven on September 21, 1916. This U-boat was a fully armed warship that was about the same length as the *Deutschland*, but was considerably less bulky because of its narrower beam and shallower draft.

October 7, 1916 found the *U-53* entering Narragansett Bay, in Rhode Island. The U.S. submarine *D-2* spotted the *U-53*, which was proceeding openly on the surface, and escorted the U-boat into the bay. Rose requested permission from the *D-2* to enter port. The *D-2* granted this permission, then transmitted a coded message to Navy headquarters about the U-boat's imminent arrival. This was no subterfuge on the part of the *U-53*, but a bold and brazen approach, for the U-boat "was flying the German man-of-war ensign and the commission pennant and carrying two guns in a conspicuous position."

Rose requested and was given a berth in the harbor. The U-boat anchored at 2:15 p.m. The commandant of the naval station "sent his aide alongside to make the usual inquiries, but with instructions not to go on board, as no communication had yet been had with the health authorities. At 3 p.m. the commanding officer of the *U-53*, Lieut. Hans Rose, went ashore in a boat which he requested and which was furnished by the USS *Birmingham*. He called on the commandant of the Narragansett Bay Naval Station. He was in the uniform of a lieutenant in the German Navy, wearing the iron cross; and he stated, with apparent pride, that his vessel was a man-of-war armed with guns and torpedoes. He stated that he needed no supplies or assistance, and

War Cruise of the *U-53*

that he proposed to go to sea at 6 o'clock."

That afternoon, before the U-boat's scheduled departure, base commandant Rear Admiral Albert Gleaves sent his aide and half a dozen other officers to board the *U-53*, with instructions to observe and memorize as much about the U-boat as they possibly could. Together they inspected the U-boat – interior as well as exterior – and conversed freely with the German officers (all four of whom spoke English carefully but not fluently) and crew. Later they compiled their mental notes in the form of a report which Admiral Gleaves submitted to higher authorities.

The *U-53* was fitted with four 18-inch torpedo tubes (two forward and two aft). "The tubes were charged and four spare torpedoes were visible. Each pair of tubes was in a horizontal plane. They could carry 10 torpedoes, but part of the torpedo stowage space was utilized to carry extra provisions. The torpedoes were short and they said their range was 2,000 yards. The guns were mounted on the deck, one forward and one aft. The forward gun looked to be about 4-inch and the after one about 3-inch – short and light. The muzzles were covered and water-tight. They had vertical sliding wedge breechblocks, with a gasket covering cartridge chamber and water-tight. . . .

A postcard picture of U.S. Navy officers visiting the *U-53* at Newport, Rhode Island.

"There were three periscopes, which could be raised or lowered, and the platform on which the control officer stood moved with the periscope; one was about 15 feet high above the deck and the others several feet lower. One of the periscopes led to the compartment forward of the engine room for the use of the chief engineer and there their was a periscope for aeroplanes.

"The complement consisted of the captain, the executive and navigating officer, ordnance officer, engineer, electrical and radio officer, and crew of 33 men."

The U-boat was outfitted with a gyrocompass and repeaters. The radio was operated by its own generator. Two wire antennas were strung atop the conning tower. "They claimed to have a receiving range of 2,000 miles." Two masts stood twenty-five feet high; they were hinged at the heel "to lie along the top of the outer surface along starboard close to the vertical side plate of the superstructure."

"There were three main hatchways – one from the conning tower to the central station, one into the forward living space, and the other into the after living space."

Rose claimed that his sole purpose in landing was to deliver a message to the German ambassador, Count von Bernstorff. It was presumed – or perhaps hoped – that this letter contained instructions from Kaiser Wilhelm that "dealt with the attitude of Germany toward peace."

Naval Intelligence officers thought otherwise. They divined Rose's appearance in port as an arrogant attempt to intimidate the Navy – and, by extension, the American people – by flaunting his ability to cross the Atlantic Ocean unassisted and to sneak undetected to within sight of American shores. Intelligence officers did not immediately comprehend Rose's eagerness to authenticate the armed attributes of the U-boat. Much to their chagrin, they learned Rose's reasons for doing so on the following day.

The *U-53* departed as promised – long before international neutrality laws required its departure. The U-

War Cruise of the *U-53*

The conning tower of the *U-53*. (Courtesy of the National Archives.)

boat disappeared in the darkness – but reappeared at dawn in the vicinity of the *Nantucket* lightship. And there the mean depredations commenced . . .

At 5:35, despite the morning haze, the *U-53* fired a shot across the bow of the *Kansan*. The American steamer hove to. According to Rose, "We get in touch with her through wireless in the Morse code. Having been ordered to bring her papers on board, she sends a boat over to us with some little difficulty. Papers show that she is plying between Genoa and Boston with a cargo of soda and no contraband. 6.15 a.m. – The steamer is released and its name and nationality noted. Wireless communication is broken off after its departure. We take a southward course to get in the main line of ocean traffic, and decide not to attack a large steamer that we see, because of the difficulty of saving the passengers."

The next steamer was not so fortunate. The *Strathdene* was registered to a British port and was therefore, according to the conventions of war, a legal target. Rose fired a warning shot across her bow. The *Strathdene* neither hove to nor reduced speed. Rose fired again, and again, and again . . . Finally, after the sixth shot, the *Strathdene* "turns and stops. 7.09 a.m. – The signal 'Leave the ship' is given, because it is clearly established that the *Strathdene* is a British boat. In neither of the two boats lowered over the side does the captain bring any papers. His crew consists of a few white people, but mostly of Chinese and Negroes. We give him the direction and distance to the *Nantucket* lightship, and they sail away. After an hour's progress they are still on the right course.

"7.43 a.m. – A torpedo is shot into the aft hold at a depth of nine feet. The steamer settles in the water but does not sink. We turn our attention to another ship that has just appeared."

Captain Wilson was less laconic in his description of the blast: "The *Strathdene* was hit apparently just forward of 'midships. The explosion was terrific. It appeared as though the entire center went upwards. The funnel collapsed and the masts fell inward. Then came a great burst of flame and she went down, head first." The stern remained afloat.

Meanwhile, the ether was flooded with radio waves from the *Nantucket* lightship. The previous morning, the steamship *Harry Luckenbach* had rammed and sunk the fishing schooner *Victor and Ethan* while most of her crewmembers were away, fishing from dories. When the fishermen returned to the spot at which their mother ship had been anchored, they found nothing afloat but a field of debris. One by one the men rowed their dories thirty miles north to the *Nantucket* lightship. By 8 p.m. every hand was accounted for: seventeen men in fourteen dories. The men spent the night aboard the lightship.

On the morning of October 8, lightship personnel were scanning the misty horizon for a passing steamer that could take the shipless fishermen to port. No sooner did a lightship crewmember spot the *Kansan* through a spyglass than the lightship received a wireless message from the steamer's angry master, wanting to know why he was stopped by a German U-boat. The lightship replied, "Know nothing about submarine," then requested the *Kansan* to take the shipwrecked anglers to Boston. The captain of the *Kansan* was in no

War Cruise of the *U-53*

mood to help. He stated that he had no time to dally, and proceeded on his way.

Lightship personnel heard booming sounds in the distance. They assumed that "some war vessels were engaged in target practice."

"8.03 a.m. – The Norwegian steamer *Chr. Knudsen*, of 3878 tons, is signaled to stop. The captain comes on board with his papers. The steamer is fair game because it is carrying gasoline to London. The captain received my orders to follow me to the steamer *Strathdene* and to leave his boat near that ship, awaiting my return so that I can tell him how to get to the lightship. He is pleasantly surprised by this message. The steamer *Strathdene* is finally sunk by grenade fire.

"9.53 a.m. – The *Chr. Knudsen* has been following us at a distance of four miles, and the crew has now left the ship. We dispatch a torpedo at a depth of twelve feet, but the ship does not sink, and we open artillery fire on her. Still no result, as the heavy cargo of oil runs out through every hole we put in the boat.

"10.54 a.m. – A third ship is sighted to the east, so we fire a second torpedo into the *Chr. Knudsen*, which finishes her."

Once again the deck log of the *U-53* was short on details. The master of the *Chr. Knudsen* did not simply hand over his vessel in resignation. He tried for an hour to outrun the U-boat. He did not stop until three shots were fired over his bow. Rose drew up alongside the Norwegian tanker and demanded the master to launch a boat and bring the ship's papers to him. After this formality, Rose ordered abandon ship. The crew launched two more lifeboats. All three remained together and rowed westward, toward the *Nantucket* lightship.

"11.30 a.m. – The steamer *West Point*, 3847 tons, is stopped by shooting across the bow, and flag signals to leave the ship are raised. The steamer gives distress signals, which have to be interrupted by force.

"11.40 a.m. – Two shots carry away the port antennae of the wireless and silence it. The crew leaves the ship in two boats. A shot in the center of the ship assures us that the boat has no concealed weapons. Its lifeboats surround us, but the captain has brought no papers with him. The ship is empty and headed for Newport News. The lifeboats are allowed to get some distance away, and the ship is then sunk by shell fire."

Ship's carpenter John Robertson told how the U-boat then took both lifeboats in tow. "The tow rope broke three times, and each time the submarine came back and took us on after it had been fixed." Rose let the tow line go when the *Nantucket* lightship came into view.

The SOS that was transmitted by the *West Point* was intercepted by the U.S. Naval Radio Service station in Boston, and was forwarded to the Navy base at Newport for immediate action. Aboard the flagship *Birmingham*, Admiral Gleaves wasted no time in scrambling a flotilla of destroyers, and dispatching them to the *West Point's* transmitted position: 40 degrees 25 minutes north latitude, 69 degrees west longitude (later given as ten miles south of the *Nantucket* lightship).

Racing to the rescue were sixteen destroyers, plus the USS *Melville* (the flotilla tender). The log entry of the destroyer *Winslow* reflects the actions of them all: "Ahead all possible speed under [all] four boilers."

Flank speed for the destroyers was 30 knots. Although the scene of activity was one hundred miles away, the destroyers reached it in less than three and a half hours.

By this time the lightship was choked with survivors: 17 fishermen from the *Victor and Ethan*, 20 crewmembers from the *Strathdene*, and 38 crewmembers from the *West Point*. Not only was there standing room only on the lightship, but there were insufficient provisions to feed an additional 75 mouths and hardly enough water to assuage their thirst. A lightship lookout spotted the steamship *P.L.M. No. 4* passing westward. The lightship's wireless operator requested her assistance. The steamer complied first by picking up a lifeboat which contained another 10 survivors from the *Strathdene*. The *P.L.M. No. 4* then pressed alongside the

War Cruise of the *U-53*

lightship and removed the rest of the *Strathdene* survivors, who were awaiting transportation to New York. This reduced the number of survivors on board the lightship to 55.

"2.45 p.m. – A tanker from New York is warned at the *Nantucket* lightship, and returns to New York.

"3.05 p.m. – A big steamer sails east past the *Nantucket* lightship.

"3.39 p.m. – The lifeboats with the crew of the *West Point* are able to reach the lightship, thanks to half-favoring winds. Our distance from the lightship is now about four miles.

"3.40 p.m. – The Norwegian vessel *Kaspana* ex *Gesto* ex *Bifrost* is stopped with shots across the bow and with signals. The captain brings his papers on board and is allowed to proceed, for the boat is headed for a Norwegian port and the cargo is largely corn.

"4.14 p.m. – We look about for the lifeboats from the steamer *Knudsen*. They are coming west, headed for the lightship. Going over, I reproach the captain for not having gone where I told him to but making me look for him."

Despite his evident anger, Rose took both lifeboats in tow and proceeded toward the lightship. The towing lines broke twice, but Rose returned for the lifeboats on both occasions. He did not cast off the lines until the lightship was in sight and within easy rowing distance. Rose wrote, "The boats are now headed for the lightship."

"4.55 p.m. – We stop the *Blommersdyk* [correctly spelled *Blommersdijk*], a passenger boat of 4850 tons, showing the Dutch flag in several places. It agrees to my demand that it bring over its papers.

"5.15 p.m. – Before this command is executed, a destroyer appears and I submerge. The destroyer is American, and is headed for the *Nantucket* lightship."

The vanguard of the Navy flotilla had arrived. The destroyers were ordered to rescue survivors, but they were given specific instructions from U.S. Naval Command with regard to the U-boat: "Do not interfere with

German submarine and her legitimate prey or send out any message regarding location or movement of submarine." This advice was designed to protect American neutrality. The United States was not permitted to meddle in the war between belligerents.

One of the first to arrive on the scene was the USS *Drayton*, which picked up the men from the *Chr. Knudsen*.

"5.30 p.m. – We rise to the surface. A great number of destroyers are approaching from Newport. The first one [the *Drayton*, then the *Jarvis*] apparently has taken on board the crews of all the steamers sunk in the course of the morning. The *Blommersdyk* sends its boat out again with papers.

"5.40 p.m. – Before the boat has reached us another steamer appears from the east. In order to prevent its coming closer, we shoot across its bows from a distance of three miles, and stop the distress signals from the *Blommersdyk*, whose papers we now look over. We find that the *Blommersdyk* is fully laden with cargo, partly contraband, and is ostensibly headed for Holland. In none of the ship's papers is the destination Kirkwall given. The officers who are sent also do not give me any such information. Only from the health papers and the American certificates on board can I learn that the *Blommersdyk* is headed for that port in the Orkney Islands. On weighing the matter, I see that I must exercise great discretion in deciding whether to sink this boat. Under ordinary circumstances I should be inclined to take the more lenient view, but conditions are such that, in order to be as easy on the feelings of the Americans as possible, I may have to let the other passenger steamer go past, because I cannot make out its nationality in the dark, yet I must bend every effort to give the impression that the presence of American destroyers is not making me submissively renounce my rights; so I decide on the harsher course, and give the signal to the *Blommersdyk*, five hundred yards away, to leave the ship. Preparations to leave are already under way.

War Cruise of the *U-53*

Captain Johan Mohr and 42 crewmembers got away in lifeboats. The destroyer *Benham* picked up the captain and 35 men; the destroyer *McDougal* picked up one lifeboat containing six men.

"Meanwhile, around the two steamers and the *U-53*, sixteen American destroyers have taken their places, so that I have to maneuver with the greatest care. When the lifeboat from the *Blommersdyk* that brought the officers with the papers goes back to its ship again, the *U-53* comes so close to the American destroyer Number 53 that I have to throw both my engines into reverse to avoid a collision. We miss each other by a bare fifty yards, and in backing I upset a tugboat whose crew had no sooner thought themselves safe on the *Blommersdyk* than they had to leave that and board the destroyer 53.

"I have told the Dutch officer that I am giving the crew twenty-five minutes to get off, – that is, until 6.30, – and that he is to lower the flag as a signal that no one is on board.

"Then I sail over to the other passenger ship to look over its papers, and to allow it to proceed on account of its passengers, thinking that it may not have enough lifeboats. I have the signal 'You can proceed' all ready to send when I realize that the boat has already been abandoned and that all the passengers have been taken on board the American destroyers. The searchlight of one of the destroyers lights for a second time on the bow of the steamer, and gives me the opportunity to see a British flag and the words '*Stephano*, Liverpool,' written there. It is a boat of 3449 tons.

"Running between the steamer and the destroyers, I return to the *Blommersdyk*, whose crew has left it but whose flag is still flying. With sirens and cries through my megaphone I make certain that there is no one left on board. A destroyer is lying in its close vicinity, and I request him in the Morse code to give way a little, so that I can sink the ship. He at once complies with my request.

"7.50 p.m. – A torpedo is discharged at a depth of twelve feet into hold number four, and the boat settles but does not sink.

"8.20 p.m. – We shoot a second torpedo into hold number three, and she slowly sinks.

"9 p.m. – The steamer has practically sunk, but a part of one side is still just sticking above the water. American destroyers go close to the wreck. Gradually all the destroyers but two disappear in the direction of Newport, and the *U-53* moves over to the *Stephano*.

"A prize crew is sent on board and sets off time bombs, but the steamer does not sink. Artillery fire is then opened, but we cannot tell what the results are.

"10.30 p.m. – The *Stephano* is sunk with our last torpedo, and we sail east. The two destroyers disappear in the west. Our homeward journey is now resumed. During the night we send a wireless message to the German News Bureau in Washington, giving a full account of the events of the day." (Author's note: I counted six torpedoes fired, not eight.)

On board the *Stephano* were 163 passengers and crew, ranging in age from ten weeks to 75 years. The only fatality was the ship's cat, which was left behind. The *Stephano* was a passenger liner of the Red Cross Line, and was returning to the U.S. from Newfoundland and Nova Scotia. The destroyer *Balch* was standing by during the evacuation of the liner. While she was taking on survivors, one of her launches towed two lifeboats full of people out of the line of fire. The destroyer *Ericsson* rescued eighty-four passengers. Both destroyers then rushed to Newport with their charges.

In one day the *U-53* sank five steamships totaling 20,345 gross tons. Not a single human life was lost, and no one was injured.

It was believed at first that the *U-53* also sank the *Kingston*, but this proved not to be true. Naval authorities later deduced that in radiograms and/or interviews, *Knudsen* was misinterpreted as *Kingston*.

The *Blommersdijk* refused to give up the ghost. Although the stern reposed on the seabed, the bow remained awash and posed a hazard to navigation. The hulk continued to pose a menace fully five days after the attack, when the Coast Guard cutter *Androscoggin* was dispatched to examine the wreck. "Captain Molloy of the cutter was instructed to blow up the wreck or mark it so that vessels may be warned of its presence."

By that time, the air that was trapped in the *Blommersdijk's* forward ballast tanks had escaped, and the ship had disappeared beneath the sea.

The audacious attacks and the arrival of survivors in Newport created a sensation. There were no stories of tragedy, but none of the survivors saved much in the way of personal effects other than money, jewelry, and small items that they could wear or carry on their persons. Gone were their luggage and clothing.

Local residents threw open their doors to the 226 men, women, and children (ten of whom were under three years of age).

Short-term nationwide repercussions were enormous. In fifteen minutes of trading, stock market values dropped $500,000,000. In 1916, half a billion dollars was a great deal of money. This was the largest drop in market value since May 9, 1901, "when Northern Pacific shares were cornered and the rest of the railroad list was slaughtered."

Overnight, marine insurance rates increased from 100% to 500%. "The advance of 500% was for vessels of belligerent countries bound for English, French, and Dutch ports."

Many shipping lines – especially foreign lines whose vessels were registered to belligerent nations – postponed departures "until the danger of attack has passed, either through the withdrawal from New England waters of the submarine or the protection of Allied warships as convoys after leaving the three-mile [territorial] limit." Other vessels changed their courses so as to avoid running afoul of the *U-53*.

A bevy of British warships proceeded northward from Hampton Roads, Virginia (at the mouth of the Chesapeake Bay). They arrived off the New England coast too late to stop the depredations of the *U-53*, but according to more than one survivor's account, suspicions were aroused that there might be as many as three U-boats operating in the vicinity. This proved not to be the case, but American and Allied intelligence could not be certain of that at the time. British airplanes were deployed from Halifax to search the Nantucket Shoals for the *U-53* and its postulated cohorts.

Ironically, the most sordid subject of debate was the legality of the attacks. Despite the outrage of the citizenry, consent among experts in international law was nearly unanimous: the attacks were legitimate. Rose complied fully with the rules of engagement by first firing a warning shot, by determining that the vessel in question was registered to a nation with which Germany was at war, and by allowing sufficient time for the crew and passengers to abandon ship before he took aggressive action. All the attacks took place in international waters.

The sole bone of contention was the sinking of the *Blommersdijk*. The Holland-American Line steamer was registered to a neutral country. The Dutch were indignant, declaring that the sinking "was absolutely illegal and contrary to maritime law. . . . We ask in astonishment . . . what reason the submarine commander could have for torpedoing a neutral vessel with a neutral cargo for the neutral population of Holland?"

The only excuse for sinking a neutral vessel was that she intended to touch at Kirkwall during her passage. The Dutch demanded that a strong protest be sent to the German government.

Diplomatic protests generally accomplished little if not nothing. They were empty and self-indulgent boasts that appeased none but the politicians who posted them. Wimpy American President Woodrow Wilson had been bleating to Kaiser Wilhelm for "strict accountability" since the sinking of the *Lusitania* (on May 7, 1915), as a result of which 123 Americans were killed (of a total of 1,198 fatalities). The Kaiser neither apologized nor promised restitution. Even if he had, all those innocent civilians would still be dead.

War Cruise of the U-53

Quite the contrary, Germany gloated over the depredations of the *U-53* in no uncertain terms. The government published encomiums with regard to U-boat warfare, and praised Rose for his prowess. To accomplish that one-day blitz against Allied shipping, the *U-53* spent more than a month in travel time: sixteen days for each crossing of the Atlantic Ocean.

Germany was bent on world domination. The sinking of enemy vessels, and the presumptuous intimidation of the American government, were but steps toward a grander goal. Germany treated foreign citizens as if they were bugs to be crushed under the heel of Teutonic superiority. There was no need to apologize for lebensraum. The depredations of the *U-53* constituted a dare which the U.S. government was yet unwilling to take.

The consequential Mexican taunt was right on the mark: "Now that the sinking of merchant vessels menaces the lives of hundreds of American citizens the Government should act energetically, because otherwise Mexicans will be led to believe that the militia and guns of the Americans are used only in demonstrations of force against the weak and not against all nations equally, as justice and right dictate."

The *Blommersdijk* proved to be a sticky thorn in the side of German aggression. An international tribunal decided that the Dutch freighter had been wrongfully sunk. Rather than antagonize neutral nations, Germany agreed to pay damages to the Netherlands for the loss of the ship and her cargo of grain.

In retrospect, the depredations of the *U-53* proved ultimately counterproductive in the achievement of its purpose. Each sinking was a straw that swayed public sentiment against the Central Powers. The seven-day wonder faded from editorial newsprint, but not from indelible American memory. The spontaneous combustion of anger led to long-term resolve to side with the Allies, in order to vanquish the enemy "over there" before that enemy could expand its scheme in the pursuit of global conquest.

SECOND MERCHANT CRUISE OF THE *DEUTSCHLAND*

The *Deutschland's* second merchant cruise was almost anticlimactic.

The submarine departed from Wilhelmshaven on October 8, 1916. The trip started auspiciously when the submarine encountered a fierce storm in the North Sea. Waves washed over the low conning tower and soaked the lookouts. Water cascaded down the open hatchway during watch changes. Seas slammed against the hull so hard that the anchor was knocked loose. The anchor crashed against the hull and "started some of the plates." It took two hours for the crew, working under horrendous conditions and in danger of being overboard, to secure the anchor.

Water seeped through the damaged plates and threatened to inundate the batteries. When salt water mixed with battery acid it formed deadly chlorine gas, so it was crucially important to keep the bilge pumps running constantly.

The storm lasted for four days. By that time the men were exhausted. The submarine had been unable to dive, so as to escape the severe surface turbulence, because of the damaged hull plates. Koenig feared that the additional pressure at depth would increase the influx of water, and that the pumps would not be able to keep up with the flooding.

After the storm abated, and the sky cleared enough to take a sextant sighting, Koenig fixed his position for the first time in nearly a week. Total forward progress since his previous fix was barely one nautical mile! The *Deutschland* had been battered backward nearly as far

Second Cruise of the *Deutschland*

as its diesel engines had been able to propel it forward.

By October 26, working in calm seas, the crew managed to patch the leaks in the hull plates – at least temporarily. There were no guarantees that the patches would hold at depth.

On the afternoon of October 31, the *Deutschland* submerged to periscope depth and entered Long Island Sound. It surfaced in nighttime territorial waters. Koenig illuminated the submarine's navigation lights. The low profile disguised the true character of the lights to an approaching dredger. A collision was barely averted as both vessels turned hard astarboard and slipped past each other within spitting distance.

The *Deutschland* dropped anchor off the Thames River. After midnight, the Eastern Forwarding Company's steamer *Efco*, which had been detailed to await the submarine's arrival, located the *Deutschland* at its temporary anchorage. She put aboard a health officer who inspected the vessel and collected its papers. He waved quarantine, and instructed Koenig where to dock.

At 2:30 a.m., on November 1, the *Deutschland* docked at the State Pier in New London, Connecticut. Once again the submarine was surrounded by vessels and barriers that prevented the few scores of reporters and curiosity seekers from getting any more than a glimpse of the hull – and then only when the gate was opened for official business. A special detail from the New London police department was assigned to guard the State Pier.

The *Deutschland* was kept under surveillance and her crewmen were held under close scrutiny throughout the time the submarine was docked in New London. Koenig and his officers and crew mostly remained aboard the *Willehad*, an interned German liner that was docked next to the submarine.

The mood of the press was somber. Most citizens looked upon the U-boat with cold indifference if not with open hostility. Koenig observed firsthand how the recent depredations of the *U-53* had altered the American outlook irrevocably. The German warning was plain: fight against us and we will ravage the merchant fleet in your home waters.

Whereas the U-boat had sought to instill a sense of intimidation, it had fomented alienation instead. Americans do not take threats lightly. History has proven – and continues to prove – that Americans react strongly to threats of foreign aggression: not by hiding their collective heads in a hole, but by harsh offensive action. Sentiment for the Central Powers was swaying toward the Allies.

It did not help matters that local stevedores were not hired to unload the submarine's cargo. Instead, the Eastern Forwarding Company imported black dockworkers from Baltimore. This action created a stir throughout the community. Violence was threatened; a picket line was intimated. Koenig hastily explained that these laborers were in the employ of the company, and were the same ones who had transferred the *Deutschland's* cargo in Baltimore.

As before, a group of U.S. Navy officers was detailed to examine the submarine. This group – thirteen in number – was tasked not just with establishing that the *Deutschland* was unarmed, but with ascertaining as much as possible about the submarine's design, construction, machinery, and so on. They arrived en masse on November 2 to conduct their examination.

This was not a cursory examination like the one that was conducted in Baltimore. These officers – and their superiors who had dispatched them – were suspicious of the true nature of the submarine. They wrote a massive report that included detailed drawings of the submarine's layout.

The senior officer of the group was Commander Yates Stirling. His astute comments were particularly telling: "The vessel could be quickly converted into a commerce raiding submarine by the mounting of several guns on the non-watertight superstructure housing within the superstructure; a certain amount of stiffening would be required. The vessel could also be readily converted into a mine-laying submarine, launching the

Second Cruise of the *Deutschland*

mines from the superstructure deck; the watertight hatches are large enough to pass a mine sufficiently large to do considerable damage.

"Furthermore, the *Deutschland* could act to a limited extent with its present equipment as a tender for several submarines. The cargo space inside the pressure hull could be utilized for the stowage of spare parts and supplies. In addition to 150 tons of fuel oil carried in the fuel tanks, several hundred more tons of fuel oil could be carried in one or more of her ballast tanks. The *Deutschland* could act, therefore, in the capacity of a supply ship for war submarines within the limit of its oil capacity, thereby permitting war submarines to remain a longer time on operating grounds than they could remain with supplies and oil ordinarily carried by themselves."

Shortly after midnight, in the wee hours of November 3, one *Deutschland* crewmember created a serious diplomatic problem when he got drunk in a local bar, assaulted a female patron, and pulled a knife on Lloyd Blanchard, a waiter who tried to protect the woman. The sailor slashed Blanchard across the arm. The sailor's companion prevented further bloodshed by dragging his inebriated friend out of the door and back to the compound.

The police, the bandaged waiter, and a rabble of reporters descended on the dock shortly afterward. Koenig invited Blanchard and the police inside the compound. Koenig suggested a payoff to quell any potential problems. Blanchard accepted the money and went away somewhat mollified.

Meanwhile, the $3 million cargo of dyestuffs and pharmaceutical products was unloaded and stored in the adjacent warehouse. The *Deutschland* also carried two other items of particular interest, to be delivered to mainland recipients. One was an English translation of *Voyage of the Deutschland*. The manuscript was rushed to the Hearst's International Library Company, in New York City. The publishing house wasted no time in typesetting and printing the book for local consumption. The American edition was on sale to the public before the end of the year.

The other item was more ominous because of its clandestine nature: new secret military codes for the German ambassador, Count Johann von Bernstorff. Oberleutnant zur See Franz Krapohl personally delivered these codes to Bernstorff in Washington, DC, along with a quantity of mail that was locked in six diplomatic pouches.

Although the pomp and circumstance of the Baltimore visit was noticeably absent, Koenig was occasionally treated with respect. Some important visitors were invited into the compound. One photograph shows Koenig shaking hands with New London Mayor Rogers.

The highlight of regard occurred on November 9. According to a newspaper account, "Fully two thousand persons attended a reception in the Municipal Building tonight in honor of Captain Koenig of the merchant submarine *Deutschland* and his crew. Officers of the Eastern Forwarding Company and members of the crew of the *Willehad* also attended. A gold watch, bearing the seal of the city, was presented to Captain Koenig, and his men received silver match cases and fountain pens."

Although visitors were not permitted through the gate onto the dock in order to see the German submarine, a great number of people poured into the city in hopes of catching a glimpse of some of its crew. The coffers of local vendors swelled with the consequential income.

After the inbound cargo was offloaded, the black dockworkers struggled with the outgoing freight. According to the newspaper, "It consists of nine carloads of nickel, averaging forty tons to a car, and ten carloads of crude rubber, averaging eighteen tons to a car, making a total shipment of 540 tons. In addition to this material the *Deutschland* now has in her hold three carloads of a chemical known as chromium and one carload of vanadium, both used in the process of hardening steel."

Second Cruise of the *Deutschland*

The cargo also included some six tons of silver valued at $140,000.

"There still remains in the warehouse of the Eastern Forwarding Company of New London a consignment of over 400 tons of crude rubber and 200 tons of refined nickel, which is apparently stored for export by another submarine."

The "other" submarine was the *Bremen*, which had failed to make its appearance.

One hundred tons of diesel fuel was transferred from the *Willehad* to the *Deutschland*, and an additional twenty-five tons were delivered in a railroad tank car.

Because of the threat of British warships patrolling beyond the three-mile territorial limit, Koenig was understandably mum about his actual date and time of departure. He was not making any announcements. Although he finally slunk away ignominiously like a thief in the night, this was the most prudent action that he could have taken.

It was 1:30 in the morning of November 17 when the *Deutschland* slipped her mooring cables and proceeded into the Sound through a blockade of press boats. It was escorted by two tugs that were owned by the T. A. Scott Company, of New London: the *T. A. Scott, Jr.* and the *Cassie*.

The *Deutschland's* unannounced departure was marred by an unfortunate incident that proved to be a portent of terrible things to come.

Preceding the submarine was the *T. A. Scott, Jr.*; following was the *Cassie*. The procession headed eastward along Fishers Island Sound. All three vessels were showing navigation lights. "The *Deutschland* was making ten knots when the trio neared Race Rock, off the end of Fisher's Island in Long Island Sound. The tug swung to port to make the passage between the rock and the island, when the full force of the flood tide brought her to a dead standstill for the few seconds it would have taken her to regain her momentum against the opposing flow of the water which runs swiftly through the narrow gut. The *Deutschland*, not yet arrived at the point where she, too, would have ported her helm, slid dead ahead and an instant later she sliced straight through the bow of the tug.

"Six men were aboard the *T. A. Scott, Jr.*: two captains, an engineer, a fireman, a deckhand, and a cook. Captain Hans Hinsch was from the North German Lloyd liner *Neckar*. He was 'in charge of the practical end of the submarine enterprise.'

"Captain Hinsch stood on the deck of the tug, behind the pilot house, a megaphone in his hand and keeping a sharp lookout for intruders. Suddenly the submarine struck the tug and the latter went to the bottom in three hundred and fifty feet of water, carrying her crew of five men with her. Hinsch jumped into the water, but the others had no chance."

Captain Hinsch's peril was acute, for he could not swim. "Again and again he sank, but each time the buoyancy of his heavy clothing brought him to the surface. There he would tread water until gravity once more pulled him below."

The *Deutschland*, having whistled a warning, backed away in an attempt to avoid the collision. "Captain Koenig and two of his crew were on deck when the crash came, but none of them was jarred enough to be thrown off his feet. The *Cassie*, crowding her engines to the utmost, raced to the rescue, lowering her small boat as she reached the spot where the *Deutschland* was sweeping the sea with her searchlight. The sea was calm and the moon gave light enough to make small objects visible. Albert Mix, Assistant Superintendent of the Scott Company, a local wrecking concern, leaned out of the boat, while those manning it fought hard to keep it still in the sea. Mix flung a life preserver and Hinsch grabbed feebly and just managed to close his hand over it. An instant later, half drowned, he had been lifted into the boat, suffering from exposure."

The *Deutschland* and the *Cassie* lingered in the area for the next two hours, hoping to find other victims afloat. Hinsch was the sole survivor.

"The stem of the *Deutschland* had been warped and

Second Cruise of the *Deutschland*

twisted by the impact. Her plates were strained and some rivets were torn loose."

The damaged submarine put back to New London.

The Steamboat Inspection Service held an inquiry. The populace wanted to believe that the German submarine was at fault. Indeed, in most maritime cases, the following vessel is held responsible in the event of a collision. But in this case there were mitigating circumstances. The tug swung out of control – admittedly, through no fault of hers – and failed to signal her turn to port. In essence, she turned unannounced into the path of the oncoming submarine that she was escorting. Captain Koenig and the *Deutschland* were found blameless.

Nonetheless, the Eastern Forwarding Company notified the T. A. Scott Company that "all damage would be settled." This despite the fact that the tug was fully insured by the Travelers Insurance Company of Hartford, Connecticut "against any damages for injuries or deaths of employees that may be awarded by the Connecticut Compensation Commission."

Neither the facts in the case nor the assurances for compensation deterred the families of the deceased from acting in true American fashion by filing suits for wrongful death against the German submarine. "Claims for damages amounting to $212,000 have been filed against the vessel and cargo."

Nothing came of the suit.

"A portable forge was rushed to her pier, experts were summoned, and the task that officials of the company declared would occupy a week or more was got under way."

After these dockside repairs, the *Deutschland* resumed her voyage on November 21.

The *T. A. Scott, Jr.* has the dubious distinction of being the first American vessel to be sunk by a German submarine off the U.S. eastern seaboard. She was only the first of many.

LIBERTY BOND CRUISE
OF THE
UC-5

The *UC-5* was a mine-laying submarine that had an exemplary history of success during its short period of operation in the North Sea. It made twenty-nine forays in less than a year. Its mines sank thirty-one vessels and damaged four others, for a total loss of more than 37,000 tons.

The worst casualty was the British hospital ship *Anglia*. She was transporting 390 wounded soldiers to Dover when she struck a mine off Folkestone Gate. The vessel sank in fifteen minutes. Despite prompt assistance from rescue vessels in removing the wounded passengers and crew, more than a hundred souls were consigned to a watery grave.

The *UC-5* was small as submarines go: it measured 111 feet in length, and had a narrow beam of 10 feet. Top speed was 6.5 knots on the surface, 5.6 knots submerged: a virtual slowpoke with a range of only 910 nautical miles. It was armed with six mine tubes, each of which held two mines, one above the other. For close-quarter defense it was fitted with a machine gun on the conning tower.

On its final cruise, the *UC-5* was under the command of Oberleutnant zur See Ulrich Mohrbutter. The night of April 27, 1916 found him trying to maneuver the U-boat to a favorable position for planting his mines off the British coast. Poor visibility, variable tides, and vessel movements conspired to drive him off his course.

Near midnight, the U-boat abruptly ground to a halt on Shipwash Shoal. Mohrbutter attempted to free the stranded submarine, but to no avail. The tide continued to rip until it tipped the hull partially onto its port side. Mohrbutter called for help on the wireless trans-

Liberty Bond Cruise of the *UC-5*

mitter.

Meanwhile, the British torpedo destroyer *Firedrake* appeared on the scene. She spotted the unidentified vessel on the sandbank, and approached to lend whatever assistance she could offer. What the lookouts mistook for an upside-down union jack flying from the masthead was not a signal of distress, but a German naval ensign. The *Firedrake* trained her guns on the beleaguered German submarine and proceeded to take the U-boat as a prize of war.

With his position untenable, Mohrbutter ordered his crew to set scuttling charges to destroy the U-boat so as to avoid capture. The submarine could not sink because it was resting high and dry, but it could be damaged enough to make it impossible to salvage.

Mohrbutter destroyed his deck log, war diary, signal books, and navigational charts. Seven demolition charges did considerable damage to the hull and interior workings. One charge blew out the Kingston valve and a portion of the hull. Another charge blew a large hole in the bottom of the hull. A third charge created several small punctures in the pressure hull. The crew set about destroying the machinery and instruments with revolver shots.

A postcard picture of the *UC-5* in captivity.

An armed boarding party from the *Firedrake* approached the U-boat in a whaler. The Germans laid down their weapons, and surrendered. Mohrbutter and seventeen crewmen were taken as prisoners of war, and transported to the *Firedrake* in the whaler.

A graphic account of subsequent events was published in newspapers on both sides of the Atlantic. "An attempt to investigate the damage was frustrated by the presence of thick, black gases and about two feet of water, but later expert examination showed that, although the submarine had laid no mines, two had been released by the force of the explosions and were foul of the bottom of the vessel. Contact between the horns, which jutted out all around the mines, and the plates of the vessel would have exploded enough to sink a battleship, and it was an act of heroism on the part of a young officer that rendered the submarine capable of being brought in as a prize.

"The officer went down in a diving suit and made the mines safe by detaching the detonators, afterward securing them in such a position that the salvers could work in comparative safety. After seventeen days she was brought into an east coast port and put on public view off the Temple Pier, Thames Embankment."

Navy personnel conducted a thorough examination of the workings of the submarine. "The captured submarine appeared to have been one of those transported in sections from Germany and put together on the Belgian coast. Her four sections are plainly marked, the hull being divided into three and the conning tower constituting the fourth part. The seams are rather roughly finished, and point to rapid assembling or none too skillful workmanship. A mere minnow in size compared with the 'big fish' possessed by both the enemy and ourselves, the *UC-5* was fitted only for mine laying.
. . .

"The whole forward section is occupied by the steel launching tubes, and they were worked either automatically from the conning tower or by a hand lever situated between the wall of each tube and the side plates of

Liberty Bond Cruise of the *UC-5*

Cutaway diagram of the *UC-5*. (From *Scientific American*.)

the ship. She was fitted with a sixteen horse power Diesel engine, driving a single screw. . . .

"A visit to the interior of the submarine was a rather disappointing experience, for her late occupants had wrecked her pretty effectively before giving themselves up. The periscope lenses and compasses had apparently been smashed with a hatchet, while revolvers had been fired into the mechanism at various other points. Rust and muddy sediment had coated everything that survived, and gave the impression of an underground cave rather than the compact mechanical model which every submarine has to be. At no point was it possible for a man of average height to stand erect. . . .

"There are one or two clever minor characteristics in the design of the *UC-5*, which have been noted by our own experts. One of them consists in the fact that every projection on deck is capable of fitting into a socket flush with the plates, so that when the ship dives her sides are smooth and offer no untoward resistance to the water."

In October 1917, the *UC-5* and a British tank were transported to the United States aboard a steamship. The hull of the U-boat was divided into three sections for ease in lifting. Their arrival was accompanied by great fanfare and publicity. According to one account:

"After the three parts of the submarine have been lifted ashore by cranes, they will be shown in a great procession headed by a brass band on Saturday morning [October 20]. Each section of the craft will be transported on a huge, specially constructed truck, drawn by forty-eight horses. The first truck will bear the bow of the boat, weighing thirty tons. The next will carry the mid-section, which weighs forty-five tons, and the third will carry the stern, a weight of thirty-seven tons.

"Because of the great weight of the three loads, the route had to be tested to make sure of the strength of the pavements over which the load was to pass. Several city ordinances regarding traffic have been nullified temporarily to make it possible to reassemble the submarine on dry land in Central Park. The trucks will move south to Manhattan Street, across Manhattan Street to 125th Street, along 125th Street to Seventh Avenue, and on Seventh Avenue to 110th Street. Then the forty-eight horses will drag their loads, the greatest which have ever been dragged along New York streets, to the Sixty-sixth Street entrance to Central Park and from there to the site in the meadow [Sheep Meadow], where the three parts are to be put together. Here Mrs. Guy Emerson, wife of the Director of Publicity of the Liberty Loan Committee, will re-christen it on Saturday, changing its name to the 'U-Buy-A-Bond.'

"A crew of Liberty Loan salesmen will be put on board, and the Kaiser's former sea terror will be transformed into one of the great factors in the Liberty Loan drive. After it has been docked in the sheep pasture, the U-boat will be opened to the public. Admission will be free to those displaying Liberty Loan buttons or otherwise proving that they are Liberty-bond holders. The Park Department has constructed a wooden stand, from which the submarine may be viewed."

And it came to pass.

The U-boat was re-examined, this time by Penni, Davis, Marvin & Edmunds: a firm of patent attorneys

Liberty Bond Cruise of the *UC-5*

From *The Illustrated History of the War.*

The mine-layer UC5 was exhibited in New York as an object-lesson in piracy and as a stimulus to subscriptions to the Liberty Loan. These official photographs show the submarine being drawn through New York, and (right) being unloaded at 132nd Street, N.Y.

that represented the Submarine Boat Corporation. William Hammatt Davis "of the firm mentioned, who has devoted years to the study of submarine patents and mechanism," conducted the examination, and "submitted a highly technical report on the subject to the Submarine Boat Corporation." He said, "His examination gave positive proof that Germany had been 'stealing Yankee brains and ingenuity and turning them against us.'"

The lawyer's findings made "charges of direct stealing by the German Government and the Krupps of patents issued to the late John P. Holland, who with the late Isaac L. Rice, formed the Holland Torpedo Boat Company" (which later became the Submarine Boat Corporation).

Davis said, "The 'lighter-than-water' principle embodied in the Holland patents 'had been snatched brazenly in all its ramifications.' It was taken for granted yesterday among those meeting the investigation that practically all of Germany's submarines – both of the offensive and mine-laying types, were built from designs prepared by Mr. Holland, and for which no remuneration had been made."

Davis specified six charges as follows:

"Steal No. 1. Design of boat almost duplicates that of the Holland type of submarine built for the United States Navy by the Electric Boat Company, even down to the characteristic spindle shape and non-water tight

The *UC-5* in Central Park. Note the staircases between the disjointed sections. (Courtesy of the Library of Congress.)

Liberty Bond Cruise of the *UC-5*

superstructure.

"Steal No. 2. The degree of submergence controlled by horizontal rudders located at bow and stern. These bow rudders are identical with the Holland type as to location, size, function, &c.

"Steal No. 3. Provisions for regulating buoyancy of boat. In the centre is a ballast tank of considerable size to which water can be admitted through a Kingston valve in the bottom of the hull. With this tank filled, buoyancy of boat is greatly reduced, allowing it to float in the so-called 'awash' condition. Tank must be completely filled to function properly, and the most involved mathematical calculations are necessary to work this point out, and was one of the fundamental laws laid down by John P. Holland.

"Steal No. 4. The 'lighter than water' principle has been snatched brazenly in all its ramifications. This Holland principle is as important to submarines as the 'heavier than air' principle is to the airplane, and is the basis of the good handling qualities of the Holland type of boat.

"Steal No. 5. A ballast tank is located on top of the main ballast tank in vertical alignment with the centre of gravity and centre of buoyancy, another of the Holland fundamental features to which the success of his submarine is largely attributed for by keeping main tank filled and using auxiliary tank for buoyancy adjustment the boat can stand practically still with only the periscope out of water and lie in wait for its prey.

"Steal No. 6. The location of these tanks involve another Holland principle. They are slightly forward of the centre, so that when the ballast tanks are empty and the boat is running on the surface it will 'trim by the stem' – the bow will be higher than the stern to offset the depressing action of bow waves, and when tanks are filled for submerging is automatically brought to an even keel."

Davis told press reporters, "I made the examination of the *UC-5* myself, and compared the design of the vessel and its mechanism with the Holland patents, and found that the Germans had utilized the devices covered by the American inventor's patents. From this it can be readily appreciated that there is nothing superhuman about the German submarines, or their achievements. It is all just plain Yankee acumen represented in the person of John P. Holland."

In the global picture, patent infringement was the least of Germany's transgressions.

Henry Carse, president of the Submarine Boat Corporation, remarked, "When one realizes that the Holland patents were filed in the German Patent Office nearly fourteen years ago, it isn't hard to understand why Germany has been so effective in her U-boat campaign, for she has stolen American brains and American ability to spread her atrocities among nearly all the nations of the world."

The Krupps steel works had rejected "Mr. Holland's offer to sell the submarine plans, but not, it would seem in the light of the latest developments, until the American inventor's ideas had been reduced to blue prints.

"In ordinary circumstances the Submarine Boat Corporation would be in a position to sue for the recovery of vast sums for the infringement or fraudulent use of the Holland patents, but relief in this direction is such a remote possibility that legal actions at the close of the war will hardly be undertaken. . . . It was pointed out . . . that judicial proceedings of any kind would have to be instituted and tried in German courts."

The will, resolve, and optimism of the American people can best be summed up by one man's statement: "What's the use of suing the Kaiser or the Krupps when the war is over? Does anybody suppose that there will be anything left in Germany to pay the big claims the American holders of the Holland patents are entitled to even if the courts there found in their favor?"

By promoting the sale of bonds, the *UC-5* did better deeds for the cause of freedom than it did for the cause of tyranny.

The submarine was scrapped after the war.

WAR CRUISE
OF THE
U-151

On May 1, 1918, in his capacity as liaison, Admiral Sims transmitted the following cablegram to U.S. Naval Intelligence: "Admiralty informs me that information from reliable agents states that a submarine of the *Deutschland* type left Germany about nineteenth April to attack either American troop transports or ships carrying material from the States.

"So far as known the Germans formed conclusions that: Nantucket Shoals and Sable Island direct to Europe.

"Second: Material transports go from Newport News to a point south of Bermuda and then to Azores and thence to destination.

"It is thought that the submarine is taking a northern route across Atlantic."

During the time of the exploits of the *Deutschland* and the disappearance of the *Bremen*, the construction of six additional sister ships was commenced. Germany then had second thoughts about whether merchant submarine service was worth the investment. Construction was halted, and the partially completed hulls were left on the ways until a decision could be made about their disposition.

Germany soon decided to outfit the submarine hulls as warships. They were designated *U-151*, *U-152*, *U-153*, *U-154*, *U-156*, and *U-157*. They were classified after the prototype as *Deutschland*-class U-boats. The *Deutschland* itself was converted from a merchant submarine to an armed U-boat, and was designated *U-155*. At that time, the *Deutschland*-class U-boats were the largest submersible warships in the world.

Each one was fitted with six torpedo tubes (four in

the bow, two in the stern), mines, two guns on deck (one trained forward, one trained aft), and a machine gun on the conning tower. Each could carry twelve torpedoes, forty mines, and fifteen hundred rounds of ammunition for the deck guns.

Fuel capacity was increased from 150 tons to 250 tons by stowing fuel in a ballast tank. The extra fuel greatly extended the range of these U-boats, enabling them to cross the Atlantic Ocean, patrol for several weeks on the American eastern seaboard, and return to Germany without refueling.

Standard complement was eight officers and sixty-five enlisted men.

Sims transmitted additional advice on May 15: "Information contained in this cable is given to me by the British Admiralty and is necessarily somewhat paragraphed for transmission, but I have every reason to believe it is authentic. There appears to be a reasonable probability that the submarines in question may arrive off the United States coast at any time after May twentieth and that they will carry mines.

"English experience indicates the favorite spot for laying mines to be the position in which merchant ships stop to pick up pilots. For instance, for Delaware Bay the pilots for large ships are picked up south of *Five Fathom Bank* Light Vessel. This in our opinion is one of the most likely spots for a submarine to lay mines."

Sims added on his own account: "There are circumstances which render it highly important that nothing whatever should be given out which would lead the enemy even to surmise that we have had any advance information concerning this submarine, even in the event of our sinking her, and that such measures as are taken by the department be taken as secretly as possible and without public disclosure of the specific reasons."

It seems that Sims wanted to protect the spies that were furnishing information, and to prevent the Germans from concluding that British intelligence was

War Cruise of the *U-151*

intercepting and decrypting their coded messages.

Sims' intelligence was borne out by actual sightings that served as tracking points of the U-boat's westward progress. On May 15, the British steamer *Huntress* escaped a torpedo attack at latitude 34° 28' north, longitude 56° 09' west. On May 19, the American steamship *Nyanza* radioed that she was being shelled at latitude 38° 21' north, longitude 70° west (about 300 miles off the coast of Maryland). Later on May 19, the American steamship *Jonancy* radioed that she was being shelled about 150 miles off the coast of Maryland. On May 21, the Canadian steamship *Crenella* sighted a U-boat at latitude 30° 50' north, 73° 50' west (about 80 miles off the Maryland coast). The U-boat fired six shots at the *Crenella* but registered no hits before the steamer escaped.

Naval intelligence collated this information on a continuous basis. By this time in the war – thirteen months after the declaration – most U.S. Navy capital ships were escorting eastbound convoys or were operating in the European theater in a support capacity. The American coast was poorly defended by a scattering of aged destroyers and small patrol boats that were thinly stretched along a thousand miles of shoreline.

Interdiction seemed unlikely.

Navy section bases were ordered to be on the alert. Naval vessels west of 40 degrees west longitude were ordered to proceed blacked out at night, and to deploy their paravanes whenever possible. (A paravane was "a device equipped with sharp teeth and towed alongside a ship to cut the mooring cables of submerged mines.") Submarine chasers were deployed to the areas where the U-boat had been spotted.

Under the command of Korvettenkapitan Heinrich von Nostitz und Janckendorf, the *U-151* reached the American coast on the night of May 24. Mines were stowed on its upper deck. Under cover of darkness, these mines were laid offshore of Cape Henry, Virginia, at the mouth of the Chesapeake Bay.

During the operation – with mines still secured to the outer deck – the U-boat submerged quickly to avoid a patrol boat, and slammed into the bottom at a depth of 45 feet. It surfaced unharmed and undetected, maneuvered for position, deployed its latent armament, then departed. On the way out to sea it was forced to dive in order to avoid an incoming warship that unknowingly approached the U-boat at high speed.

The U-boat announced its presence on May 25 by firing a shot across the bow of the 3-masted schooner *Hattie Dunn*.

Captain Charles Holbrook held no suspicions when he heard the shot. He never expected to see a U-boat barely twenty miles off the *Winter Quarter* lightship. When he noticed the U-boat approaching, he ingenuously thought that it was an American submarine. Not until the U-boat drew alongside the schooner did he comprehend the terrible reality that war had reached the eastern seaboard.

Von Nostitz must have been angry at Captain Holbrook's apparent ignorance, for he asked the schooner's skipper if he wanted to be killed. Captain

The gun is aimed at the *Hattie Dunn*. (Courtesy of the Naval Photographic Center.)

War Cruise of the *U-151*

Holbrook explained about the mistaken identity.

Captain Holbrook later deposed, "The second officer in command came aboard and demanded my papers and articles and gave us ten minutes to leave the vessel, and he obtained the articles and papers and also took the vessel's chronometer. There were four or five other Germans that boarded the Schooner and they took off the forward hatch and placed a bomb in the forward hold on the port side and also hung a bomb on the outside of the port side of the vessel.

"In the meantime, the Commander of the submarine sighted a four-masted Schooner, named the *Hauppauge*, approximately three (3) miles away and proceeded immediately to destroy the *Hauppauge* and in the meantime, the German officer in command of the *Hattie Dunn* together with his boat crew left to complete the destruction of the Schooner *Hattie Dunn*, and I together with my crew of six men beside myself, was ordered into my vessel's boat and one German who was fully armed was placed in the boat with us. Then the German officer who was in command of the boats proceeded toward the submarine, which was approximately three (3) miles away and after we had been rowing about ten minutes and about two or three hundred yards away from the Schooner *Hattie Dunn* the bombs exploded causing the vessel to settle by the head and when last seen the stern was protruding out of the water and the box was submerged."

Thus the *Hattie Dunn* earned the dubious honor of being the first vessel to be sunk by enemy action in American waters since the War of 1812.

Captain Holbrook: "Then we rowed three miles and then we were taken alongside the submarine and the things taken out of our boat, the plug pulled out, and a man with a hatchet got in and stove one plank down through the bottom and we were ordered below."

The captain and crew were taken aboard the U-boat and held as prisoners.

Captain Holbrook was given a receipt for his vessel, which read (in translation), " 'Protocol' On May 25th,

1918, at 10:10 A.M. the American 3-masted schooner "Hattie Dunn" K C P M [the vessel's signal letters] was destroyed by his Majesty's submarine at 37 24' North latitude and 75 05' West longitude. The Commanding Office, v. Nostitz, Naval Captain."

This location lay off the coast of Virginia, slightly south of the eastern extension of the Maryland border.

The captain and crew of the *Hauppauge* were treated in similar fashion. Captain Sweeney, master, sighted the U-boat from a distance of five miles, and heard three shots. He elaborated: "We tacked ship and headed in about northwest for the shore. This brought us broadside to the German submarine, who immediately fired a shot which landed about 225 feet away. We kept going at a speed of about 4 or 5 knots, and a second shot was fired, which passed through the ship's side about 5 feet above the water; a third shot passed through the vessel's wake about 75 feet astern. The shots were fired in sequence of about four or five minutes. We stopped the schooner in latitude 37° 27' N., longitude 75° 09' W. and shortly after the submarine came close to us. An officer aboard the submarine called to us:

" 'Leave your ship immediately.'

"The submarine then pulled away from the ship, 50 feet or more, and ordered us to come alongside. We obeyed and went aboard. The commanding officer asked me for the ship's papers, and when I told him they were on the ship he replied:

" 'Well, we have to have the papers.'

"They took me back to the schooner for the papers; they also took three bombs with them which they placed aboard the *Hauppauge*. We had just returned to the submarine when the bombs exploded and the *Hauppauge* sank at 11.30 a.m.

"There were no casualties. . . . Upon boarding the submarine we found the crew of the *Hattie Dunn* sunk a short while before."

Captain Sweeney was given a receipt for his vessel; the receipt was nearly identical to the one that was

War Cruise of the *U-151*

given to Captain Holbrook.

Shortly afterward, the *U-151* chanced upon the American schooner *Edna*, Captain C. W. Gilmore. "About half past 1 on May 25 we heard a gun fired and a little later a shell struck in the water about a half a mile from us. We had heard firing inshore about an hour or so before. About a minute after the first shot there came another shot which fell about 50 feet away. I then ran up the American ensign; he had run up a German flag. He was standing about 4 or 5 miles northwest. I hauled down the jibs and hove to. The submarine then came toward us towing a yawl boat belonging to one of the schooners he had sunk before; finally he came alongside. Two German officers and four men came over the *Edna's* railing; they shook hands with us and greeted us just the same as they would have done men on one of their own naval vessels. They ordered us to lower our boat and gave us 10 minutes to abandon ship, saying that they were going to blow her up. They asked me where I was from, where I was bound, and what my cargo consisted of. The officer in charge took me into the cabin and said he wanted me to come below and that he wanted my papers. When we got below he said to me:

" 'Now, don't get excited; if you want to change your clothes and get everything of value to you, we are going to be around here an hour.'

"He took possession of all my official papers, which I had encased in one envelope. When I came from below I noticed that they had placed some little black tubes about 10 inches long and one-half inch in diameter, which looked like sticks of dynamite and which were tied to ropes extended over the side of the vessel abreast of the main hatch.

"Twenty minutes after the German officer and his crew had boarded the schooner, and after I had had time to have everything of value placed in the lifeboat, he ordered us to proceed over to the submarine, and laughingly said:

" 'You will find some of your friends over there.' "

The "friends" were the skippers and crewmembers of the *Hattie Dunn* and *Hauppauge*. There were now twenty-three American prisoners on board the U-boat. The prisoners were well fed. Said M.H. Saunders, mate of the *Hauppauge*, "The food was good. In the morning we had rolls and fresh butter. The butter was fine. The bread was black and came in loaves about 3 feet long. We had cognac nearly all the time." They also had meat stews, roast meat, and wine. They were given cigars to smoke on the upper deck. The men must have been cramped for sleeping space, although no one complained about it.

German bomb crews had much to learn about the robust construction of American schooners, for the *Hauppauge* and *Edna* settled deep but failed to sink completely.

The Clyde Line steamer *Mohawk* discovered the hull of the *Edna* the following day. She took the schooner in tow, but the schooner's towing bitts carried away, so she was abandoned. "Later she was picked up by the tug *Arabian* and towed to Philadelphia, arriving May 29. An investigation made by the aide for information, fourth naval district, disclosed the presence of two holes, 20 to 30 inches in diameter, in the vessel's hold just above the turn of the bilge, evidencing an external explosion. A time fuse was found, the extreme end of

The salvage of the *Edna*. (Courtesy of the National Archives.)

War Cruise of the *U-151*

which had been shattered by an explosion. Thus, the naval authorities received the first visual evidence of the work of an enemy raider."

The *Hauppauge* was later discovered capsized and adrift, and was subsequently salvaged.

Von Nostitz's strategy in not releasing his victims was to keep his presence in American waters unknown, so as not to tip his hand to the Navy until after he transacted other business in secret.

The next piece of business was the sowing of another minefield, this one at the entrance to the Delaware Bay. On May 26, under the cloak of darkness, von Nostitz ordered mine-laying operations to recommence. As before, mines that were stowed on the upper deck were planted in shallow water. The presence of numerous merchant ships caused a few anxious moments, forcing the U-boat to submerge and surface several times.

After this operation, the U-boat worked its way north by running on the surface when no other vessels were in sight, and by running submerged in order to avoid detection after a vessel was sighted.

The other piece of business was cutting underwater telegraph cables. Both Captain Holbrook and Captain Sweeney noticed "a mysterious device on the deck of the submarine" which they later described for naval authorities. Their description matched intelligence reports, which stated, "Submarines 'U-converted mercantile type' are especially fitted with submarine cable-cutting devices."

May 28 found the *U-151* sixty miles southeast of New York Harbor. Prisoners later reported that on that day the U-boat "gave a sudden lurch and listed on beam end." The next time the prisoners were permitted on deck for fresh air, the grappling device had disappeared.

The U-boat had cut two cables from New York: one to Europe and one to Central America. Telegraphic communications were halted for a month or more. The cable ship *Relay* repaired the European cable on June

25. The Central American cable was repaired on July 4.

The *U-151* lurked unseen and, so von Nostitz hoped, unheralded. After working his way north to deploy mines and cut telegraph cables, he planned to proceed farther north to the Gulf of Maine. Thick continuous fog influenced his decision to turn south instead. In this direction he found clear skies. June 1 was spent in reaching a position off the coast of southern New Jersey.

The real coming-out day for the all-purpose U-boat was June 2. This was the day on which the undersea raider successfully mounted one of the most destructive forays of the entire U-boat campaign. With its mines sowed and its cable-cutting mission accomplished, the *U-151* was now prepared to come out of hiding.

Shortly after dawn, lookouts on the *U-151* spotted sails on the horizon. The U-boat changed course in order to overtake the schooner, which turned out to be the *Isabel B. Wiley*. The U-boat fired a shot across the schooner's bow. Captain Thom Thomassen, master of the *Isabel B. Wiley*, gave the order to heave to. The crew hauled down the jibs. Before the U-boat reached the schooner, however, German lookouts sighted a steamship. Without even signaling to the *Isabel B. Wiley* – which could not possibly escape from the much faster U-boat – the *U-151* set a course to intercept the SS *Winneconne*. The steamship was transporting coal from Newport News, Virginia to Rhode Island.

On the *Isabel B. Wiley*, Captain Thomassen accepted his fate fatalistically. "I ordered the steward to get some provisions to put in the lifeboat and directed the engineer to get some oil and gas for the engine. Without waiting orders from the German commander the entire crew got into the lifeboat and we pulled off about 100 yards, waiting for the submarine to return."

The U-boat fired a warning shot across the *Winneconne's* bow. Captain Waldemar Knudsen, master, "tried to make for shore." The U-boat fired again. This

War Cruise of the *U-151*

time the shell sailed overhead and plowed through the rigging, then burst only a couple of hundred yards in front of the steamer. Captain Knudsen then thought better of trying to escape. He gave the order to blow off steam. "The submarine came closer ready for action and then launched a small boat. An officer and two men came on board and gave orders to leave the ship immediately, as they were going to sink her. I asked him how long they were going to give us, and he said he would give us one-half hour. He asked me where the chronometer was, and I told him it was my private property, and he said I could take it. He took the ship's log, ship's register, and ship's papers. We launched the two boats and the crew got in. The chief mate and I were still on board and were under the impression that we were to go aboard the schooner, but he told us to launch the small boat and go alongside the submarine, which we did. He placed four bombs on our ship, one on the fore deck, one on the aft deck, one in No. 1 hatch, and one in No. 3 hatch."

The boats reached a safe distance from the steamer before the fuses burned down and the bombs exploded, at about three minute intervals. The *Winneconne* settled slowly by the stern, then slipped beneath the surface and was gone.

The *Winneconne's* lifeboats hovered near the U-boat like a brood of ducklings next to their mother. They were soon joined by the lifeboat from the *Isabel B. Wiley*. Von Nostitz saw his opportunity to rid himself of the crews of the *Hattie Dunn*, *Hauppauge*, and *Edna*. He ordered his prisoners into the lifeboats, and told them to shove off.

Twelve of the ex-prisoners were distributed among the *Winneconne's* three lifeboats, which were already crowded with the twenty-six men of the steamer's crew. Nineteen men wound up in the *Isabel B. Wiley's* lifeboat: all eight of the schooner's crew plus eleven ex-prisoners (the crew of the *Hauppauge* and the mate of the *Hattie Dunn*). Captain Thomassen: "I informed the captain that I did not have sufficient water to take care of the extra men, and he gave me a large keg of water."

Von Nostitz also gave them provisions.

The Germans returned to the *Isabel B. Wiley*, which had drifted quite a ways off, and offloaded supplies that they needed to fill the larder that had been depleted by their erstwhile prisoners. Then they placed demolition charges on board, and sank her.

The four lifeboats were left to their own devices. Captain Thomassen's lifeboat was the only one equipped with a motor. "I consulted with those in the other three lifeboats and concluded that, as I had the only power lifeboat, it would be best for me to make for shore as soon as possible, with a view of hailing some ship and have them advise the location of the other three lifeboats and to send them help. I instructed the other three lifeboats to remain where they were."

Overloaded with nineteen men, Captain Thomassen proceeded westward at seven knots. The thirty-eight men in the other three lifeboats decided to row rather than to wait. They had not made very much headway when they heard explosions in the distance – the death knells of the U-boat's next victim.

The *U-151* proceeded south. Shortly before noon it came upon the American schooner *Jacob M. Haskell*: Norfolk, Virginia to Boston, Massachusetts with coal. The U-boat fired a warning shot across the bow. According to Captain William Davis, master, "A few minutes later a second shot was fired across the ship's bows and the approaching submarine displayed the international signal 'Abandon Ship.' We made arrangements to abandon, and dropping the boats into the water prepared to take the crew off. While we were doing this, a rowboat containing one officer and six heavily armed seamen rowed alongside. The men came aboard the schooner and the officer demanded the ship's papers, log book, and crew list, which were delivered. The captain then directed the men to hurry and get the crew off. During this time, the bombing party had placed four bombs over the ship's side – two forward, one on each side, and two aft, one on either side.

War Cruise of the *U-151*

The bombs were about 6 inches in diameter and 14 inches in length. They were hung so that the bombs themselves rested about 2 feet under the surface of the water and alongside of the schooner's hull. The men went about their work in a business-like manner: the officer was so polite that he almost got on our nerves. Each seaman was armed with two automatic revolvers and a long, vicious-looking knife."

Although Captain Davis was quoted as stating "boats" (in plural form), in actual fact the *Jacob M. Haskell* was equipped with a single motor launch. It was this motor launch in which the eleven crewmembers made good their escape. The boat was bobbing nearby in the gentle swells when the bombs detonated, one after another. Apparently the Germans did not think that the schooner was sinking fast enough. They pumped a six-inch shell into her hull to speed her demise. The *Jacob M. Haskell* then "disappeared with all sails set. As we were starting on our way, the boarding officer called out: 'Good luck. The New Jersey coast is just 40 miles away. Better go there.' The submarine proceeded slowly on her way due east. Later we heard firing coming from the general direction in which the submarine had proceeded."

The *U-151* later changed course to the southwest, and bore down upon the American schooner *Edward H. Cole*. Like the *Jacob M. Haskell*, she was transporting coal from Norfolk to Boston. By this time it was mid afternoon. Mate Robert Lathigee had the watch. Karl Karlson, the helmsman, called Lathigee's attention to a submarine that began circling the schooner at high speed.

Lathigee: "We both believed it was an American craft with some Naval Reserve cadets on board, who were trying to have some fun with us sailors of the merchant marine. I thought that it would be a good idea to have a little fun with our skipper, who had turned in for a nap in his cabin, and I yelled down the skylight, 'Tumble up on deck lively, Cap! There's a big German submarine close astern, getting ready to attack us.'

Then I took the marine glasses and looked through them at the stern of the U-boat, where her ensign was flapping limply against the short flagstaff. For a moment or two I could not make out her nationality, and then a gust of wind came and blew the ensign straight so that I could see that it was a German flag, and then I shouted in earnest to Captain Newcombe, 'It's no joke this time. By gosh, she is a German submarine!' "

Captain Humphrey Newcombe hurried topside, clearing sleep from his eyes. The U-boat "came up then about 150 feet off us and told us to clear away the boats, as they were going to sink us, which we did. An officer and some of the men lowered a boat from the submarine and came on board and demanded the ship's papers and took them, and while in the cabin he told me we had seven and one-half minutes to clear. His men had already placed bombs on the ship, two on each side, and I believe there were others. He told me to get some clothes and supplies, but we were too busy getting the boats cleared to do it: we had no water or compass in the boat. I went down into the cabin and got a few papers, licenses, barometer, etc., and showed them to the officer and asked if it was all right. He said, 'Sure, go ahead.' We got into the boat and pulled away, and about 16 minutes after we left, the ship sank."

Once again, the use of the word "boats" in plural form was a mariner's convention. Eleven men crowded together on the benches in the schooner's sole lifeboat. They took turns at the oars.

Newcombe: "About an hour after this we were about 4 miles away from the submarine, which had not moved, when the steamer hove in sight. The submarine opened fire, firing five shots. The steamer turned around and headed in the opposite way and stopped. About 15 minutes later we heard an explosion, such as we heard on the *Cole*."

The steamer was the *Texel*, owned and operated by the United States Shipping Board. She was carrying sugar from Puerto Rico to New York. After a warning

War Cruise of the *U-151*

shot passed over the deck forward of the funnel, her master, Captain K.B. Lowry, "proceeded to maneuver the vessel in a manner to elude the enemy as prescribed by the United States Navy Department. . . . I immediately ordered the helm hard starboard, as to bring the aggressor directly over the stern. When the vessel had assumed this position I steadied and ordered all possible speed. The vessel at the time of the attack was running at her maximum speed. A second shot was fired when the vessel had assumed her new position at right angles to her former course. This shell was of the shrapnel variety and exploded on the water to starboard of the vessel."

At this point in the captain's narrative there comes an unexplained circumstance. He thought he saw another enemy submarine surface in front of him. It is certain from German records that the *U-151* was the only U-boat operating in the western Atlantic at the time. The next U-boat on the Atlantic treadmill did not arrive off the American coast until more than one month later. What Captain Lowry actually saw cannot now be ascertained. A third shell struck the water close to the starboard side, and sprinkled the bridge with splinters. The working boat was carried away and the starboard wing of the upper bridge was shattered. Facing an impossible situation, Captain Lowry brought his ship to a halt. He had enough presence of mind to toss overboard the ship's register, the manifest, and the Navy instructions, so these valuable documents would not fall into enemy hands.

Deck Engineer William Laufer described how Able Seaman Patrick Huston remained heroically at the helm during the bombardment. "Pat had a close call on the first shot from the submarine. It tore away one side of the pilot house not five feet from him, and there was a regular hail of shell and splinters over him. But Pat is Irish, and he stuck right at the wheel, keeping the *Texel* nosing right along in her course. The shrapnel crashed all around the pilot house, but Pat stuck until the skipper ordered the engines stopped and he swung around awaiting the arrival of the U-boat skipper and his boarding party. I ran up to Pat and found him cussing a long splinter that had stabbed through the back of his hand well under the skin. He was fighting mad and wanted to take a crack at the Germans."

Huston treated the incident with aplomb, and with a touch of humor that was tempered with mild-mannered anger. "That wheelhouse sure looked like a sieve when I got outside and on deck. Guess I was lucky, but I will get square some time with those birds for what they did to my new serge coat."

The *U-151* circled the *Texel* twice, sidled close to the freighter's stern, then sent a boarding party to arrange for the vessel's destruction. Captain Lowry: "Three bombs were set at the base of each mast; bombs were also set in the engine and fire room, but as to the numbers I can not say. When all the bombs were set, the lieutenant ordered me to leave as they would explode in 10 minutes. As he proceeded to leave, I did as ordered."

The crew of thirty-six (and a pair of kittens) abandoned the freighter in two lifeboats: one under command of the captain, the other under command of the mate. The lifeboats had barely rowed away from the steamer's side when the bombs exploded. The *Texel* went down by the stern while listing to starboard. The time was 5:20 p.m. The *Texel*'s lifeboats shaped a course for the New Jersey shore. An hour later, the captain heard four shots "which probably signified that he [von Nostitz] had encountered another victim."

Let us pause for a moment in order to recap the situation. The score of the *U-151* so far for the day was five vessels sunk. The sea was littered with numerous survivors in lifeboats. There were eight lifeboats in all: one from each of the three schooners that were sunk that day, three from the *Winneconne*, and two from the *Texel*. These lifeboats held the crews of eight vessels (counting those from the attacks on May 25). Thus the number of men cast adrift totaled 112.

At 5:25 p.m., lookouts on the *U-151* spotted another steamship. The U-boat took off in pursuit.

War Cruise of the *U-151*

At 5:30, just when the motor lifeboat from the *Isabel B. Wiley* ran out of gas, the Ward Line steamer *Mexico* hove into the lifeboat's view and effected the rescue of the nineteen men who were waving frantically. The next morning, at 7:30, the southbound *Mexico* transferred the survivors to the northbound *Santiago*, which then transported the men to New York, which they reached at two o'clock on the afternoon of June 3.

This rescue reduced the number of people adrift to 93, occupying seven lifeboats. The *Mexico* wasted no time in sending an alarm about the recent U-boat casualties, and about the other lifeboats in the area. The wireless message was received by shore installations and relayed to Naval authorities. It was also intercepted by the *U-151*. Thus von Nostitz knew at once that his position had at last been compromised.

The steamship that the *U-151* was chasing was the *Carolina*, owned by the U.S. Shipping Board but operated by the New York & Porto Rico Steamship Company. She was proceeding from Puerto Rico to New York with 333 men, women, and children: 216 passengers and 117 crewmembers. Her holds were sweetly laden with sugar. The *Carolina* also intercepted the radio transmission, which gave the position of the attack. Captain Barber, the *Carolina's* master, realized that at that precise moment he was steaming very close to the spot at which the *Isabel B. Wiley* had been sunk.

"I immediately ordered all lights closed down on my ship. I ordered the chief engineer to open her up all he possibly could and steered due west by the compass. . . . I just got my vessel steadied on the new course and scanned the horizon to find the submarine, when I saw the conning tower and two guns on my starboard quarter distant 2 miles. Although the weather was quite hazy at the time, I could make out the outline plainly. She seemed to be rising in the water."

The log of the *U-151* confirmed the captain's description. The U-boat submerged after intercepting the *Mexico's* radio transmission, so as not to give itself away, but continued to stalk the *Carolina* while traveling at periscope depth. Following the liner's radical change in course, the U-boat surfaced and raced at high speed after its intended victim. Shortly after 6 p.m., the *U-151* fired its gun at the retreating steamship. The shot fell short and cleaved the *Carolina's* wake.

Captain Barber: "The second shot went overhead and landed straight ahead about one-half ship's length, the third shot landing quite close to amidships on the starboard side. I had already ordered the chief wireless operator to send out a wireless SOS that we were being attacked by gunfire from a German submarine. After the second shot I stopped my ship, ported my helm, and brought her broadside onto the submarine. I hoisted the signals 'I am all stopped,' and the American ensign.

"Realizing the uselessness of trying to escape, not having the necessary speed, I at the time gave the wireless operators orders to send the foregoing dead reckoning position broadcast, but thinking that if I sent it out he [von Nostitz] would possibly shell the ship, and having many women and children aboard the ship, I recalled the order. Later the chief wireless operator informed me that the submarine had wirelessed under low power the message: 'If you don't use wireless, I won't shoot.' Our ceasing to use the wireless, I presume, was the reason for his stopping firing."

Von Nostitz did not take the captain's action for granted. He jammed the *Carolina's* signal with his own radio. Nonetheless, the *Carolina's* initial transmission was intercepted by the U.S. destroyer *Walke*. The *Walke* relayed the message to Navy shore facilities, and proceeded at twenty-four knots to the scene of the attack. According to the *Walke's* war diary, "The *Carolina's* maximum radio range was ascertained to be 300 miles and her probable position puzzled out of her somewhat garbled SOS as Lat. 39. Long. 73." The *Walke* was then some seventy-five miles north of Montauk, New York. She could not expect to reach the *Carolina's* calculated position until dawn – which, as it developed, was too

War Cruise of the *U-151*

late to render any assistance.

Captain Barber: "After the third shot was fired, the submarine bore down on my starboard bow and when he got nearer I saw he was flying the signal 'A.B.,' abandon ship as quickly as possible. I had already ordered a boat full out and now I ordered all hands to leave the ship. The women and children were put into the boats first and the men entered after the boats were lowered."

The *Carolina* was abandoned in an orderly fashion. Everyone donned life preservers. The passengers proceeded to their lifeboat stations precisely as they had during a previous fire drill. The crew lowered nine lifeboats without a hitch. The tenth boat – lifeboat No. 5 – snagged one rope in the falls while the other rope ran freely through the block. The boat upended and dumped its occupants into the sea. Men and women struggled to remain afloat in the water until they were hauled back on board. One man, who was accidentally left on the ship, jumped overboard and was picked up by the captain's lifeboat.

"After I had seen everyone off the ship into the boats, and after I had destroyed all the secret and confidential papers, I, myself, got into the chief officer's boat, this being the only boat left alongside. Upon clearing the ship's side, about 6:30 p.m., I was ordered by the submarine commander, both in English and by signals with the hand, to make for shore." The last sign of life seen aboard the *Carolina* was a small white dog. He was left behind.

It is interesting to note that many survivors – from all nine vessels that were destroyed by the *U-151* – reported on the ability of the German officers and crew to speak educated English.

Captain Barber: "I collected all the boats near me and moored them head and stern one to the other. Being eventually joined by all the boats except the motor lifeboat and lifeboat No. 5, we pulled to the westward and out of the line of gunfire as much as we possibly could."

Von Nostitz noted in his log, "As the visibility is

decreasing and radio traffic of warships can be heard in the vicinity, it is decided to sink the steamer with torpedo. Port tube fired while on surface. Torpedo turns 4 points to starboard and then to port immediately after leaving the tube, once more to starboard, broached and sank."

Several passengers and crew of the *Carolina* observed the launching of this torpedo, assumed that it struck the ship, and that it was primarily responsible for sinking her.

Captain Barber described the follow-up action. "When the boats were clear, the submarine then ranged alongside the ship on the port side at what seemed a short distance off and at 7.15 fired one shell into No. 2 hold, lower port, as near as I could judge. She then fired another shell into the wireless room and another into the vicinity of my own room behind the pilot house. The submarine proceeded around the ship's bow and seemed to watch her sink from there. The Germans did not board the steamer as far as I could see.

"The ship remained steady about 20 minutes then listed to port, gradually sinking on her port side, and finally sank at 7.55 p.m. with the ensign and signals flying. Great clouds of fire and steam arose as she went down."

At this point the *U-151* diesels out of the picture as far as the present situation is concerned.

The threads that we must follow now are those that weave through the stories of the lifeboats that were left adrift on the broad Atlantic Ocean more than fifty miles from shore. Of the eighteen lifeboats cast to the ocean's caprices by von Nostitz, only one had so far been recovered (from the *Isabel B. Wiley*). But now the word was out that there were survivors to be rescued. Mariners were on the lookout – not only for survivors but also for enemy submarines.

At 8 p.m., the SS *Bristol* picked up the eleven men from the *Edward H. Cole*. Only minutes after the rescue, a state of agitation erupted on board the steamer. Witnesses swore not only that they spotted a German

War Cruise of the *U-151*

U-boat in the distance, and kept it in sight for half an hour, but that it launched a torpedo that narrowly missed striking the retreating steamship. The *U-151*'s log notes no such attack, and, as noted previously, no other U-boats had yet arrived off the American coast. Naval interrogators were at a loss to explain the incident.

This rescue reduced the number of lifeboats left adrift to sixteen: three from the *Winneconne*, one from the *Jacob M. Haskell*, two from the *Texel*, and ten from the *Carolina*. The total number of occupants was 418, all of whom spent the entire night at sea. The *Winneconne*'s lifeboats remained in contact with each other throughout the hours of darkness, as did the two boats of the *Texel*. The lifeboat from the *Jacob M. Haskell* was on its own. Of the *Carolina*'s lifeboats, eight were roped together under the captain's command, while the motor dory took lifeboat No. 5 in tow. At first, the dory's motor would not start. Chief Deck Engineer Christian Nelson transferred from lifeboat No. 5 to the dory, and worked on the motor until he got it going. He remained aboard the overcrowded motor dory. These two boats soon got separated from the other eight.

The weather that day was mild, the winds were light and variable, the sea was intermittently covered by haze. Clear skies and smooth seas continued until midnight, at which time storm clouds moved into the area. The survivors were then exposed to heavy seas accompanied by cold rain and lightning. Severe squalls passed through with irregularity. Waves washed over the gunwales, soaking everyone and making them miserable.

When the storm arose, Captain Barber "ordered the boats to put heads to seas, riding to sea, anchored until the squalls passed. Then we resumed our voyage to the westward, attached in the same manner as before."

During one of these squalls the towing line, connecting lifeboat No. 5 to the *Carolina*'s motor dory, was severed. The motor dory turned around in the splash and spray and, miraculously, located the lifeboat in the dark. The towing line was then re-secured. Later the rope broke again, and once again the motor dory reversed its course and managed to relocate the lifeboat. After the rope broke for the third time, the motor dory overturned in the process of searching for the drifting lifeboat.

Thirty-two people suddenly found themselves fighting for their lives in the middle of a nighttime thunderstorm. Passenger J.M. McCaffery graphically described events leading up to and during the catastrophe. He was especially critical of the crew. "We could not make the Spaniards or Niggers work, they said they had just been working in the hold and were tired, and would not work, or help us. There was also a huge light haired man, one of the crew, I think he was Norwegian or a Swede. He was one of the nineteen of us saved, and he sat on the back seat with the Spanish girls. He would not work either, but just sat with the girls. At night the thunder squall came up, which lasted four hours or more, the wind blew very hard, and our boat turned over at the beginning of it, and we were all thrown into the water. The Purser, the four babies, two women and some of the others were lost immediately. We found one of the Spanish girls that was saved [Elona Donato Virola], clinging to two dead bodies, and an old Frenchman with two life preservers, who was so crazy at this time that he did not know what he was doing, kept taking his life belts off and putting them on repeatedly.

"We could have easily righted the boat had it not been for the niggers and Spaniards. We found them by the aid of the flashes of lightning, which made it continuously light. For a time we would cling to the side of the boat and get it partly bailed out with our caps, without the aid of the niggers and Spaniards, we would then try to get into the boat, all the same side at once, the boat would then upset, this must have happened nearly twenty times. If there had not been so many of them, and if I had had any help I would have thrown them overboard to save the rest of us, as they refused to help. Finally we all got into the boat, but the niggers,

War Cruise of the *U-151*

Spaniards nor the big Swede would [not] help bail the boat out, he would keep with the girls all the time."

McCaffery was obviously suffering from the trauma of his ordeal at the time he gave this statement to Naval examiners, shortly after his rescue. No doubt it must have been a harrowing experience for all, especially for those who were shocked to incapacity by the terrible life-threatening events. Thirteen men, women, and children met their maker during the bitter nighttime travails.

The first of the remaining survivors to be rescued on June 3 were those occupying the motor launch from the *Jacob M. Haskell*. Mate George Gilliatt told the story: "After putting off from the submarine we headed for the New Jersey coast, and passing Barnegat Light in the early evening, made fast to a fish trap about 11 o'clock. We remained there until daylight. During the night a thunder squall came up and we were thoroughly drenched. At daylight we started our engine again and soon sighted the *Grecian*. We raised an oar as a signal of distress and the steamer hove to." They had spent nineteen hours in the lifeboat.

Next to be discovered were the three lifeboats from the *Winneconne*. On board these boats were not only the men from the steamship, but the crews of the *Hattie Dunn* and *Edna*. At 8:30 in the morning, after some twenty-two hours at the oars, they were picked up by the Mallory Line steamer *San Saba* at a point some twenty-five miles off Barnegat. The *San Saba* transported the men to New York, where they arrived that night.

At 11 a.m., Captain Barber "sighted a schooner standing to the northward and sent the second officer's boat to intercept her. We saw her haul down her jibs and heave to. I ordered all the boats to proceed to the schooner which proved to be the *Eva B. Douglas*. Captain G. Launo, Master of the schooner, and his wife and daughter received us with fine courtesy and placed all their supplies and stores at our disposal."

Whether this event falls under the definition of "rescue" is open to debate. The *Carolina's* eight lifeboats held 254 people: 160 passengers and 94 crewmembers. Most of them remained in the lifeboats, which were taken in tow. The schooner's resources must surely have been strained by the presence of so many hungry survivors. The only saving grace was that the *Eva B. Douglas* was provisioned for a six months' cruise to South America.

Later that day, the British steamship *Appleby* came across the *Carolina's* partially flooded motor dory. The nineteen survivors were taken aboard. These people were cold, wet, thirsty, and hungry, having lost all their provisions when their lifeboat capsized in the storm the night before. Off the Delaware breakwater, the survivors were transferred to the pilot boat *Philadelphia*, which transported them to Lewes, Delaware, where they arrived on the morning of June 4.

Meanwhile, both lifeboats from the *Texel* as well as lifeboat No. 5 from the *Carolina* had managed to remain afloat throughout the devastating squalls. The occupants rowed, and rowed, and rowed some more. The general routine was to take one-hour stints at the oars – for the women as well as for the men aboard the *Carolina's* lifeboat. It is difficult to understand why, with the large number of lifeboats spread across so vast an area of ocean, they were not all discovered on June 3. The area was not only a highly traveled shipping lane, but sub chasers and patrol craft had been dispatched to search for survivors and enemy submarines. The fact that these lifeboats were not observed by any of the vessels that were on the lookout also explains how the *U-151* managed to avoid detection. The vastness of the ocean is often underestimated.

Captain Lowry, the *Texel's* master, related the following strange occurrence. "We rowed steadily, seeing nothing, until 11:30 A.M. June 3rd, when a hydroplane came off shore, dropped in the water alongside the boats, asked us who we were, to which I replied that we were survivors of the torpedoed steamer *Texel*. He told me to wait and he would go ashore for help. However, I kept on rowing on my former course throughout the

War Cruise of the *U-151*

day. No help arrived."

The *Texel's* men had by this time run out of fresh water. The only food they had to eat was hardtack.

Frank Nelson, the *Texel's* first officer, described the hydroplane as "a Zeppelin, an airship." He told how the two boats then "got separated, the Captain's boat and mine, and pulled a long way before we joined together again. . . . We burned a blue light to keep together, and the life savers on the beach saw us, but they didn't come out. They stayed on the beach."

Captain Lowry used Absecon Light to guide the boats to shore. At 11:30 that night, the men rowed through the inlet and beached their boats at Atlantic City. They were met by Ensign Kelly, "who provided food and accommodations for the crew during our stay at that port." The survivors had rowed steadily for more than thirty hours.

Nine lifeboats full of *Carolina* survivors spent a second night at sea. For twenty-four hours the *Eva B. Douglas* clawed toward shore against light and variable winds. Not until 11 a.m. on June 4 – one full day after she had taken the *Carolina's* lifeboats in tow – did she drop anchor outside Barnegat Inlet. Captain Barber sent one lifeboat ashore. Chief Officer C. W. Hoffman, who was in command of this lifeboat, was met on shore by Coast Guard personnel. Hoffman explained the situation, then sent a telegram to the *Carolina's* owners, requesting assistance in the form of a tug.

Shortly thereafter, the *S.P. 507* fortuitously appeared from the south. Ensign Thomas Packard, skipper of the Section Patrol boat, offered to tow the *Eva B. Douglas* and the lifeboats to New York. Captain Barber accepted the offer. The entourage did not reach New York until 4 a.m., June 5. By that time, everyone was understandably exhausted from the ordeal. Waiting to greet the weary survivors were the Red Cross "and other relief societies that gathered about the dock. Hot coffee and sandwiches were provided when they arrived at the pier as well as blankets." There were also ambulances, medical aid, and "supplies of every kind."

Private automobiles provided transportation.

The New York & Porto Rico Steam Ship Company felt so grateful for the relief that was furnished to the *Carolina's* passengers and crew, that the company donated $10,000 to the Red Cross.

Now only one lifeboat remained unaccounted for: lifeboat No. 5, under the command of Chief Engineer John McLaren. This was the boat that had dumped its occupants in the water upon launching, and had later been cast adrift from the motor dory when the towing rope parted in the storm.

According to a deposition given by fifteen of the twenty-nine survivors from lifeboat No. 5, "the rope broke and we lost the motor boat then. We didn't see her any more. She went away from us. Then we proceeded under oars, rowing ourselves, and we just kept up to the head of the wind that night. During the night, while we were keeping it to the wind, as we hadn't any definite point, we heard 'Help' at different points. As we raised this lantern there was 'Help', 'Hello', etc., in the water, wherever it was. We couldn't trace it, as we saw no other lights. We had one lantern at that time and as we would lift this lantern we would hear this and we couldn't see, it being so indistinct. We didn't know whether they were in difficulties or what it was. Naturally, seeing this lantern, perhaps they thought we were some ship or something.

"Next morning we went on our course, that is, west. Mr. Johnson suggested to Mr. Lewis, the chief engineer [sic], and the chief engineer decided, and we steered west, a couple of points north at that time. We kept to that course all day and we rowed and rowed, and then last night we decided to row all night, every man to take an hour at the oars or do the best we could, which every man did and tried to do his best, and we kept proceeding all night, the night being very calm and Monday being very calm, too, and Monday night."

The deposition failed to mention one incident that must have lost its importance in the company of more serious events. The drenched survivors were still suf-

War Cruise of the *U-151*

fering from the cold of the night when, on Monday morning, as if by divine intervention, a bundle floated past the lifeboat. A man pulled the bundle aboard with a boat hook. It was a bundle of blue chambray shirts. Even though the shirts were wet, they provided an extra layer of protection against the elements. The people – men and women alike – wasted no time in donning their newfound garb.

"Between two and four this morning we sighted a steamer at a distance of say five or six miles. We saw the mast-head lights. Then we burned five rockets, distress signals. On the last one that we burned, maybe they saw a reflection from the mast that we carried, she sort of closed her lights down gradually. From that until the time of the last rocket we fired was about fifteen or twenty minutes or half an hour, we could see no more lights. Whether he had gone over the horizon or had doused his lights we can't say. He may have thought we were a periscope or something in the water, from that pole we had.

"At daybreak this morning [June 4] the first thing we sighted was a sailing vessel, three master, we believe, on the offing. She was beating on the wind, away from us, beating to the southward. Then a little while afterwards, we will say half an hour to be sure, we saw another sailing vessel, and then Mr. Johnson here discovered land. He saw houses and Mr. Bennett got up and saw houses, too, and gradually the outline of the shore formed, etc., and we kept coming right up and kept rowing and plugging until we got through."

On June 4, Atlantic City was enjoying the annual Shriner's convention. A multitude of Shriners, vacationers, swimmers, and sunbathers romped the white sandy beach and waded playfully in the waves. Hundreds of visitors thronged the boardwalk seeking amusement. On the street, the Lu Lu Temple Band and Drill Patrol were in parade. The time was 1:45 on a lazy Tuesday afternoon. Except for the knowledge that survivors from the *Texel* had landed the night before, and that an enemy submarine had sunk their ship, to the people on holiday the war must have seemed more than three thousand miles away, on the other side of the Atlantic.

Beach Patrolman Edward Shaw observed a speck on the eastern horizon. Memories differ as to precisely what he remarked to a fellow lifeguard. It was either "This looks like another boat load of survivors" or "There comes a boatload of people from one of those torpedoed ships."

When the people near him looked to where he was pointing, they saw a lifeboat bobbing in the distance. Captain Alex Miller of the Life Guard force raised binoculars to his eyes. He was able to discern that the object was indeed a boat, and that it was "moving very slowly." Miller and three other lifeguards launched two surfboats "and went out to meet the boat. They found two men at the oars and they were so played out that they could hardly move the boat. The two life savers' boats took the *Carolina's* life boat in tow and helped pull them to shore."

According to another account, which is corroborated by a photograph, "the boat neared the shore unassisted." Possibly, the lifeguards towed the lifeboat until they reached the outer breakers, then released it to land on its own.

The exhausted survivors kept pulling at the oars. Gradually, people on shore began to realize the historic importance of the event that was occurring before their eyes. "A mighty cheer went up from the throngs on the beach and boardwalk." The band quit playing "Where Do We Go From Here, Boys" and struck up "The Star Spangled Banner." "Pleasure seeking hundreds on the Boardwalk stopped, looked, caught the significance of the strains of music filling the air, and then started with a rush for the beach. Bathers stopped romping. They gazed, spellbound for an instant, then took up the shout of welcome that burst from the crowds.

"Beach guards launched their boats and bent their backs as they tore through the combers toward the yawl. Excited Shriners in the full regalia of the order,

War Cruise of the *U-151*

rushed waist deep into the surf. Other visitors, fully attired, were in up to their knees and never noticed it. The guards swept alongside the craft, lifted out two women who had collapsed from the reaction and started back to shore. Others transferred some of the passengers into their boats and leaving one man to take them to the beach, leaped into the yawl and tore the oars from the exhausted hands of the men who were still battling gamely, with fast waning strength, and pulled the others into shallow water where willing hands helped them to the beach and up into the hospital tent, where Dr. Charles Bossert, chief surgeon of the lifeguard forces, was ready with a corps of volunteers to administer stimulants."

After forty hours of continuous rowing, the survivors could not have landed at a better place than at the foot of South Carolina Avenue, for that was precisely where the hospital tent was located for the resuscitation of overconfident swimmers.

"As the yawl shot up on the sands under the powerful drive of the life guards, the strains of music swept out from the instruments with renewed strength. Men and women stood with bared heads. Some were shouting, others stood with tears streaming down their cheeks, tears [not] of grief, but happiness over the res-

A postcard picture.

SURVIVORS OF THE STEAMSHIP CAROLINA COMING ASHORE ON THE BEACH AT ATLANTIC CITY, N.J.

cue and scene before them. Others were swearing, spilling their wrath at the Kaiser. The play of emotions as revealed by the faces was undescribable [sic].

"A little girl not more than 12 or 13 was the first lifted ashore. She was dripping wet, but smiling, and she blew a kiss to the crowds that cheered her as she was carried into the hospital tent. 'I'm all right. Help those other people. Just give me a coat. I'm cold,' she said as friendly hands reached out to give her assistance. A big six-foot Shriner peeled off a gold lace trimmed green velvet coat that topped off his brilliant raiment and flung it about her shoulders. She smiled her thanks.

"Two frail women, biting their lips in their determination not to give away to the strain that had made them almost frantic, were carried in. They were dressed in heavy blue overalls and jumpers men of the party had taken off and given them during the cold hours of the two terrible nights they had fought with the seas off the coast. [The correspondent did not know about the bundle of chambray shirts the survivors had recovered.] One fainted, as a sudden blast from the band carried the strains of the national anthem to her.

"The other for the first time seemed to realize that she was in the hands of friends once more when she heard the music. 'We're saved,' she said simply, then fell unconscious into the arms of Dr. Bossert."

One man and three of the eight women were removed to the Atlantic City Hospital, where they were treated for shock, exposure, and near starvation. These were Felix Capdeville, Caroline Higgins, Gertrude Lucian, and Charlotte Perkins. The rest were taken to the Hotel Thurber, where they met and commiserated with the survivors of the *Texel*. Later, the women were cared for "in private homes of the members of the Red Cross, and the men are being taken care of by the Community Service Committee with headquarters at the Morris Guards armory."

Two female survivors aboard lifeboat No. 5 described their adventures with uncommon pluck. Said Rachel Hamilton, "So long as a Porto Rico boat had to

War Cruise of the *U-151*

be sunk by the Germans I am glad I was on it. I would not have missed it for anything in the world. When I am sure that all the people in the other boats are safe the whole tragedy will be dispelled so far as I am concerned. My daughter thought it was quite a lark."

Mrs. A.L. Seymour added, "And when we came ashore you had the band playing for us just as if you knew we were coming."

Prowling destroyers recovered the bodies of four people who drowned when the *Carolina's* motor dory overturned. They saw no signs of the elusive U-boat.

In retrospect, it is remarkable that of the 448 men, women, and children who were cast adrift on June 2, 1918, only thirteen perished. The death toll could have been much higher.

Germany had hoped that the U-boat threat would influence the United States to reconsider its policy of aggression against the Central Powers. Americans were not intimidated. If anything, the events leading up to and concluding on June 2 only solidified their resolve. The call to arms became a shout against the tyranny that was spreading along foreign shores, and which threatened to overtake the world like a devastating plague.

Meanwhile, the destructive presence of the *U-151* continued to be felt.

On the afternoon of June 3, at the mouth of the Delaware Bay, an underwater explosion blew a hole in the hull of the brand new tanker *Herbert L. Pratt*, 7,145 tons. She was transporting a full cargo of crude oil in bulk from Tuxpam, Mexico to the refineries in Philadelphia, Pennsylvania.

Captain H. Bennett ordered the lifeboats swung out in preparation for launching. He also transmitted an SOS: "*Overfalls* Lightship Delaware Breakwater have struck a mine or am torpedoed."

Three Section Patrol boats intercepted the transmission and proceeded to the scene: the *Miramar*, *Georgiana*, and *Edorea*.

When Captain Bennett determined that the ship was in no immediate danger of sinking, he turned toward shore with all possible speed. The tanker was underway for only fifteen minutes before she began to settle by the head. When forward motion ceased, he ordered the men out of the engine room.

The crew barely escaped in four lifeboats before the bow slipped beneath the surface. But the captain had accomplished his goal of reaching shoal water. The bow struck bottom at sixty feet but the stern stayed high and dry.

The pilot boat took on the crew, and landed them at the naval base at Lewes, Delaware, none the worse for the experience. Captain Bennett boarded one of the guard boats to make a report. This boat later took him to the naval base.

The *Herbert L. Pratt* cost $1.5 million to build. Her tanks were filled with 78,000 barrels of Mexican crude. Salvage operations commenced on the following morning: "The salvage was taken in hand at once by Lieut. Commdr. Walter M. Davis, U.S.N., aided by the U.S.S. *Tasco*. He employed a Merritt & Chapman diver named Anderson with diving crew and equipment. The ship lay with her bow on bottom and her stern out of water. Anderson descended into the pump room and moved

The *Herbert L. Pratt* prior to salvage. (Courtesy of the National Archives.)

War Cruise of the *U-151*

certain valves; he also connected extensions to certain vent pipes from the forward tanks, bringing them above water, so that the forward tanks could be pumped out. The task was hazardous. The *Tasco* then supplied steam, and the *Pratt's* pumps pumped her forward tanks clear of oil. By afternoon of the 4th, Davis decided to pull on the *Pratt's* stern. The pilotboat *Philadelphia* was employed for this, and after 15 minutes the *Pratt's* bow came up from the bottom and she floated. She was then towed to shore and beached."

Some 65,000 barrels of oil were saved. The tanker was pulled off the beach on June 5. She was towed to Philadelphia that same day. She was then repaired and returned to service.

Extensive minesweeping operations cleared the mouth of the bay without any additional casualties. During the week, four of the infernal devices were found and destroyed by gunfire. On June 10, one mine was found on the beach.

The Navy acquired a fleet of fifty-nine minesweepers by purchasing and converting commercial fishing vessels, private yachts and motorboats, and harbor tugs. This ragtag fleet periodically swept the channels that led to principal ports along the eastern seaboard.

Most of the mines that U-boats planted were never found. They either sank, or they broke free of their moorings and drifted out to sea.

By this time, the *U-151* was wreaking havoc off the coast of Virginia. At 6 p.m. on June 3, the U-boat overtook the American schooner *Samuel C. Mengel*, Captain Hans Hansen. She was transporting cocoa beans from the west coast of Africa to New York City, and had been at sea for fifty-three days. She was practically becalmed when the U-boat fired a warning shot at her. The schooner reefed her sails.

The U-boat drew alongside the *Samuel C. Mengel*. A seven-man boarding party used a pontoon boat to reach the schooner. The boarding officer, who said that his name was Kohler, examined the ship's papers while the rest of the Germans placed bombs and cleaned out the pantry; they were particularly eager to steal soap.

Kohler shook hands with crewmembers as they abandoned ship in a lifeboat, and exclaimed, "Send [President] Wilson out here and we will finish him in 10 minutes. Wilson is the only one prolonging the war."

The men in the lifeboat hoisted sail and rowed westward. They were about two miles from the schooner when they heard the bombs detonate. They spotted an eastbound steamer a couple of hours later, but were unable to get the ship's attention. They spent the night alone upon the sea. The next morning, at 6:30, they were picked up by the Danish steamer *Paris*, which landed them at New York.

The next afternoon, the SS *T. M. Werner* happened upon a wrecked sailing vessel "drifting on her starboard side with masts and sails in the water and with a large hole in her port side forward. The Captain sent a boat over in charge of the First Mate, Hans Hagedorn to investigate and see if anyone was aboard but no sign of life was found." They identified the *Samuel C. Mengel* by a life-buoy on which the name was written. The hulk was left adrift.

At 6:45 on the next morning of June 4, the *Edward R. Baird, Jr.* was luffing along without concern when what appeared to be a sub chaser swung into the schooner's lee and fired a shot through the foresail. Captain R.R. Coulborn wasted no time in letting the schooner heave to.

The *U-151* circled its prize and stopped on the weather side. An armed boarding party put out in a collapsible boat. While a German officer demanded the ship's papers and manifest, a bomb squad hung two explosive charges along the outer hull amidships, port and starboard, and two more inside. They also dropped the sails. The officer gave the schooner's crew five minutes to gather clothes and provisions, and to abandon ship.

The Germans had hardly finished their nefarious

War Cruise of the *U-151*

work when a steamer was sighted on the horizon. The boarding party returned to the U-boat, while the crew of the *Edward R. Baird, Jr.* got away in a dory.

Five minutes later the timed fused detonated. The explosion blew out the schooner's sides in great clouds of smoke and fire. Von Nostitz noted in his log, "Schooner is sunk. Sinking not observed. During the sinking a tanker with brightly painted hull, bearing 250°, is sighted."

The *U-151* chased after the French tanker *Radioleine*. The French had been in the war a lot longer than the isolated Americans, and their ire was up as well as their weapons. As the master swung his vessel toward Hampton Roads, Virginia, in order to outrun his adversary while heading for a friendly port, a trigger-happy gun crew fired at the U-boat as soon as it came within range.

Von Nostitz accepted the challenge and returned round for round. Nearby, the U.S. torpedo boat destroyer *Hull* heard the exchange of shots, and charged full speed ahead into the fray. On the way to battle, the *Hull* intercepted the *Radioleine's* SOS on the wireless. Then the *Hull* spotted the French tanker racing away from her pursuer in a zigzag pattern, firing as she went. Enemy shots splashed near the tanker.

When the *Hull* reached the vicinity of the battle, von Nostitz thought better of crossing guns with an armed warship. The *U-151* submerged and slunk away under water.

About an hour after abandoning ship, the crew of the *Edward R. Baird, Jr.* was spotted by the *Hull*, and was rescued. The *Hull* searched in vain for the U-boat, then "went close aboard schooner which was still afloat to determine if she could be saved. Executive Officer of this vessel went on board with crew of schooner; found deck awash and holds full of water from bomb, holes in side; vessel floating due to cargo of lumber."

The *Edward R. Baird, Jr.* was deemed unsalvageable, and left adrift. The *Hull* took her crew to Norfolk, Virginia where they were debriefed by Naval Intelligence. The Coast Guard duly filed its report, claiming the vessel as a total loss. The value of the hull was given as $18,000, that of the cargo as $12,000. The *U-151* was given credit for the sinking; the schooner's tonnage counted as part of its wartime record.

Five days later, on the morning of June 9, the American steamship *Harvey H. Brown* was nearing the end of her voyage from Boston, Massachusetts to Sewall's Point, Virginia when she spotted a three-masted schooner "sitting upright, her decks all under water, but her cargo of lumber on deck visible. Her sails were hanging overboard, let go by the run." The location was "56 miles E.S.E. from Cape Henry."

Captain R.H. McLean kept his ship in motion, circling the partially sunken schooner while four men put off in a lifeboat and inspected the hulk. Finding her situation stable, they tied hawsers onto the *Edward R. Baird, Jr.* and lashed her to the steamer's side. The tow to Sewall's Point took the rest of that day and most of the next. At 10:30 p.m. on June 10, the *Harvey H. Brown* docked with her charge still afloat and in no immediate danger of sinking.

The Aid for Information of the 5th Naval District filed a report to the Office of Naval Intelligence (ONI) that stated, "An above-water examination of subject did

The *Edward R. Baird, Jr.* is lashed to the side of the *Harvey H. Brown*. (Courtesy of the National Archives.)

War Cruise of the *U-151*

not disclose any signs of shell fire, etc. Her interior, however, showed signs of raiding, all nautical instruments and records being gone."

Von Nostitz had taken the schooner's logbooks, and Captain Coulborn had retrieved his valuable navigational instruments when the *Hull* had taken him back to inspect his vessel.

Captain Coulborn was soon reunited with his precious schooner, and the *Edward R. Baird, Jr.* was dewatered, repaired, and returned to service.

Meanwhile, after submerging to escape from the *Hull*, the *U-151* eventually surfaced when the coast was clear and continued to patrol the shipping lanes off Virginia. At 4:15 on the afternoon of June 4, von Nostitz spotted the Norwegian freighter *Eidsvold*. He fired a shot across her bow. Captain J. Johnson issued the order to stop the engines, then hoisted the ship's signals and the national ensign, to show that the vessel belonged to a neutral nation.

Von Nostitz insisted on examining the ship's papers. Captain Johnson, along with a mate and three sailors, put off in a small boat and rowed for the U-boat. Captain Johnson climbed onto the steel hull to present his papers. When von Nostitz learned that the cargo of Cuban sugar was bound for New York City, he explained politely that the freighter must be sunk.

Captain Johnson: "The submarine took the ship register, certificate of nationality, bills of lading, manifest and American bill of health, leaving me the crew list and Cuban bill of health."

Captain Johnson pleaded for time to abandon ship because, in addition to the crew, his wife was on board. Von Nostitz spoke in German that was translated by one of his lieutenants, saying that he would give him all the time he could. Captain Johnson returned to the *Eidsvold*, ordered the lowering of the ship's boats, and gave the crew fifteen minutes to gather their clothing before shoving off. Louis Daniel, the *Eidvold*'s French cook, had the foresight to take "13 loaves of bread and one sack of mixed canned meats."

According to Captain Johnson, as soon as they were far enough away for their own safety, the Germans "fired 4 shots into her starboard side, and then turned around and fired 3 shots on the port side, all shots taking effect on the water line."

Daniel stated, "We saw the ship going down. She listed on the port side and then she kept filling up and went down head first. The last thing I saw was the Norwegian flag flying from the stern."

Captain Johnson: "After leaving the vessel we divided the crew between the boats, our motor boat wouldn't work, so we set sail in two lifeboats, towing motor boat steering south by west, wind about north east."

The U-boat dogged them until dusk, staying a couple of miles behind, "Evidently for the purpose of waiting for some vessel to come along and try to pick us up, when the vessel would become easy prey for the submarine."

After dark, the twenty-four men and one woman were left alone in the great open sea, a hundred miles from land. With crewmembers taking turns at the tiller, the boats sailed all night long in a gradually dying wind. The surface was placid, the temperature mild. In the morning they heard detonations from the south. After breakfast they tried to fix the motor boat which, with its engine inoperable, was holding them back. They gave up on it about nine o'clock. The crew reapportioned themselves in the two lifeboats, and the errant motor boat was cut adrift.

Then, "we started rowing, keeping west by north, with stops for rest and meals, until 2:30 pm, when a steamer was sighted to the southward."

After a great fanfare of waving jackets, the crew bent to the oars and pulled for the steamship until "about two miles off she altered her course and bore down toward us and proved to be the SS *Proteus*."

The survivors had been in the lifeboats for more than twenty hours. The Morgan Line passenger vessel picked up the *Eidsvold's* crew and transported them to

New York.

The explosions that the *Eidsvold's* crew heard were from the bombing of the *Harpathian*, which at that moment was steaming slightly south of the Virginia border off the coast of North Carolina.

The *Harpathian* was a British steamship whose black gang consisted of twenty-nine Chinese who were not sailors, but shovelers: their job was to shovel coal into the furnaces under the boilers. Twelve officers and crewmen handled the rest of the duties.

According to the official report, "The *Harpathian* was sunk without warning by a torpedo from an enemy submarine at 9:30 a.m. June 5, . . . sank in about seven minutes. All hands were saved. One member of the crew, a Chinaman, was struck between the eyes by a piece of the torpedo that sunk the ship. The captain did not see the submarine till after the ship was hit, and only a few of the crew saw the torpedo before it struck.

"The crew got away safely in the boats. The submarine commander called the boats alongside and asked if all were saved and if any were sick; he also asked if they had food and water. The Chinaman was given treatment [his wounds were bandaged] aboard the submarine and was then returned aboard the lifeboat. The submarine commander gave each boat a bucket of water and asked the captain of the vessel if he had sent a wireless and on being told that there had been no time, gave the boats the course to the nearest land."

The crew of the *Harpathian* did not make it to shore on their own. Instead, they spent all day and night at sea. After more than twenty-five hours adrift, they were picked up by another British steamer, the *Potomac*. They reached Norfolk, Virginia on the sixth.

After sinking the *Harpathian*, the *U-151* stopped the American whaler *A. M. Nicholson* around 4 o'clock in the afternoon. Captain J. T. Gonsalves, master of the whaler, pleaded with von Nostitz not to sink his whaler because it would ruin him financially if his vessel were destroyed. It contained $30,000 worth of sperm oil. Von

Nostitz pondered over the master's predicament. After a brief consultation with his officers, he graciously decided to let the *A. M. Nicholson* go free.

The Norwegian freighter *Vinland* was not so lucky when she was stopped a couple of hours later. She was transporting Cuban sugar to New York.

According to the *Vinland's* master, Paul Bratland, "A German submarine sent a shot over the ship which landed 300 yards on the other side. The submarine was about 3-1/2 miles away and one point abaft the port beam. I went aboard the submarine and they told me to get the boats ready as quickly as possible. I went back to my ship and told every man to get as many clothes as he could. About the same time one German officer and four or five men came aboard. They took two bags of sugar. After that they placed a bomb on the outside about 2 feet below the water line. It was cylindrical in shape and pointed at both ends and they dropped it down with a piece of rope. The attitude of the Germans while aboard was very nice; they said they were going to give us as much time as they could and it was 20 minutes after they came aboard before we left the ship.

"One of the men struck a match and lighted the fuse it being a fuse bomb and it exploded in about five minutes."

These men spent twenty-three hours adrift before they were rescued by the U.S. destroyer *Walke*, and transported to Cape May, New Jersey. The destroyer did not land the men, but signaled for a Coast Guard

The *Vinland* is settling by the stern. (Courtesy of the Naval Photographic Center.)

War Cruise of the *U-151*

vessel to take them ashore. "The men were immediately taken to the Wissahickon Naval Barracks Hospital at Sewell's Point, several miles up the ocean side of the cape. . . .

"When the crew came ashore they had two dogs with them, but the naval officers would not permit the men to take them to the barracks with them, and the sailors were compelled to abandon them."

On June 8, the *U-151* surfaced three-quarters of a mile from the Norwegian freighter *Vindeggen*, and fired two shots across her bow. The freighter was carrying wool, copper, and salted skins from Chile to New York. Captain Edward Ballestad, master, described subsequent events:

"We lowered the port-side boat and it went over to the submarine with the ships papers. During the work of lowering the starboard boat some Chinamen jumped into it and it capsized and one of the Chinamen was drowned. At 7.30 a.m. we sighted another steamer and the submarine proceeded down to the eastward and ordered us to follow."

The *U-151* overtook the *Pinar del Rio*, an American freighter that was transporting 25,000 bags of Cuban sugar to Boston, Massachusetts. Captain John Mackenzie ignored the warning shots and tried for half an hour to outrun the U-boat before yielding. The U-boat fired continuously but none of the shots struck the freighter, all of them hitting the water forward of the bow. Because of the consistent accuracy of the shots, the crew was of the opinion that the U-boat was firing warning shots, and was not trying to hit the freighter.

Von Nostitz noted in his log: "Upon approaching and bearing to lee of steamer, a heavy sea washed 4 men of the crew overboard. It was possible to rescue several people in spite of the very heavy swell. Worthy of note is the service of both our guns during this heavy sea, which frequently washed over the gun crews."

The *Pinar del Rio* hove to. As the U-boat drew alongside, Second Engineer Walter Burrows took half a dozen snapshots of the *U-151* with a Kodak camera.

The *U-151* as seen from the *Pinar del Rio*. (Courtesy of the National Archives.)

The crew was ordered to abandon ship. They launched two lifeboats. After the boats pulled away, the U-boat sank the freighter by gunfire, then rushed back to the *Vindeggen*, abandoning the survivors of the *Pinar del Rio* to their fate.

Captain Mackenzie and seventeen men occupied one lifeboat. The chief officer and fifteen men occupied the other. Land was a hundred miles to the west. The lifeboats raised sail and set a course for the American shore. A heavy sea was running and a great deal of spray was blown over the men. They spotted the *Vindeggen* in the distance and, because the *U-151* stopped alongside but did not sink her, mistook the freighter for either a decoy steamer or a U-boat supply ship.

Due to different sailing characteristics, the boats got separated during the day. After ten hours, the Norwegian steamship *Taunton* picked up Captain Mackenzie and his men, then cut the lifeboat free.

The other lifeboat sailed all day, all night, and all the next day. They sighted land at around 2 o'clock in the afternoon of June 9. Four miles from the beach they met the steam-schooner *Mary Olsen*, which was bound for Cuba. The survivors clambered aboard and the captain gave them supper. Then they got back into the lifeboat and sailed for shore. They landed safely at Nags Head, North Carolina.

War Cruise of the *U-151*

The survivors of the *Pinar del Rio* created quite a stir when they told ONI their suspicions about the decoy steamer or supply ship. On the other hand, ONI was ecstatic when Burrows had his film developed and gave them a set of prints. It was standard operating procedure to ask survivors to describe the U-boat, and to draw pictures of its appearance. Now they had an actual photograph.

Captain Ballestad: "At 11.30 the submarine came back to us. It was the intention of the submarine to sink the ship right away but when they found out we had copper they decided to bring it over to the submarine." They used the *Vindeggen's* lifeboats as lighters, and enlisted the *Vindeggen's* crewmen to do the work.

"At 9 a. m. on the 9th they commenced bringing copper to the submarine and they continued until 8 p.m. Next day they began work again at 5 in the morning and continued until 11" in the morning.

J. Ugland held a master's license, but shipped aboard the *Vindeggen* as second mate in order to obtain passage for himself, his wife, and their young child. While the copper bars were being transferred, he and his family were quartered in the captain's cabin of the U-boat. This afforded him ample opportunity to observe the interior layout.

The U-boat took on seventy tons of copper bars. In order to compensate for the extra weight, the German sailors threw ballast iron and trimming weights overboard. The U-boat also discharged some of its water ballast.

When the U-boat had as much copper as it could afford to carry, Ugland and his family were placed aboard a lifeboat. Captain Ballestad: "The submarine commander gave orders that the ship should be sunk and said he would tow us to port. They planted bombs and in seven minutes the ship disappeared. The submarine then proceeded westward with the boats in tow. At 6.30 p.m. another steamer was sighted and the captain of the submarine gave us orders to cast off the ropes and sail in a westerly direction."

The *U-151* chased after the Norwegian freighter *Henrik Lund*, Captain Axel Kaltenborn (or Kaltenburn). She was bound from Norfolk, Virginia to Rio de Janeiro, Brazil with a cargo of coal, copper tubing, and iron plates. Because a U-boat was known to be operating in the area, the Captain of the Port had issued specific instructions to Captain Kaltenborn:

"You are directed to clear Cape Henry about two hours before dark, and run at greatest speed to obtain the best possible offing before morning. Direct your course nothing to the southward of East true until well off shore, then haul down for your destination, avoiding the regular steamer tracks. Give vicinity of Crooked Island passage a wide berth. Darken your ship completely at night and do not use running lights unless in danger of collision. Use zig zag courses if attacked by enemy.

"German submarines may display running lights to entice you near them, therefore, avoid all vessels showing running lights. Regard all vessels, especially small sailing craft with suspicion. Do not approach closely to floating spars, or any suspicious object. In case mines are sighted, do not pass between them."

Ordinarily, these instructions would have kept the *Henrik Lund* out of the way of the *U-151*, which had been operating fairly close to shore. But because it was on its way home, it had shaped an offshore course that coincidentally intersected with the course of the freighter, about 175 miles east of the mouth of the Chesapeake Bay.

The U-boat fired a shot across the freighter's bow.

Captain Kaltenborn: "I stopped immediately because I saw it was no use to try to escape. I had all the life boats manned and had the men stand by and the submarine came near and lay alongside with both of his guns pointing towards me. We all went in the boat and my boat went over to the submarine and I went on board and showed my papers and he told me I was to be sunk. Then he told me that I could go aboard my ship again and get more clothes. He went with me;

War Cruise of the *U-151*

also the Officer 2nd in command and we went back to my ship and I went to my room and got my clothes. While I was getting my clothes they put bombs on the ship and blew her up. It took a long time before the ship went down. She went a little forward and then turned over. It was dark and we did not actually see her go down."

Once again the boarding officer claimed that the cargo consisted of contraband. The Germans absconded with one hundred bottles of beer from the pantry. Captain Kaltenborn returned to the U-boat. During casual conversation, one officer stated that he was offended by American newspapers referring to Germans as Huns. Another officer pointed to a shipping register, in which red ink was used to cross out the ships that the *U-151* had sunk. He said that it had sunk fifty-three vessels since the U-boat had been built. "That is our Bible. We are trying to make that book as thin as possible."

Instead of casting the crewmen adrift in lifeboats, von Nostitz towed the two boats back to where he had left the lifeboats of the *Vindeggen*.

Captain Ballestad: "The submarine picked us up again and towed us till 8.30 p. m., when they sighted another steamer and cast us off again and submerged. They did not say how many tons of copper they took from my ship, I should say about 70 or 80; they estimated the value at about 1,000,000 marks."

The steamer sighted was the *Brosund*. Captain Kaltenborn had a flashlight on his person. He kept flashing the light until the Danish steamer spotted the beam, and hove to. She took aboard the sixty-eight officers and men from the four lifeboats of the *Vindeggen* and *Henrik Lund*, and transported them to New York.

When these survivors were interviewed, ONI was able to discount the theory of a decoy steamer or supply ship; they realized that the *Vindeggen* had been mislabled. Better yet, they had an accurate description of the U-boat's interior courtesy of Ugland. His description tallied closely with the descriptions that ONI had obtained from the survivors of the *Hattie Dunn*, *Hauppauge*, and *Edna*.

U-boat sightings were now becoming common. Not every sighting was real. As if in expectation, people were seeing U-boats where none existed, or were mistaking other vessels for U-boats. Survivors often stated that they first mistook the U-boat for an American sub chaser, because their profiles were similar. Many vessels put their stern to anything that they could not positively identify.

Two sightings that were definitely confirmed were those of the British steamers *Llanstephan Castle* and *Keemun*, on June 13. Captain Chope, master of the *Llanstephan Castle*, sighted an unidentified vessel at a distance of ten miles and approaching fast. He kept watching it until he was certain that it was a U-boat. He turned away. The U-boat played cat and mouse by changing course back and forth. Captain Chope's suspicions were already aroused. The steamer was armed, and the gunner was keeping the U-boat in his sights. He clearly saw two deck guns on the U-boat as it turned away.

The *Keemun* hove into view. Captain Chope raised warning flags that the *Keemun* did not answer. Chope then transmitted a warning by wireless, and gave his vessel's position. About that time the U-boat commenced firing upon the *Keemun*. The *Keemun* was also armed (as were all British merchantmen). The steamer returned fire from a distance of 7,000 yards. A running battle ensued in which neither steamer nor U-boat scored any hits. The *Keemun* outran the U-boat, firing her last shot from a distance of 11,000 yards, at which time the U-boat "came to a standstill."

At five o'clock in the morning of June 14, the *U-151* happened upon the Norwegian bark *Samoa*. She was transporting wool and copper ore from South Africa to Perth Amboy, New Jersey. Different official records gave three different names for the *Samoa's* master: Peter Dahl, Christian Dahl, and Pierre Christian Dare.

War Cruise of the *U-151*

Von Nostitz fired a shot across the *Samoa's* bow, then gave the signal to abandon ship. After the men got into two lifeboats and shoved off, the boats approached the U-boat. A German lieutenant inquired if the lifeboats were adequately provisioned. The master told him that they had only bread and water. The lieutenant gave him fifteen minutes to return to the bark and secure some food. This was accomplished by the boat under the command of the first mate, Frithjof Olsen.

The master was uncertain of his position after a long journey from the opposite hemisphere. He asked for the latitude and longitude. Not only did the lieutenant comply with the master's request by giving him a paper with the *Samoa's* position, but he used his wireless to send a call for help before departing from the scene. He also gave the master a receipt for the bark, stating that she had been "destroyed by a German Navy vessel."

After the lifeboats were well clear of the bark, the U-boat pumped three shells into the *Samoa's* hull. The bark sank after the third shot. The U-boat departed.

The men were abandoned some two hundred miles off the Virginia coast: a long way to go in open boats, even though they were equipped with sails. The fifteen survivors sailed and rowed westward for thirty-eight hours before the schooner *George W. Truitt, Jr.* picked them up.

The *Samoa's* end. (Courtesy of the Naval Photographic Center.)

The *Samoa's* odyssey was not yet over. The survivors were in the process of hauling the lifeboats aboard the schooner when the U.S. destroyer *Paul Jones* arrived. The *Samoa's* men transferred to the destroyer. They were fed well on the way to Hampton Roads, Virginia. They were then transferred to the submarine tender *Fulton*. After that, a launch from the destroyer tender *Bridgeport* took the men ashore as charges of a chaplain named Ayers. The chaplain was instructed to escort the men to the Office of Naval Intelligence at Old Point Comfort, and not to let anyone – especially newspaper reporters – talk with them until after they had given statements to the officer in command.

What followed was like a scene out of the Keystone Cops. No one wanted to take responsibility for the men, and no one wanted to feed them. They sat in the launch in the hot sun all day long, with no food or water, while Ayers tried desperately to find someone at ONI to take charge of them.

Ayers: "I took the Collector [of the Port], Mr. Hamilton, aboard the boat and introduced him to the captain and first mate of the *Samoa*. Mr. Hamilton seemed at a loss to know what to do with the refugees as he had no place to put them and stated that he had no available funds or authorization to feed and lodge them. He said that if he took them, it would simply be to turn them over to the Inspector of Immigration."

Ayers made a series of nonproductive phone calls. Boats that were supposed to be sent for the men never arrived. Finally he flagged down a tug "and transferred my passengers aboard. The tug was in command of a regular tug captain who seemed to be acting under the instructions of a Warrant Officer who had been sent out from the Commandant's Office to get the survivors. I asked the tug captain if he had food enough to give these men their supper and he replied that he had the food but he did not want to take the responsibility of feeding them if he did not know where the pay was coming from."

War Cruise of the *U-151*

This was not a nice welcome to America, especially for shipwrecked sailors who had been bringing a much-needed cargo to a country that seemed to be bound by red tape and official inhospitality. Ayers was persistent. He asked the tug captain "if he proposed to let these men go hungry rather than take a chance at the cost of a bit of food to feed them. He replied that he guessed that he could feed them. I then shoved off, leaving the captain and crew of the *Samoa* aboard the tug in charge of the Collector of the Port."

About an hour after the *U-151* sank the *Samoa*, it stopped the Norwegian bark *Kringsjaa*, en route from Buenos Aires, Argentina to New York with a cargo of flaxseed. After turning over the ship's papers, Captain Gunwald Magnusdel asked that the U-boat tow his lifeboats toward land. Lieutenant Kohler refused, but transmitted a message in which he requested assistance for the beleaguered seamen, who could hear the wireless crackling.

The *Kringsjaa* was sunk by gunfire.

The men spent the night at sea. At 5 a.m. they spotted a tanker that was "hove to." Boatswain Oscar Johnson: "We immediately made for her, but upon her sighting us she started ahead in a N. direction at full speed." The men then spent all day and another night at sea. They were picked up on June 16 by the U.S. destroyer *Patterson*, which landed them at Cape May, New Jersey. There they were transferred to the pilot boat *J. Henry Edmonds*, which landed them at Lewes, Delaware.

The *U-151* now proceeded directly for home. On June 18, without warning, it fired a torpedo into the hull of the British liner *Dwinsk*. She was traveling from Brest, France to Newport News, Virginia, in order to pick up troops and munitions for the Western Front. On board were 153 men: officers and crew numbering 148, plus five U.S. Navy personnel. The location of the attack was approximately 400 miles north of Bermuda, and about 600 miles southeast of New York.

The torpedo struck adjacent to the engine room. The blast disabled the engine. The wireless transmitter was "shaken to pieces" and its condenser was broken. The liner lay dead in the water and was unable to transmit a call for help. The hull took a gradual list to port and commenced to settle by the stern.

In orderly fashion, the men launched seven lifeboats, each filled to about half capacity. Lieutenant Commander H. Nelson, master, was the last to abandon ship. The U-boat surfaced twenty minutes after the attack, found the *Dwinsk* abandoned, approached the drifting lifeboats, and took in tow lifeboat #3, Second Officer J. Coppin in command. Coppin was brought aboard the U-boat, where he was interrogated. The U-boat drew close to the *Dwinsk*, and hastened her sinking by firing a number of shells into her side. Coppin was ordered back into his lifeboat, which was then released.

Intermittent rainsqualls passed through the area. The state of the sea was Force 3 on the Beaufort scale: gentle breeze (8 to 12 miles per hour), large wavelets, crests beginning to break, and scattered whitecaps. The lifeboats hoisted sail and headed west-northwest under trying conditions. They were soon separated by the vagaries of the wind.

The *U-151* headed east-northeast. It proceeded slowly on the surface for a couple of hours, until lookouts spotted a westbound steamer that sported four funnels. The U-boat submerged and moved into position to attack.

The four-stacker turned in the direction of the lifeboats, proceeding at such high speed that the U-boat could not draw closer than one mile. It launched a torpedo at the unidentified vessel.

The steamer was not an unarmed merchant vessel, but the U.S. destroyer *Von Steuben*, which was returning to New York from Brest, France after escorting an eastbound convoy. It was shortly after noon when she happened upon the cluster of lifeboats. She adopted a

War Cruise of the *U-151*

zigzag approach as she drove in to rescue survivors. From a distance the lifeboats appeared to be unoccupied.

A lookout reported a torpedo approaching fast from the port side. The skipper ordered all engines full speed astern and the wheel hard astarboard. Gun crews manned their guns and commenced firing at a periscope. The *Von Steuben* barely slowed and turned in time to let the torpedo pass a few yards ahead. She then circled toward the U-boat, firing her guns and delivering a withering depth-charge attack.

Aboard the *Von Steuben*, it was presumed that the *U-151* was using the lifeboats as decoys to lure unsuspecting vessels to their doom. If that was the case, von Nostitz attracted the kind of attention than he wanted to avoid. He crash-dived to 130 feet. As depth charges started detonating overhead, he descended to 200 feet, then to 260 feet.

The *Von Steuben* zigzagged northward at flank speed, leaving the U-boat and the lifeboats astern.

The *U-151* surfaced to assess damage. The close explosions had damaged the air intake trunk. In addition, "the bow tank and the telephone buoy were crushed by the water pressure."

Von Nostitz steered again for the boats, this time catching up with lifeboat #6, which was lagging behind the flotilla because of the boat's poor sailing characteristics. Von Nostitz hailed First Officer Robert Pritchard, who was in command. He asked for the name of the four-stacker, and wanted to know if it was an auxiliary cruiser. Pritchard had recognized the vessel as a *Von Steuben*-class destroyer, but pleaded ignorance and refused to divulge the true nature of the vessel, claiming that she was too far away to identify.

The *U-151* then departed.

The survivors of the *Dwinsk* were left to their own devices. Their suffering must have been enormous. For some, days and nights passed with no sign of relief appearing on the horizon. The men were plagued with rough seas and heavy rain. If there was any saving grace to their dire situation, it was that they were able to collect rainwater to supplement their drinking supply. For food, most men had only one biscuit per day.

On the evening of June 19, the British schooner *Mowen* picked up lifeboat #7, with 17 survivors. These men were landed at Bermuda on June 22.

On the morning of June 21, the American steamship *Edwin F. Luckenbach* (or *Edgar F. Luckenbach*) picked up lifeboat #3, with 18 survivors. These men were landed at Newport News, Virginia on June 23.

Four hours later, the passenger-freighter USS *Siboney* picked up two lifeboats: one with 18 men and the other with 28 men, including the master of the *Dwinsk*, Lieutenant Commander H. Nelson. These men were landed at New York on June 22.

Five days later, on June 26, the schooner *James M. Marshall* (or *George M. Marshall*) picked up lifeboat #11, with 24 men. These men were landed at Shelbourne, Nova Scotia on June 27.

What all these men endured can best be described by the survivors of lifeboat #6.

According to Lieutenant (jg) R. P. Whitemarsh, "The condition of boat #6 was deplorable. The sail was a mass of ribbons and holes, while the hull leaked to such an extent that two men were kept continuously at work bailing her out. The beef for boat provisions was left in four barrels on board ship. Water was stale and pilot biscuits were mouldy [sic]."

The day after the *Dwinsk* was sunk, these men sighted a steamer through the heavy rain. According to Pritchard, they fired a red flare as a signal of distress, "but the steamer did not reply to our signal. All that day heavy rain."

None of the lifeboats had any cover, so the occupants were exposed all the time to the weather.

The next day passed without any vessel sightings until evening. Pritchard: "We showed five red lights but no reply. On our starboard beam a large bark steering westward but failed to see the boat."

War Cruise of the *U-151*

The following day: "Favorable weather wind northeast sighted another steamer at dusk on our starboard side, showed lights again but no reply. Sailed along all night."

The day after: "About 5:30 A. M., sighted boat right ahead on nearing it discovered it was #3 life boat of our ship, the crew apparently been picked up. We went alongside the boat and took sail and compass out of it and steered away on our westward course." They also obtained a tin of biscuits that had been left behind.

By noon the wind increased to a moderate gale. The "sea rose very high. We reduced sail and at 4 P. M., took in sail running before wind and sea under bare poles. At 5 P. M. gale raising furiously with heavy sea. About 6 P. M. sea rolled over starboard quarter washing Cadet [Eugene] Currie overboard, filling the boat to the gunnel [sic]."

Currie's body was not recovered. With the lifeboat barely awash, the men bailed desperately to get rid of the water. They were all thoroughly soaked.

The gale abated toward midnight. There followed a day with moderate wind, then two days with variable winds and calms. Another gale struck the following night. The day afterward, the wind died down and the rain slackened somewhat.

In the morning of June 28 – fully ten days after the loss of their ship – the troop transport USS *Rondo* hove into view and rescued 20 famished and dehydrated survivors, some of whom were barely alive.

According to the *Rondo's* official report, "The survivors in this boat were in a pitiable condition from exposure, lack of food and water, after ten days battle with wind and wave. . . . One man, D. Walker, chief baker, fell unconscious on deck as a result of exposure and hunger, and was immediately taken to the sick bay and is now doing nicely. The others were in a more or less weakened state, but otherwise in good health."

The seventh lifeboat was never found. Its 23 souls must have suffered terrible hardships that eventually overcame them when their food and water gave out, and no one came to their rescue.

Four men were unaccounted for. Although Captain Nelson thought that no one was killed in the explosion, and that no one was left on board when he abandoned ship, it is likely that they were carried down to Davy Jones's locker with the *Dwinsk*.

Such were the true horrors of the U-boat war.

Meanwhile, on June 22, the *U-151* fired a warning shot at the Belgian freighter *Chilier*, Milford Haven, England to New York in ballast. "She was armed with 'an old French 90-mm. gun, which could be loaded with powder and cartridges,' and with this antiquated piece she fired several ineffective shots at the submarine before she surrendered."

The guns of the U-boat were larger and fired with greater accuracy. One shell struck the starboard lifeboat and punctured one of the watertight tanks, "which rendered it almost useless."

Captain Edward Delmee, master, hove to and gave the order to abandon ship. Twenty-five men boarded the port lifeboat; six men boarded the starboard lifeboat. By the time they ascertained that the starboard lifeboat was unseaworthy, the U-boat had drawn close enough to engage in conversation. The men requested time to return to the ship and launch the small auxiliary boat. Permission was granted. Permission was also granted to take additional tins of biscuit from the ship, as well as a sextant and chronometer. Both lifeboats rowed back to the *Chilier* to accomplish these tasks.

The *Chilier* settling by the stern. (Courtesy of the Naval Photographic Center.)

War Cruise of the U-151

The Germans made several trips in their own boat to take flour and preserved meat from the *Chilier*. They placed bombs in the hold of the freighter.

According to Captain Delmee, "About a half hour after they left the ship the bombs started to go off, about a dozen in all, at intervals of about four minutes. The ship's bow rose out of the water and she sank stern first and the submarine fired two shots from its forward gun into the bottom of the *Chilier*. . . . About a minute later she sunk, stern first."

The U-boat headed east; the lifeboats headed west. The lifeboats sailed in consort throughout the night, with the smaller boat connected to the larger boat by means of a line. The next morning they encountered storms. Due to the strain that was induced by the waves, the connecting line broke several times. On each occasion, the larger boat waited for the smaller boat to catch up, then secured another line.

After the final break, the smaller boat fell behind and before it could catch up, it capsized. Captain Delmee: "They were only a short distance from us at the time, but we could not aid them because of the heavy sea that was running. . . . We saw one of the men trying to swim to our boat but he soon disappeared and the smaller boat drifted away, bottom up, with two men on it." All six men perished.

Captain Delmee: "We had very little to eat, a biscuit at mealtime, and a quarter of a cup of water a day. The weather was extremely bad. We rowed most of the time to keep ahead of the seas and in calm weather drifted."

The *Chilier* taking the final plunge. (Courtesy of the Naval Photographic Center.)

The survivors suffered from thirst and hunger for days, until they were picked up by the SS *City of Savannah* and taken to New York.

The Norwegian steamer *Augvald* fell afoul of the *U-151* on June 23. She was traveling in ballast from La Pallice, France to Baltimore, Maryland. The U-boat fired a shot over the freighter from four miles astern. Captain Hans Haea, master, gave the order to stop the engine. The U-boat drew alongside of the *Augvald*, and waited patiently while the crew abandoned ship in two lifeboats, fourteen men in each.

One lifeboat was under the command of Captain Haea. The other was under the command of the Chief Officer August Immundasen.

The U-boat sank the *Augvald* by firing 25 to 30 shots into her hull.

What followed for the survivors was eleven days of great hardship. On June 25, the chief officer's boat capsized during a fierce storm. Third Engineer Johan Tolsen and Boatswain Andersen drowned, and all the food was washed away. The surviving crewmembers struggled to right the boat and bail out the water. The boat capsized again that afternoon; this time the compass was lost. Once again the men righted the boat and bailed. During the night, the boat capsized for the third time. Immundasen drowned and the oars were lost.

Now there were eleven. They had nothing: no food, no water, no oars – nothing at all but their soaked clothes. According to Chief Engineer Alfred Pedersen, "We saw many steamers, but not one would pick us up. Two of them were very close but they wouldn't pick us up either. Our boat was full of water and they could see us standing in water but they didn't pick us up."

One steamer hove to and observed the men in the lifeboat from a distance of a mile and a half. This steamer was camouflaged with different colors. The men waved their arms and shirts to attract attention. The steamer raised a Norwegian flag, then took off on a zigzag course.

War Cruise of the *U-151*

The men ate "small bits of seaweed and little fish that were caught in the seaweed." At first they had plenty of rainwater, but after the storms passed they had nothing to drink but seawater.

Another steamer approached to within a mile and a half, stopped her engines, and lay still. She then got up steam and circled the lifeboat twice, but made no attempt to rescue the men. She left the men to their fate.

The men were eventually picked up by the British steamship *Haverford*. The other lifeboat was never found.

The *U-151* attacked other vessels by gunfire, but unsuccessfully. It made its way safely back to Germany. Von Nostitz and the U-boat survived the war.

Once again Germany badly misjudged the American character. The U-boat attacks along the eastern seaboard did not dissuade Americans one iota from fighting the war.

Quite the contrary, military enlistments were stimulated so much on the day after the *U-151* made its presence known, that Army and Navy recruiting centers were overwhelmed and working extra hours. They were breaking enlistment records that had been established after the declaration of war more than a year before. Not only did applicants arrive at recruiting stations as early as six o'clock in the morning, but the line stretched halfway along the block.

These men were not as eager to earn $35.90 per month as they were to defend their country against foreign aggression.

Furthermore, the U.S. did not recall any warships from convoy duty or from the European theater, as Germany had hoped. As Americans always do under adverse conditions, they knuckled down to vanquish the enemy in his home territory – suffering the sniping pawns in order to strike at the king.

WAR CRUISE
OF THE
U-156

While the *U-151* was working its way home, the *U-156* was outward bound under the command of Kapitanleutnant Richard Feldt. The *U-156* was a *Deutschland*-class U-boat. Unlike the sister ships that followed, the *U-156* possessed only two torpedo tubes instead of four.

Feldt took the northern route through the North Sea around the British Isles, and may very well have crossed paths with von Nostitz. Feldt did not wait to cross the Atlantic Ocean before commencing hostilities. He was about 200 miles northwest of Ireland when he torpedoed and sank the British steamship *Tortuguero*, on June 26, with the loss of 12 lives.

Feldt disguised the *U-156* as a merchant vessel by erecting a false funnel. He proceeded westward for nine days without encountering a vessel on which to try his disguise. Finally, on July 5, his course intersected that of the USS *Lake Bridge*.

The *Lake Bridge* had previously operated as a commercial freighter named *War Rifle*. The United States Shipping Board chartered the merchantman at the outbreak of war, and changed her name. The Navy then commissioned her to transport mines for deployment in what came to be known as the North Sea Mine Barrage. The *Lake Bridge* was returning from Scotland to Hampton Roads, Virginia, on her first voyage as a mine transport, when she ran afoul of the *U-156*.

The U-boat charged directly toward the unsuspecting freighter. Not until it opened fire from a distance of six miles was its true nature unmasked. The *Lake Bridge* was defensively armed. Her gun crew wasted no time in returning fire. A running gun battle raged for

War Cruise of the *U-156*

half an hour. Neither vessel was struck, although one shell from the U-boat exploded so close to the freighter that chunks of metal were flung onto her deck.

The greater speed of the *Lake Bridge* enabled her to outdistance the U-boat.

The *U-156* spotted the *Marosa* on July 7. The Norwegian bark was transporting coal from Newport News, Virginia to Buenos Aires, Argentina. Feldt fired a warning shot across the bow of the bark. Captain Andreas Nyhus, master, gave the order to heave to. Both lifeboats were lowered. The crew abandoned ship and rowed toward the U-boat.

Captain Nyhus gave his log book and ship's papers to the first officer. After examining them, the officer returned the crew list, the passports of the crewmembers, and the captain's pocketbook (which contained $40 in currency). The crew was permitted to return to their ship and collect provisions, water, and personal belongings.

According to Chief Officer S. E. Holte, "They gave us a course, but told my captain to steer to westward and some one on board the submarine shouted, 'Good trip and God bless, you are 800 miles from land.' We then steered NW. by W. to gain north of the Gulf Stream."

A boarding party ransacked the *Marosa* and took whatever they wanted, using the vessel's gig to transfer their pillage to the U-boat. Then they set scuttling charges.

By that time darkness had fallen. The *Marosa's* lifeboats drifted in the vicinity overnight. In the morning the men spotted a sailing vessel and, hoping for a quick rescue, rowed toward her. Their hopes were soon doused because the ship was abandoned. The *U-156* stood nearby, so the *Marosa's* men turned away.

Holte: "Heavy rain, squalls, a very rough sea, and a westerly wind had set in by this time. The next day we saw nothing, and the day after that we saw nothing. The next morning there was a light southwesterly breeze, and we sighted the barque *Sorkness*. . . . They picked us up, took our boats on board, and carried us

200 miles toward the Nova Scotia shore."

In those days, Norwegians may well have been the greatest sailors in the world. Certainly they tramped the globe grandly in the prosecution of their ocean-going trade. The *Marosa's* crewmembers were so comfortable on the sea and so confident in their abilities that they decided to strike out on their own.

Holte: "We shoved off again in our two boats, loading up with provisions again, and during the next two days we saw several fishing vessels from Newfoundland. We held our course and kept the boats together so that they would not get lost in the fog. A large British man-of-war came up to within 10 yards of us and nearly ran us down. They saw us and altered their course. She was using her siren constantly. Our boats got mixed up with the propeller wash. They never answered our signals and at the time one could not see more than 200 feet ahead on account of the fog. We landed on the night of the 16th, at 11 p.m., at Cranberry Island."

On the morning of July 8, the *U-156* forced the *Manx King* to heave to by firing a shell so close to her that fragments landed on the deck. She was a Norwegian full-rigged ship that was en route from New York to Rio de Janeiro, Brazil. Captain Rasmus Halversen, master, "protested against the seizure of his vessel, pointing out that she was of neutral register." The submarine officer insisted that the type of cargo (oil, cotton, barbed wire, sheet iron, wax, and shoes) was contraband and that the vessel must be destroyed.

The definition of contraband was fluid and self-serving. Initially it was defined as arms, munitions, and specific articles of military value. This definition was too constraining for Germany, so the Kaiser gradually broadened the definition for the sake of convenience. The definition reached the peak of absurdity when Germany claimed that food was contraband because it might conceivably be eaten by soldiers, and that cotton could be woven into uniforms, and that iron could be used to manufacture weapons, and that oil could be used to lubricate military vehicles, and so on.

War Cruise of the *U-156*

According to the German definition, everything that was raised, grown, or produced constituted contraband.

Feldt permitted the crew of the *Manx King* to provision their lifeboats before he cast them adrift and set scuttling charges. This was the vessel that the crewmembers of the *Marosa* found abandoned.

The lifeboats stayed together and sailed north-northwest through choppy seas until they were out of sight of the U-boat. Then they changed their course westward. They sailed all night and much of the next day. At about three o'clock in the afternoon they were picked up by the British steamship *Anchisis*.

While these intrepid Norwegian sailors were making their seagoing peregrinations, the *U-156* reached the American coast and proceeded to conduct the first phase of its depredations against Allied shipping: it laid minefields in shipping lanes and harbor approaches.

The only casualty that resulted from these mines occurred on July 19. Calamity came suddenly and without warning at 11:05 a.m., when a tremendous explosion stove in the hull adjacent to the port engine room of the U.S. armored cruiser *San Diego*. Two men were killed instantly by the blast: Frazier Thomas, Machinist's Mate Second Class, and James Rochet, Engineman First Class. Only moments before, Thomas Davis, Engineman Second Class, had closed himself in the port shaft alley on his way to oil the bearings.

Lieutenant J. P. Millon was standing watch in the watertight space between the port and starboard engine rooms. The concussion blew him into the starboard engine room, right over the man who was working the starboard throttle. Robert Hawthorne, at the port throttle, was knocked from his station into the centerline bulkhead.

The forward end of the engine was blown clear off its base, and was displaced inward. Within seconds, a great inrush of coal-saturated water spurted into the port engine room. Severed steam lines hissed raucous-

The *San Diego* was the largest U.S. Navy warship that was lost during World War One. (Courtesy of the National Archives.)

ly, spewing superheated water into the compartment in thick, scalding clouds. The bulkhead separating the port engine room from Number 8 fire room was buckled, and the door was blown inward and twisted sideways. The engine stopped of its own accord.

On the bridge, Officer of the Deck Lieutenant F. S. Irby "felt a distinct jar, the bridge vibrating considerably." He immediately gave the order to close watertight doors. The quartermaster sounded the warning siren. Irby told the bugler to sound submarine defense (general quarters), and sent a messenger to the radio room.

Above, in the exposed wheelhouse, Captain Harley Christy rushed to the engine order telegraph and rang for full speed ahead on both engines, at the same time calling for hard right rudder. The port engine annunciator did not answer. The ship took an immediate ten degree list.

Lieutenant Commander Gerard Bradford, the Executive Officer, left the bridge to ascertain the extent of the damage. The first sign of trouble he saw was in the dynamo room, where water was leaking up from flooded compartments below. On the port side, one machine was operating with its armature half in the water. The ventilating ducts were pouring a continuous stream of water into the room, as were the voice tubes in the cen-

War Cruise of the *U-156*

tral station. Bradford asked Chief Electrician Frank Boot to divert power to the boat cranes.

Ensign John Hildman rushed to the depth charge racks on the stern, and cast off the auxiliary lashings in preparation for word from the bridge to drop the 300-pound charges.

From his station in the charthouse, Lieutenant Frank Kutz raced to the forecastle and gave instructions to have the life rafts lowered to the deck. As soon as he was certain that his orders were being carried out, he dropped down to the berth deck to check on the closure of hatches and ports. He ran into Bradford, who was emerging from the dynamo room dripping with water, and was told to make a report to the captain on the bridge.

With water lapping over the supports of the switch board, Boot was pulling power from the lights in order to keep electricity flowing to the boat cranes. Fuses continually blew out as short circuits developed from submerged equipment. Lights winked out all over the ship.

Lieutenant V. R. Greiff was the ship's radio officer. All attempts to send an SOS were frustrated. The main radio set was knocked out of commission due to the blast interrupting the power leads: the motor-generators were located on the port side of the berth deck. As the ship was not equipped with emergency batteries, Greiff switched the transmitter to a 110-volt outlet in the radio room, but by the time he made the connections, the power source failed.

Irby told the quartermaster to call the engine room on the telephone or voice tube; he received no answer from below. The navigator on the bridge, Lieutenant R. J. Carstarphen, leaped down the stairs to the chartroom in order to obtain the latest position.

Christy climbed down from the wheelhouse to the bridge, and relieved Irby so the lieutenant could take his submarine defense station at the starboard 6-inch gun. The list to port was too great for the elevation mechanism: the barrel would not point at the horizon.

Although it was impossible to direct an attack against an enemy that remained unseen, Irby pulled the percussion firing pin anyway and shot a round into space.

This was the first time in the *San Diego's* career that her guns were fired in anger.

With the ocean gushing into the inoperative port engine room, Lieutenant Millon gave orders to close the watertight doors that separated the port engine room from the starboard engine room. The door was jammed. In only half a minute the port engine room was full to overflowing. Millon found the door between the starboard engine room and Number 7 fire room operating smoothly, so he stepped through the doorway and closed the door behind him. When he opened the door between fire rooms seven and eight, he was met with inrushing water. He closed the door, then gave the order to open the feed stops in order to keep the water in the boilers and prevent an explosion. He then told the men to abandon the fire room.

If Thomas Davis was still alive, he was trapped inside the shaft alley.

By this time the engine room was a cacophony of steam that was escaping through broken and tortured pipes. Despite Captain Christy's order for full speed ahead, the annunciator bell in the engine room rang for all stop; then, a few seconds later, for full speed astern: the chain linkage had been knocked askew by the blast.

Millon and the only other man who was still working the engine (George Stockton) did their best to comply with the erroneous order. Torrents of water poured through the unsealed centerline hatchway. When the water stood four feet deep over the floor plates, Millon and Stockton hurried to carry out last minute shutdown procedures: Millon alerted the bridge on the annunciator that he was stopping the engine, while Stockton closed the proper valves.

The two men climbed the catwalks and escaped into the berth deck at a level above the waterline and the armored deck. The door leading to the passageway had been carried away by the blast. Tom Humphrey reported that the deck plates in the machine shop were buckled as well. Lieutenant C. J. Collins, Engineer Officer, appeared at that moment to inspect for damage before reporting to the captain. It was his opinion that, as the top of the evaporator room was the deck of the machine shop, the door between the port engine room and the evaporator room must have carried away as well.

Topside, Lieutenant Irby jumped from the casemate to the gun deck, but when he tried to reach the berth deck to check the closure of the watertight doors, he found the engineer's log room filled to the top with seawater. Because the ship was still rolling to port, inrushing water flooded the berth deck. Another watertight door was broached by the pressure, allowing the overflow to cascade through the armored hatchway into the starboard engine room: it was now being flooded from above as well as from below.

Captain Christy remained at the conn, digesting damage reports. The turn to the north steered the *San Diego* toward shoal water; she stood only ten miles from shore. Without motive power the ship slowly lost headway.

Knowing that the barely moving ship could not get out of range of her own depth charges without suffering damage, Ensign Hildman secured the depth charge racks. He tied the safety forks with line so they could not be released by sudden jars.

The starboard 6-inch gun crews fired their guns at what they thought was a periscope. Shells winged across the ocean at anything that remotely resembled a U-boat. The 3-inch guns joined the fracas as well. On the port side, the water was lapping at the lower part of the gun-port shutters.

With the main radio off line, Lieutenant Greiff carried the field set to the badly tilted boat deck, connected the antenna, and tried to start the backup gasoline engine. The trip up the ladder had spilled gasoline out of the carburetor and flushed the oil out of the bearings. The engine would not start. The ship was completely without power.

Captain Christy quietly gave the order to abandon ship.

Word passed quickly through the echelons. Men poured out of darkened corridors and below-deck compartments in answer to the call, swarming onto the main deck in order to don life preservers and canteens. Some of them struggled to launch boats by hand. There was no confusion. The abandonment might have been just another drill.

Lieutenant Irby descended to the port-side gun deck, carrying an armful of life belts. One gun crew was still standing at their stations, firing the gun although the muzzle was nearly under water. Irby had to pull some of the men away from the breech, and order them overboard. The men took the life belts and simply stepped through the gun port into the water.

So rapidly was the *San Diego* rolling that by the time Irby climbed the ladder to the boat deck, it was even with the surface. Other gun crews left their posts only after they could no longer fire their weapons. Counting all the guns, about forty shots had been fired.

Lieutenant Greiff's duties called for him to throw the code books overboard. He left the malfunctioning radio set and headed directly for his cabin safe where most of the secret information was stowed. Water had risen so high in the ward room, and the angle of the deck was so severe, that he could not open the heavy steel door. He was forced to leave the code books in the safe.

One set of operational codes, in lead-covered books, was tossed into the sea; another set was saved.

As the ship heeled sharply, all manner of loose gear slid down the decks and splashed into the water. Guy wires snapped, and one by one the smokestacks broke off and crashed into the sea. One of the smokestacks crushed the port motor sailor.

Acting Pay Clerk J. D. Gagan removed currency from his safe: $20,305 of government funds, and $720.11 of sailor's safe-keeping money. Left behind

War Cruise of the *U-156*

was $5 in gold, some $700 in silver, and approximately $38,259 in currency.

The ship was rolling even faster now. Two whaleboats, a dinghy, a wherry, and two punts were launched off the steeply canted deck. Life rafts were cut free and slid into the water. Anything that would float was tossed overboard, including a hundred kapok mattresses, fifty wooden mess tables, loose hammocks, and a pile of lumber that was being carried as deck cargo.

Almost leisurely, more than one thousand men stepped into the water and swam away. They clambered onto whatever floating jetsam was available. D. Easdale, ship's carpenter, walked overboard when the ship sank from under him. Ensign Hildman merely floated off the cabin hatch.

The *San Diego* stood nearly on her beam ends.

Machinist's Mate Andrew Munsen was struck on the head by one of the rafts, and was killed. Engine Man Clyde Blane drowned. Seaman Paul Harris was the last lookout to start down from the crow's nest in the forward mast; he was apparently still inside the cage when the mast hit the water, and was dragged down with the ship.

Only two men were left aboard. Bradford went over the port side. Captain Christy, in the age-old tradition of the sea, was the last man to leave his ship. He jumped from the nearly vertical bridge and climbed down a ladder to the boat deck, then slid down a line to the protrusion of the still-dripping armor belt. As the *San Diego* continued to capsize, Christy walked across her freshly cleaned bottom like a logger balancing on a rolling log. He kept pace with the ship that was rolling under him, dropped from the armor belt to the starboard bilge keel, then jumped to the docking keel. He hesitated and surveyed his ship, to make certain that no one else remained on board. Then, saluting his command, he jumped eight feet into the water.

Men in the rafts cheered as the captain and the executive officer left the ship. Christy was without a life vest. He swam a short distance from the settling cruiser, and was picked up by a motorized whaleboat.

It took another five minutes for the ship to turn completely upside down, in a symmetrical position with the keel inclined about ten degrees to the horizontal, with the forward end elevated. The *San Diego* sank slowly by the stern, without appreciable suction.

Total time from explosion to the last sight of the inverted hull was twenty minutes.

Remarkably, only six men perished.

In the water were 1,177 survivors: 49 officers, 9 midshipmen, 63 marines, and 1,056 enlisted men. Everyone was in excellent spirits. They sank "The Star Spangled Banner" and "My Country 'Tis of Thee." When the U.S. ensign was hoisted on the sail boat, they cheered the stars and stripes. The men's love of their ship did not end with her sinking. They were true patriots to their service and to their country.

Captain Christy ordered Lieutenant Clarkson Bright to take the dinghy to shore to alert the Navy of the *San Diego*'s plight, and to request rescue vessels to pick up the men. Two hours later, Bright and twenty sailors landed through the surf at Point o' Woods. As Coast Guard Station No. 82 was nearby, authorities of the Third Naval District soon learned of the disaster.

The first Navy vessel to depart for the scene of the sinking was the destroyer *Perkins*, followed by the torpedo boat destroyer *Preble* and the torpedo boat *Shubrick*. Soon a small flotilla of boats was underway: Coast Guard cutters *S.P. 740*, *S.P. 966*, *S.P. 251*, and submarine chasers *SC-55*, *SC-56*, and *SC-59*. Later, more boats joined the hunt.

Lieutenant Bright and the sailors were treated handsomely by local residents, who gave them food, clothing, and drink. That afternoon they were taken to New York City by automobile.

Meanwhile, Captain Christie was not sitting idle. He had the whaleboat's mast stepped, and hoisted sail. The whaleboat then carved a circuitous course through the survivors, picking up the sick and injured. Two steamships were sighted to the south. The whaleboat tacked toward the smoke and soon intercepted the *Malden*, Captain H. R. Brown, and the *Bussum*, Captain Brewer. Despite the possibility of a U-boat's presence in the vicinity, both captains unhesitatingly came to the rescue. Shortly thereafter, the *F. P. Jones*, Captain Dodge, hove into view and joined the operation.

Every man of the *San Diego's* crew was picked up before district headquarters at Sayville knew of the casualty. The three vessels searched the area until 3 p.m., then proceeded to New York City with the survivors: 708 on the *Bussum*, 370 on the *Malden*, and 78 on the *F. P. Jones*.

Representatives of the American Red Cross met the beleaguered crewmen with comfort kits, sweaters, socks, pajamas, watch caps, and 1,200 blankets. Since the men lost everything they owned except what they were wearing, the gifts were sorely needed. Later, the crew was given quarters aboard the USS *Maui*, a troop transport.

At the same time, the hunt was on for the dastardly U-boat that sank the *San Diego*. No one reported seeing a submarine, either its wake or its periscope. Yet, because the explosion on the *San Diego* occurred around frame #78, which was abaft the point of the ship's greatest beam, it seemed unlikely that a mine could have caused the explosion.

It was five o'clock before the *Preble* arrived at the approximate position of the sinking. *Preble* reported "considerable wreckage floating around, in center of which there was what appeared to be a smokestack at an angle of 45 degrees, and perhaps two or three feet out of the water." She picked up five Carley Life Rafts and a punt.

By this time the sea was a beehive of activity, with sub chasers and mine sweepers crashing through the waves in search of signs of the enemy U-boat. Seaplanes (or, as they were called at the time, hydroaeroplanes, or hydroplanes) buzzed in the air. Seaplane No. 7 spotted what it thought was a U-boat; it flew close enough to the *Shubrick* for the pilot to shout a verbal warning, then flew off to make an attack.

The plane dropped an aerial torpedo over the suspected U-boat, which was submerged, but the torpedo failed to explode. The plane then returned to the slower-moving torpedo boat, and dropped a box containing a message at her stern. Seaman Second Class William Queenan jumped off the *Shubrick's* fantail to recover the box. The message read, "Submarine – follow us."

Shubrick made off at full steam; she signaled three of the sub chasers to follow. General quarters was sounded and the ship prepared depth charges. All the men on the torpedo boat saw what looked like the wake of a submarine. The *Shubrick* made a run on the spot and dropped a depth charge which did not detonate. She circled, and dropped another depth charge; this one exploded, as did two more that were launched from the Y-gun of the *SC-56*.

The men then reported seeing an object very much like a periscope rise momentarily seven feet above the surface, then disappear. *Shubrick* circled again and discharged her last depth charge right on target. She then fired her port battery at the location.

The *Perkins* arrived and saw the spot where bubbles were frothing the surface, and where oil stained the blue ocean with rainbow colors. She dropped a pattern of four depth charges, none of which exploded.

SC-55 fired her Y-guns. The *Preble* steamed into the fracas and fired her Y-guns as soon as she came abreast of the still-visible wake. Both charges detonated. She circled three times, each time dropping another deadly can of explosives on the rising bubbles. She also fired her deck guns at what appeared to be a periscope.

The progression of bubbles appeared to be moving in a straight line, so the *Perkins* chased the apparently moving object with shells from her forward guns. When the bubbles maintained a stationary position, the *Perkins* let go her anchor and dragged over the spot, hanging on a submerged object for a while.

Then a pair of mine sweepers came in and swept the

War Cruise of the *U-156* 143

sea. They caught the object in their wire, and held onto it all night long. Five more mine sweepers worked their wires. Two groups of sub chasers prowled in the vicinity; they picked up what they thought was a moving submerged object, but lost track of it.

In the morning, two more mine sweepers formed a loop over the object that had been caught by the first two, the idea being to secure the object in case it turned out to be a U-boat. They maintained their position for the rest of the day. Other mine sweepers dragged up three mines, all of which were exploded by gun fire. With enemy mines now known to exist, sub chasers raced back and forth to warn ships of the danger.

The whole area was a mass of floating wreckage, much of which resembled floating mines. Cautious skippers did not draw near anything without shooting at it first. In retrospect, these pot shots may seem wasteful, but in light of the situation as it was perceived, the tactic was sound. No one knew what manner of infernal machines the Germans had left. It was only after the objects that were fired upon failed to explode that they were approached and identified: paint drums, pickle kegs, coffee tins, and water breakers.

The location of the object that appeared to be a smokestack, which was angled at forty-five degrees, was lost. The wreck that the mine sweepers were holding turned out to be a coal barge; a diver from the *Perkins* identified it without question the following morning.

Three miles to the south, the *S.P. 427* located a wreck that turned out to be the *San Diego*. A diver examined the hull on July 20, and made positive identification. The armored cruiser lay upside down in 120 feet of water. It was never salvaged.

By this time, the *U-156* was several hundred miles away, attacking the fishing fleet between Maine and Nova Scotia. But in the meantime it created havoc off the coast of Cape Cod, Massachusetts.

On July 17, the troopship *Harrisburg* spotted the U-boat southeast of Cape Cod. After remaining in full view for ten minutes, Feldt strategically withdrew under water without offering to fight.

July 21 once again found the *U-156* off Cape Cod, only this time within three miles of shore. Feldt spotted the tug *Perth Amboy* and her string of four barges. In order to save his torpedoes for larger and more valuable targets, Feldt surfaced and commenced to shell the helpless tug and tows.

The *Perth Amboy* was a steel-hulled tug that measured 138 feet in length. Her owner was the Lehigh Valley Railroad, which routinely employed her in towing coal-laden barges from New York to ports in New England, after which she returned with barges in ballast. On this passage, the tug's barges were the *No. 703*, the *Lansford*, the *No. 766*, and the *No. 740*. Only the *No. 703* carried cargo (paving stones); the other three barges were empty. Tug and tows were southbound from Portland, Maine via Gloucester, Massachusetts to Whitestone, New York.

Altogether, there were forty-one people aboard the tug and her tows: seventeen or eighteen on the *Perth Amboy* (the records are unclear), the remainder on the barges. The people on the barges included three women and five children. It was common practice for barge masters to take their families with them on coastwise voyages.

In the excitement and confusion of the attacks and subsequent escape, the recollection of events differed slightly from person to person.

According to Captain James Tapley, skipper of the *Perth Amboy*, by 10:30 in the morning he had reached a point about two and a half miles north of the Orleans Coast Guard Station when "an enemy submarine about two miles Eastward fired three shots without effect. The fourth shot carried away the Pilot House and Master's room and set it afire."

Second Mate Albert Thorsen thought that the first shot "missed us going over our heads, then the second and more shots followed in such quick succession that

War Cruise of the *U-156*

I could not count nor see where they went. I hurried into the pilot house and was there about a minute when a shell exploded in the forward part of the boat and destroyed the pilot house and the master's room, setting them afire. The Captain and a deck hand were in the pilot house with me when the shell hit us. Neither the Captain or I were hurt but the deck hand was shot in the right arm, I think by a piece of shell."

Assistant Engineer Hollis Pettengill recalled that the first two shots fell short, and that the third struck the pilothouse.

Manuel Gomes, the steward, thought that the third shot struck the pilothouse. "Then I was shot in leg and arm."

First Mate Rufus Fossett concurred. He was in bed "when the first shot burst. This woke me up and I went on deck, only pants and under shirt on. The third shot took the pilot house. I was struck on the arm and the hip."

John Zitz took a moment to retrieve his money from his locker, then grabbed a life preserver on his way topside. He arrived in time to be struck by shell fragments in the right knee and the middle finger of his right hand. He met John Bogovich, who had been struck on the arm by "a fragment of a shell." Zitz learned from Bogovich that he was the deck hand at the helm when the shell struck the pilothouse. Bogovich told him that the first shot "dropped on the port side of the tug but not very close. The second shot went over the pilot house. The third shot went through the pilot house and was the shot that injured him. He did not remember anything after that."

The deck was littered with broken glass and splinters of wood. Because the tug was unarmed and was therefore unable to defend herself, Captain Tapley ordered abandon ship. The crew wasted no time in launching the lifeboat. Everyone clambered aboard. Bogovich's wound was so severe that Zitz had to help him to board the boat. Some crewmembers manned the oars and commenced to row out of the line of fire. Once clear, others held aloft an oar to which they secured a piece of canvas, and waved it in imitation of a white flag of surrender. The tug continued to burn.

The U-boat redirected its aim at the barges, starting with the one that was closest to the tug, then working its way back along the string. First struck was *No. 703*. Captain Peter Peterson, master, heard the detonation of the shell that struck the *Perth Amboy*. He realized "that something was serious and that the tug was afire." Then a shell struck his barge forward. He ordered abandon ship.

Then came the *Lansford's* turn. Captain Charles Ainsleigh, master of the barge, made the same decision that Captain Peterson made: abandon ship. Captain Ainsleigh's 11-year-old son reportedly ran to his cabin and returned with a small American flag. Then Captain Ainsleigh, his wife, his two children, and his crewmembers departed safely in the lifeboat.

Next was the *No. 766*. "The third barge in the line, the smallest of all, proved a hard mark and the German gunners occupied half an hour in disposing of her." Everyone abandoned ship during the thirty-minute barrage. There were no injuries or loss of life.

Last struck was *No. 740*. Captain Jose Pereira was "tipped back in his chair on the deck" with his wife and 11-year-old daughter Mamie when the shooting began. He stated that after the U-boat fired at the tug and the first three barges, "They began firing at me. The first shot hit in the bow of my barge and she began to list. The next shot exploded just off the stern of my barge. I jumped in the dory taking the other fellow who is my nephew whose name is Joas Laiton, age 19 yrs. with me and we rowed to shore as fast as we could, being constantly shelled by the submarine with explosive shells which scattered shrapnel all about us."

According to Captain Pereira, "When we had pulled a few rods a shot struck the barge, her boiler exploded, and she sank in two minutes. About a half mile from shore the motorboat *Ina* came out and towed us in safely. I saw another shot strike *Barge 766* and I think her

War Cruise of the *U-156*

boiler exploded also for she sank quickly."

The shelling did not go unnoticed by people on the beach. The booming of the submarine's gun, and the explosions as its shells struck their targets, drew a crowd of summer vacationers to watch the spectacle. Someone placed a telephone call to military authorities and reported the one-sided battle.

The Naval Air Station at Chatham responded by dispatching aeroplanes. "At 10:54 a.m. sent two flying boats and at 11:15 a.m. sent 29 machines for combat. Plane 1695, pilot Ingard flew over submarine at 400 feet, dropped bomb which failed to function, plane 991, pilot Lieut. Eaton flew over submarine at 11:22 a.m. and dropped bomb from altitude of 500 feet. Bomb hit water about 100 feet off starboard quarter of the submarine and failed to function. Submarine was on surface and fired four shots at seaplanes with her main battery. She then submerged and was lost by planes because of thick smoke."

The shells that the U-boat trained high at the oncoming biplanes failed to strike their gnatlike targets, but they created an historic side effect when they struck inland beyond the beach: these shots constituted the first enemy attack upon American soil since the War of 1812.

By this time – some three-quarters of an hour after the opening shot – three of the abandoned barges had sunk. The U-boat submerged to periscope depth after the aerial attack, but surfaced shortly after the biplanes departed the area, and recommenced its attack against the tug and the still-floating barge. Feldt concentrated most of his fire on the remaining barge, which he eventually sank.

The unequal battle lasted for an hour and a half before the *U-156* submerged and left the area. Witnesses estimated that it had fired between fifty and sixty shots. Some witnesses on the tug and the barges believed that the U-boat had launched as many as three torpedoes at their vessels before firing its deck gun, but this seems unlikely.

The U.S. Navy, Boston Group, deployed a submarine chaser and the submarine *N-2* to proceed to the scene of the catastrophe. By the time the warships arrived off the coast of Cape Cod, the *U-156* was long gone. Similar orders for the destroyers *Wickes* and *Bell* were canceled before their departure.

Thirteen men were wounded in the barrage of shell fire, but none of them died.

The crew of the *Perth Amboy* rowed ashore at the Chatham Coast Guard Station. Three boats from the barges landed at Nauset Harbor. Dr. James Callanan and Dr. Danforth Taylor dressed the wounds of the injured. Newspaper reports stated the likelihood that Bogovich's arm would have to be amputated.

The sinking of the barges represented an aggregate loss of $90,000. The *Perth Amboy* was worth $100,000. The tug remained afloat with fire still raging through her wooden deckhouse. Because the towing lines had not been cast off or severed, the *Perth Amboy* was held in place "by the sunken barges, one of which with a load of stone made an effective anchor."

Some of the shell damage to the *Perth Amboy*. (Courtesy of the National Archives.)

War Cruise of the *U-156*

On July 22, Captain Tapley returned to the *Perth Amboy* with salvage vessels of the Lehigh Valley Marine Fleet. The tug's upper structure was badly burned and riddled with shell holes, but the hull, engine, and boilers were undamaged. The tug *Lehigh* towed the hulk to Vineyard Haven, Massachusetts for temporary repairs. Later she was completely refurbished at a cost of $50,000.

While the *Perth Amboy* was being salvaged, the fishing schooner *Robert and Richard* was enjoying a good catch off the coast of southern Maine. She had been fishing for two weeks, and her holds were crammed with more than 100,000 pounds of halibut, cod, hake, and cusk. On board were twenty-two men and one boy. The skipper and part owner was Robert Wharton.

The crew was eating a mid-day meal when a shell screamed overhead and landed in the water nearby. The men and boy rushed out of the cabin. When they saw the approaching U-boat, they jumped into their dories and rowed away.

A German officer ordered Captain Wharton to approach the U-boat. After questioning him, the officer ordered the skipper to row him and three men to the fishing vessel. The boarding party placed a bomb in the water under the hull. They also requested a pair of oars for the U-boat's dory. Captain Wharton then returned the Germans to their undersea craft.

The survivors heard the explosion and witnessed the sinking of the fishing vessel. The five dories stuck together throughout the afternoon, sailing and rowing toward land, which was one hundred miles away. After sunset they got separated in the dark. Dawn found two dories within sight of each other; each of the other three appeared to be alone on the wide, wide sea.

One dory rowed and sailed all day long. At 7 p.m., this dory landed on the beach at Kennebunkport, Maine.

Next to be rescued were the pair of dories under the command of Captain Wharton. They were off Portland light when the SS *Snug Harbor* found them and picked them up.

The other two dories spent a second night at sea. The tug *Standard II* rescued four men and the boy from one dory. An unnamed motorboat rescued four men from the fifth dory. There were no casualties.

August 2 found the auxiliary schooner *Dornfontein* transporting a cargo of lumber from St. Johns, New Brunswick to South Africa. She was on her maiden voyage. Captain Charles Dagwell and his crew of eight men observed the U-boat in the distance. They thought it was a tug until it fired a shell across the bow of the schooner.

The *U-156* drew alongside the *Dornfontein* and ordered her men to board the U-boat. The crewmembers were taken down below while Captain Dagwell was kept topside.

Dagwell: "We were about five hours on the submarine during which time the crew of the U-Boat robbed us of all we had on board worth taking." The Germans absconded with all the provisions they could find, as well as spare clothing.

They then torched the schooner by setting fires to her cabins and cargo.

The men were ordered back into their dory. They spent the rest of the day and all night at sea. At 6:30 in the morning of August 3, they men landed safely at Gannet Rock Light.

The still-smoking hull of the *Dornfontein*. Note the boat tied to the bow, and men standing on the bowsprit and amidships. (Courtesy of the Naval Photographic Center.)

The Germans did as poor a job of burning as they sometimes did of bombing. Twenty-four hours after they set the *Dornfontein* afire, the smoke was observed from Grand Manan Island, New Brunswick, "indicating that she was still afloat." The still-burning vessel was towed to Eastport, Maine with her hull and engines still intact, and with four hundred thousand board feet of lumber that was reclaimable. The motor schooner was later repaired and returned to service.

With no large targets in sight, Feldt next determined to devastate the fishing fleet.

About noon on August 3, the *U-156* attacked the fishing schooner *Muriel*, Captain Eldridge Nickerson in command. Nickerson did not give up easily. He turned his taffrail to the U-boat and crowded on all possible sail. For an hour he led the chase at a speed of ten knots. Not until the U-boat fired a shell across the *Muriel's* bow, and another across her stern, did he heave to and await the U-boat's approach.

The twenty-two men abandoned ship in four dories. Captain Nickerson and the three men in his dory were taken aboard the U-boat. A boarding party ransacked the schooner for provisions, and tied a bomb to her sounding lead, which was then placed under the stern. The *Muriel* sank by the head about two minutes after the bomb detonated.

The crewmen rowed their dories for the rest of the day and all of that night. The sea was choppy, the wind was fresh, and the sky was clear. The men were hungry and tired when they landed at Yarmouth, Nova Scotia at 7 o'clock in the morning.

Although official records are mysteriously meager, after scuttling the *Muriel*, the *U-156* disposed of the *Sydney B. Atwood* in similar fashion. The sole surviving archival reference is the transcription of a telegram, which states: "On August 3, when west (true) of Seal Island 30 miles, the American schooner, *Sydney B. Atwood* was sunk by bombs placed aboard her by an enemy submarine crew." There is no elucidation about what happened to the crew. The lack of mention implies that the crew survived their suffering.

At 4 o'clock that afternoon, the *U-156* sank the *Annie Perry* "by a bomb placed under the said schooner's stern." This incident also occurred about 30 miles east of Seal island, Nova Scotia. Once again, the Germans ransacked the fishing vessel for provisions.

Captain James Goodwin and eighteen men rowed all night in dories. They reached Seal Island at 4 a.m., then departed for Wood's Harbor, which they made that evening. The men were "greatly exhausted from cold and lack of food." They spent four days at Wood's Harbor, recuperating from their ordeal.

Next to suffer the same fate was the *Rob Roy*, at 6 p. m. Captain Charles Freeman Crowell and ten of his men rowed for twelve hours to reach Seal Island.

Depredations against the fishing fleet continued on August 4. After more than a week at sea, the *Nelson A.* was returning home with a catch that consisted of 7,000 pounds of halibut and 70,000 pounds of "mixed fresh fish." The U-boat drew alongside the fishing vessel and ordered the crew to abandon ship. Captain John Simms and seventeen men launched four dories.

Captain Simms: "Acting under instructions of the commander of the submarine, I took one dory with two men alongside the U-boat. We rowed the German Commander and two men over to the *Nelson A*. They had with them several bags, containing bombs, I suppose. The Germans went aboard and ordered me to come with them. They took our log line and hauled one end of it under the ship's stern, making it fast to the main rigging. They then proceeded to keel haul on one of their bombs. It was evidently timed, as the Germans seemed in no hurry to leave the ship."

The eighteen survivors rowed to shore without incident.

On August 5, the *U-156* captured and bombed the Canadian fishing vessels *Agnes G. Holland* and *Gladys*

War Cruise of the *U-156*

H. Hollett within an hour of each other.

Captain Cluett, master of the *Gladys H. Hollett*, had this to say: "They ransacked us from stem to stern, and even took my clothing, watch and nautical instruments. Myself and men were allowed to take with us nothing but the clothes we had on."

All these reports of "ransacking" imply that the U-boat was low on provisions, and needed victuals to feed the sailors during the homeward journey.

The survivors reached a buoy at eleven o'clock that night, to which they moored until dawn. Then they rowed ashore. There were no fatalities.

The U-boat took off as soon as the bombs were placed in the hold of the *Gladys H. Hollett*. It should have hung around to observe the vessel's complete destruction. The hull rolled onto its beam ends, but refused to sink. It may be that she was supported by her full cargo of herring. The vessel was successfully towed to port.

It appears that the reason that the U-boat departed so expeditiously was that she spotted a lucrative target in the distance – one that was far more valuable than a 203-ton fishing vessel. This was the 4,868-ton *Luz Blanca*.

The Canadian tanker had departed from Halifax, Nova Scotia at seven o'clock that morning. She was proceeding southward in ballast at ten and one half knots. Her destination was Tampico, Mexico, where she was scheduled to pick up a cargo of oil. Three hours and forty minutes later found her some forty miles from port when, without warning, a torpedo struck her after port quarter below the waterline.

Captain J. Thomas brought his vessel to a halt in order to ascertain the extent of the damage. Number 8 tank was breached and was quickly filling with water, and the shaft alley was flooded.

The wireless operator transmitted an SOS and an SSS. SOS was the standard signal of distress; SSS was the newly adopted Morse code that meant "I am being attacked by a U-boat." The warning was intercepted by the *F. Q. Barstow*, a tanker that was following the *Luz Blanca* by about one mile. Although no U-boat was in sight, the *F. Q. Barstow* immediately put about and headed back for the protection of Halifax Harbor.

Captain Thomas had the engine restarted. He decided to return to Halifax for repairs. The *Luz Blanca* was proceeding at nine knots when, two hours and twenty minutes later, a U-boat was spotted on the surface at a distance of four to five miles to port. It commenced to fire upon the tanker.

The *Luz Blanca* was armed with a single 12-pounder that was mounted aft. The torpedo blast had lifted the gun deck, "rendering it impossible to use gun to advantage." Nonetheless, the gun crew wasted no time in returning fire as best as they could manage.

Captain Thomas ordered emergency speed in hopes of outrunning the U-boat, even if the machinery was damaged in the attempt. Speed was increased to eleven and one half knots.

A raging gun battle ensued for more than an hour. The speeds of the two vessels were closely matched, but the tanker was outgunned. When the Germans realized this, the U-boat dropped out of range of the tanker's gun, then proceeded to lob shells at the tanker until one struck the after deck. Two men were killed by the blast. The tanker lost way and gradually came to a halt, leading Captain Thomas to suspect that the propeller had been shot off.

Thirty-two surviving crewmembers abandoned ship in three lifeboats. They were hardly clear when shells started pummeling the tanker's hull. In all, the U-boat fired approximately sixty rounds: thirty before the tanker came to a halt, and another thirty afterward. Four or five hits were registered afterward, setting the empty tanker afire.

The *Luz Blanca* later sank. The *F. Q. Barstow* escaped destruction.

Two lifeboats were picked up by a submarine chaser, which transported the survivors to Halifax. Captain Thomas and seventeen men were unaccounted for until

War Cruise of the *U-156*

the following day, when "the third boat finally made the Halifax Light Ship and were later brought to Halifax."

On August 7, the *U-156* stopped the freighter *Elizabeth von Belgie*. An examination of her papers established to the satisfaction of the Germans that she was operating for the Belgian Relief Fund.

Belgium became occupied territory after the German army invaded the country on its way to France. Because of the British blockade, the Belgian citizenry became sorely pressed for food. In October 1914, a group of Americans organized the Commission for the Relief of Belgium. Herbert Hoover was one of the organizers; he became the head of the CRB. With incredible energy, Hoover solicited tens of millions of dollars by means of private subscription. This money was used to purchase food and charter vessels for its delivery. The CRB operated with the sanction of the German government, under the proviso that none of the provisions was used for military purposes.

On August 8, the *U-156* stopped the Swedish freighter *Sydland*. Captain Alexandre Larson had been in command of the *Sydland* since the beginning of the war. The freighter's chief occupation was in delivering wood pulp to America and general cargo to Sweden.

According to official records, "The *Sydland* was taken over in Bagen, Norway, by the Allied Government in charter, and was proceeding to Hampton Roads, Va. for further orders. The Captain understood that the ship was to be used in the Belgian Relief Service." She carried no cargo to Hampton Roads, Virginia.

After firing a warning shot across the freighter's bow, the U-boat used International Code flags to signal, "Bring your papers on board."

Captain Larson and three crewmembers put out in a small boat. "The Prize Officer and six men of the submarine got into the boat and rowed back to the *Sydland* with the Captain, and asked the Captain if he had any license from the German government to show that the

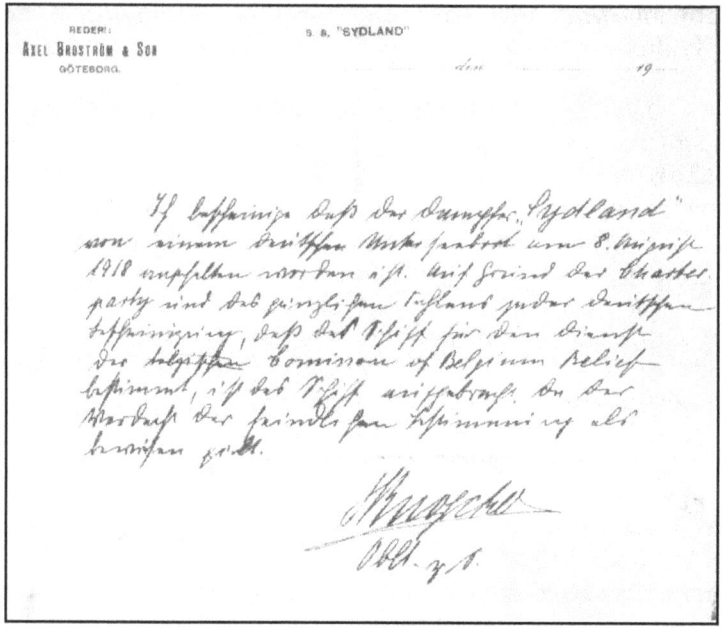

Oberleutnant zur See J. Knoeckel signed this receipt for the *Sydland* before giving it to Captain Alexandre Larson. (From Publication No. 1.)

Sydland was a Belgian Relief Ship. As the Captain could not produce the necessary German papers, the Prize Officer returned to the submarine and at 4.10 P.M. came back to the *Sydland* with papers from the Commanding Officer of the submarine stating that the *Sydland* must be sunk."

Captain Larson protested to no avail. He then "demanded a paper from the Prize Officer showing for what reason he was about to sink the vessel. After a little conversation he gave the Captain a document."

The *Sydland's* crew abandoned ship in two lifeboats, with fifteen men in each. The boats became separated. Two days later, each boat was picked up by a different vessel.

The prize crew placed scuttling charges which sank the freighter.

War Cruise of the *U-156*

On August 9, the British freighter *Penistone* departed New York for Bordeaux, France with a cargo of sugar. She was last in the right column of a convoy that consisted of more than two dozen merchant vessels plus their escorts. At ten o'clock on the morning of August 11, southeast of Nantucket Island, a torpedo exploded against the starboard hull of the engine room. Fourth Engineer Cadivor Howells was killed instantly by the blast, three firemen were badly scalded by steam, and the engine room and fire room were flooded.

The vessel forward of the *Penistone* was the Brazilian freighter *Guaratuba*. She sounded a warning by tooting six blasts on her whistle, commenced to zigzag, and raced away from the *Penistone* at high speed. Joseph Martin, the *Guaratuba's* signalman, spotted the U-boat's periscope in the distance. The French naval gun crew fired two shots "which passed about a foot above it." *Penistone* Apprentice Seaman J. S. Clark thought the shell missed "by about 50 yards."

The U-boat submerged.

The convoy scattered. Escort vessels made no attempt to rescue survivors, but stayed with the convoy in order to provide protection against further U-boat attacks.

The airwaves crackled. The *Penistone's* wireless operator, W. H. C. Holloway, transmitted a distress call that was intercepted by the Siasconsett Radio Station in Massachusetts. Escort cruiser USS *Columbia* radioed a situation report to the Office of the Chief of Naval Operations in Washington, DC. Messages were sent to land-based sub chasers to leave port and engage in rescue operations.

As the *Penistone* began to sink, the surviving crewmembers abandoned ship in three lifeboats. The *Penistone* settled until her main deck was nearly awash, "and then she hung." Two hours later, when Captain David Evans saw that the *Penistone* had stopped settling, he decided to reboard his command to determine if the vessel could be saved. His lifeboat was approaching the *Penistone* when the *U-156* surfaced nearby.

Captain Evans was ordered to go on board the U-boat; the rest of the men stayed in the lifeboat. A boarding party used this lifeboat to reach the freighter. The Germans took a chronometer and a bundle of clothes (or bedding) before they placed three scuttling charges to hasten the sinking of the vessel.

Captain Evans had abandoned ship so hastily that he had neglected to throw overboard a number of sensitive documents. These documents included routing instructions, 415 Diversion Code, and Mercantile Tables 18 and 19. It could be surmised that the bundle of clothing or bedding was used to conceal the stolen documents. Upon investigation, ONI conceded that these secret codes might have been compromised.

The lifeboat was released but Captain Evans was kept on the U-boat as a prisoner.

Three lifeboats were left adrift: one with sixteen occupants, one with thirteen occupants, and one with nine occupants. The lifeboats got separated after dark. After rowing for three days, two lifeboats with twenty-nine occupants landed at the Highland Radio Station, on Cape Cod. All the men were suffering from exhaustion. A doctor was called to treat the burn victims, who were suffering more horribly than their companions. The boats and their survivors were then towed to Cape Cod by Coast Guard cutters.

Sub chaser *SC-2840* rescued the nine men in the third lifeboat, and landed them on Nantucket Island, Massachusetts.

Captain Evans was kept prisoner for six days. He was given a kit with a hammock and a thin mattress. He was quartered in a compartment with the forty seamen. He ate well, deposing afterward that all the food was kept in tins, even the bread. He was allowed topside when the U-boat was underway and no other vessels were in sight.

On August 16, the *U-156* fired two torpedoes at the British steamship *Lackawanna*. One torpedo passed

War Cruise of the *U-156*

some twenty feet astern; the other was "diverted by gunfire." The U-boat then engaged the *Lackawanna* in a running gun battle. The U-boat fired approximately forty shells at the freighter, but failed to make a hit, due in part to a smoke screen that made it difficult for the German gunners to sight their target. The *Lackawanna* fired about twenty shells in return. The last shell struck close to the U-boat, after which it submerged. The *Lackawanna* escaped undamaged.

The *San Jose* was not so fortunate the following day. The Norwegian freighter was traveling in ballast from Bergen, Norway to New York City. The vessel was unarmed and unable to defend herself, was too slow to outrun a U-boat, and carried no radio to call for help.

Captain Hans Thorbjornsen thought that he had nothing to fear from a German warship, as he was under government charter to deliver foodstuffs for the Norwegian Food Commission.

The U-boat opened fire with its forward gun. The lone shot struck a few fathoms on the port side of the *San Jose*. The freighter stopped her engine and continued to steer the same course. The *U-156* hoisted International Code flags which signaled for the captain to bring the ship's papers to the U-boat.

The captain and five men rowed to the U-boat. The German officers examined the documents. After a discussion that lasted half an hour, and despite Captain Thorbjornsen's protests, the Germans decided to sink the *San Jose*. A boarding party placed scuttling charges while the merchant sailors launched two lifeboats.

The lifeboat under the command of the captain had thirteen occupants. The lifeboat under command of the first mate had twelve occupants. Before they left the scene, the Germans put Captain Evans, master of the *Penistone*, aboard the captain's boat.

The lifeboats sailed and rowed northward for twenty-five hours, until they were picked up by the British steamer *Derbyshire*.

August 20 found the *U-156* on the Newfoundland

Banks off Nova Scotia. Around noon, it fired a shot across the bow of the Canadian fishing vessel *Triumph*. Captain G. Myhre stopped the trawler's engine and ordered the crew to abandon ship. The men grabbed some boxes of biscuits, launched their dories, and tried to make good their escape.

The U-boat ordered the men to come aboard. Instead of scuttling the 124-foot-long steam trawler, the Germans converted her to a surface raider by arming her with two rapid-fire 3-pound guns, plenty of ammunition, and high-explosive bombs. A prize crew took command of the *Triumph*.

In German hands, the *Triumph* decimated the unsuspecting fishing fleet in a single afternoon. One after another she stopped and bombed the *Lucille M. Schnare*, *Francis J. O'Hara*, *A. Piatt Andrew*, and *Pasadena*.

Meanwhile, the *U-156* stopped and bombed the *Uda A. Saunders*.

The sea was speckled with dories whose occupants found themselves fifty miles from shore with no food or water. The records do no enumerate the number of men who sailed with each fishing vessel, but by way of example the *Francis J. O'Hara, Jr.* had eighteen fisherman including the skipper, the *A. Piatt Andrew* had twenty-four, and the *Pasadena* had seventeen.

The average number of dories for each fishing vessel was six. Thus approximately one hundred men were adrift in about thirty rowboats. Again by way of example, the men of the *Uda A. Saunders* rowed for eighteen hours before making landfall. The men of the *Francis J. O'Hara, Jr.* were luckier: they were picked up by another fishing vessel.

Only because these fisherman were so hardy, and were so capable at handling small boats at sea, was there no loss of life. Fair weather helped.

The *Triumph* fired a shot over the bow of the fishing vessel *Sylvania* at 5:30 in the morning of August 21. The fishermen stopped baiting their trawls. After the standard preliminaries, twenty-three men took to sea

War Cruise of the *U-156*

in nine dories while a German boarding party sank the fishing vessel with bombs.

The survivors determined that their number could handle seven dories better than they could handle nine. The men reapportioned themselves and let two dories go adrift. All day long they sailed and rowed toward land. The dories became separated after dark.

At 2 o'clock the following morning, the fishing schooner *Catherine Burke* picked up two dories containing seven occupants. These men were later transferred to the Canadian patrol vessel *Restless*, which transported them to Sydney.

During that day and the next, the other five dories showed up at a number of places in Nova Scotia: one at Arichat, two at Grand River, and two at Louisburg.

One group of seven survivors deposed with elaboration: "Shortly after midnight we saw St. Esprit light and landed on Guyon Island about 10 o'clock a.m., the 22nd of August, 1918. And were taken care of by the Lightkeeper of the Island. After getting something to eat the lightkeeper came with us and we landed at Gull Cove, Gabarus Cape, N. S., Where we were taken care of by the residents. We reported to a Magistrate at Gabarus, N.S. and were instructed to proceed to Louisburg, N.S., to report to the American Consular Agent at that Port. We were brought to Louisburg on Friday the 23rd of August in a motor boat, by two of the residents of Gabarus."

Throughout their peregrinations, two dories containing seven men chanced upon a dory that was occupied by survivors of the *Notre Dame de la Garde*. The French fishing vessel had been fishing on the Grand Banks for nearly three months. Her holds were crammed with 604,000 pounds of fish. On August 22, she was approached by both the *Triumph* and the *U-156*, each of which was flying an American flag.

The enemy straddled the *Notre Dame de la Garde*: the *Triumph* on one side and the U-boat on the other. The French fishing vessel was armed with two millimeter guns of an old design, but it was deemed prudent not to attempt to use them.

The crew was set adrift in dories, and the fishing vessel was sunk by means of scuttling charges.

According to an official telegram, "Five of the crew were landed at Gabones near Quechie and all were sent to the French Agent at North Sydney. None lost and no further news."

A newspaper article gave the number of survivors as 27: "After a hard row 18 landed at Gabarous, five at Forchu, and the remaining four at St. Esprit, all finally reaching North Sydney on Friday last."

On August 25, at 1:30 in the morning, the *U-156* spotted the British steamer *Erik*. She was proceeding with sixty tons of stone in ballast, from St. John's, Newfoundland to Sydney, Nova Scotia. Her navigational lights were darkened, but a nearly full moon made her hull stand out in stark relief against the horizon. The closest point of land was St. Pierre, about 70 miles away.

The U-boat fired seven rounds in rapid succession. The first shot knocked out the wireless apparatus. The second shot knocked down the smokestack and burst the main steam pipe. Two shots missed, but three more struck the steamer and damaged all but one lifeboat. Captain William Lane and four other men were wounded by pieces of shell and flying debris. Captain Lane brought the *Erik* to a halt.

The *U-156* drew alongside the *Erik*, and ordered the crew to come aboard. Because the only serviceable lifeboat could hold but four people, the boat had to make a number of trips to transfer everyone. The *Erik* was scuttled with bombs.

A doctor treated the men who were wounded. They were then given coffee, brandy, and cigarettes. Feldt told the men that he would put them aboard the first vessel he came across that had enough boats to accommodate them.

"About 6 a.m., the submarine sighted the Newfoundland schooner *Willie G.* The submarine went alongside the *Willie G.* and the submarine commander

War Cruise of the *U-156*

inquired regarding the number of boats she carried. On being informed that she only carried six small dories, he said that these were not enough to accommodate the crew of the *Eric* [sic] and the crew of the *Willie G.* and that therefore he would send the *Eric's* [sic] crew aboard the *Willie G.* and would not sink her, as he had intended doing. This was done, and the *Willie G.* brought the crew of the *Eric* [sic] to St. Pierre, arriving there about 10 a.m. on August 26."

At St. Pierre, Captain Lane had a shell fragment removed from his side. "An Engineer has a wound in the breast and a finger gone."

While the *Willie G.* was headed for St. Pierre, the *U-156* drove into a flotilla of fishing vessels. In quick succession the Germans placed bombs aboard the *E. B. Walters*, *C. M. Walters*, *Verna D. Adams*, and *J. J. Flaherty*.

They ransacked the *E. B. Walters* before setting off the scuttling charges, "even going through the chests of the crew in the forecastle." They also took a large quantity of canned goods.

Captain Mosher, master of the *Verna D. Adams*, thought that the Germans removed canned goods from his ship's stores before scuttling her.

The twenty-five men of the *J. J. Flaherty* headed for land in eleven dories. These men and the crews of the other three fishing vessels were obliged to spend the night in their dories.

The crews of all four schooners "rowed from the place of the sinkings to St. Pierre. Some of them were picked up by a small steamer [*Terranova*], transferred to a St. Pierre tug [*St. Pierre*] and reached St. Pierre about 7:30 p.m. on the same day. The other members of the crew reached St. Pierre at various times during the morning of August 26, 1918. There were no casualties."

More than a quarter million pounds of fish were lost during these raids against the fishing fleet.

Samuel Wiley, the American consul in St. Pierre-Miquelon, took charge of the men from the *J. J. Flaher-*

ty, which was owned and operated by Americans who resided in Gloucester, Massachusetts. He wrote, "I made arrangements at once to have the men lodged in a boarding house. The best possible arrangements, under the circumstances, were made for their comfort. As there were about 110 men from ships sunk by submarines who had arrived the same day, to say nothing of crews of numerous French and Newfoundland fishing vessels which were held in port on account of the proximity of the submarine, it was necessary to lodge all the men in one large room, a sort of auditorium forming part of the hotel or boarding house. They were provided with mattresses and sufficient bed coverings by the Marine Department of the colony, and they report that they have received an abundant supply of well cooked, substantial food.

"Some of the men had been able to save some of their clothes. The others wore the oil-skins or overalls they wore while fishing. I supplied the men with such articles of clothing as I judged to be necessary for their comfort.

"As there is never a large food reserve in this colony, and the existing stock of flour was alarmingly low, the Administrator, after consulting with the British consul and me, cabled to the Naval authorities at Sydney, Nova Scotia, requesting that a steamer be sent here immediately with a cargo of flour, and to aid in the transportation to Sydney of the men from the vessels sunk by submarine."

Wiley's request for flour and transportation was met with approval. A stock of flour was brought by a small steam trawler that was armed with a 3-inch gun and depth charges. The French mail steamer *Pro Patria* transported the crew of the *J. J. Flaherty* to Sydney.

Wiley: "I have given the master of the *J. J. Flaherty* a letter of identification of himself and crew to the American Consul at Sydney, Nova Scotia, who will repatriate the men. I have also provided the Master with six dollars and twenty-five cents for ferry fare for himself and crew from North Sydney, where they will be

War Cruise of the *U-156*

landed, to Sydney where the Consulate is located."

The parting shot of the *U-156* occurred on August 26. Thick fog shrouded the fishing banks some seventy miles southwest of St. Pierre-Miquelon. The U-boat emerged from the fog next to the fishing schooner *Gloaming*.

According to Captain Frederick Richard, master, "I was ordered to lower a boat and go alongside and all hands were ordered to leave the ship, which was done, and we rowed about 1 mile distant when we heard the explosion of bombs and saw the vessel sink.

"I landed with 21 men of my crew at Pointe Platte, Miquelon on August 27, 1918, at 6 a.m. We left the following day in our boats for St. Pierre where we arrived at 7 P.M. and found the 3 remaining members of my crew of 24 had safely landed 3 hours previously."

Captain Richard noted that the schooners *Athlete* and *Annie Parker* were fishing near them at the time of the sinking. For a while it was feared that both had been sunk by the U-boat. They escaped detection because of the fog.

The *U-156* lobbed shells at the USS *West Haven* on August 31, in mid-Atlantic. The troop transport was armed, and brought her guns into action against the U-boat. Neither vessel was hit. The U-boat ceased firing and turned away.

This was the last time the *U-156* was seen.

Records of the final days of the *U-156* are understandably sketchy. The last message that Feldt transmitted was received by the U-Cruiser Unit on September 24. It read, "Shall pass new English Barrage area on route 1660 on 25 September after 2014h. Can reach Skagen Reef Light-ship with greatest speed by the evening of 27 September at the earliest. Where can rendezvous take place?"

U-Cruiser Unit responded with the following instructions: "Follow planned route only by day and in calm weather. Note carefully large balls of glass which carry mines. Radio entry by Skagen south of new barrage area. Rendezvous will then be radioed."

The *U-156* did not make it through the North Sea Mine Barrage. In what might be the final irony, it is possible that it was sunk by a mine that was transported by the mine carrier *Lake Bridge*, with which the U-boat had tangled on its outgoing passage. Even more ironic, it is possible that it was sunk by a mine that the *Lake Bridge* carried *after* she escaped from the *U-156*. Perhaps if the U-boat had sunk the mine carrier, it would have made it through the mine barrage. No one will ever know.

Kapitanleutnant Richard Feldt went down with his ship. The log and all the records of the *U-156* were lost, clouding some of its activities with mystery.

The date on which the *Triumph* was scuttled remains unknown. The fishing vessel was last seen by fishermen on August 22, when she was used in consort with the U-boat to stop the *Notre Dame de la Garde*. She was not seen on August 25, when the *U-156* stopped the steamer *Erik* and four fishing vessels.

Captain Lane, the *Erik's* master, reported seeing life buoys with the name *Triumph* painted on them, when he and his crew were inside the U-boat.

From this information it can be inferred that the *Triumph* was likely scuttled on August 23 or 24.

The *U-156* did not radio for instructions on September 27, after it was supposed to have passed the lightship that guarded Skagen Reef. From this in can be inferred that it was sunk on or about September 26 – after its final transmission of September 25, and before it was supposed to make its next transmission on September 27.

According to Publication No. 1, "Twenty-one survivors were landed on the Norwegian coast shortly after the signing of the armistice." This unlikely sentence fails to account for where the U-boat survivors spent the preceding month and a half – between the probable date of loss of September 26, and the date on which the Armistice was signed (November 11, 1918).

U-boats generally tried to pass through the mine-

War Cruise of the *U-156*

field during the hours of darkness, so they could travel on the surface without being seen. In this scenario, it is possible that crewmembers who were topside at the time the U-boat struck the mine, could have survived. It is also possible that some crewmembers managed to escape from the U-boat through open hatches before it sank.

I have been able to unearth only one archival document on which the statement in Publication No. 1 could be based. It states, "It is now known that the *U.D. 156* was damaged and sunk in passing through Cattegat Minefield about November 15; the 21 survivors were interned in Haugsholne, Norway."

The misidentification (*U.D. 156* should be *U-156*), misspelling (Cattegat is spelled Kattegat, the body of water that lies between Denmark and Sweden, but the minefield was in the North Sea, between Scotland and Norway), and misnaming (there is no Norwegian city called Haugsholne, although there is one named Haugesund) are telling. The document is not an official document, but a typed summation of all U-boat activity in American waters: one that is undated but which could not possibly have been written until after the war ended.

Other errors exist. For example, the sinking of the *Sydland* is credited to the *U-117* instead of to the *U-156*. Granted that the deck log of the *U-156* went down with the U-boat so that confirmation from that source is not possible. But according to the log of the *U-117*, it was three hundred miles away from the *Sydland* on the date of her loss. On August 8, the *U-117* did try to fire a torpedo at the last vessel in an eastbound convoy consisting of twenty-two vessels, but the torpedo misfired: it stuck in the tube, worked itself free of its own accord, and missed its intended target. Droscher did not take credit for sinking any vessels that day.

Worse yet, what could the *U-156* possibly have been doing for nearly two months between September 26 and November 15, during which time there was no radio communication? I cannot hold much faith in a source that is so easily impeachable. If that was the only document on which the sentence in Publication No. 1 was based, then that sentence is subject to extreme doubt.

Because no authenticated information about these putative survivors has ever come to light, the loose language of this story appears to be more apocryphal than plausible.

The short career of a U-boat that began with such notoriety, ended in mystery and virtual anonymity.

This picture of the *U-140* was taken after the war. The view is facing forward at the aft end of the conning tower. (Courtesy of the National Archives.)

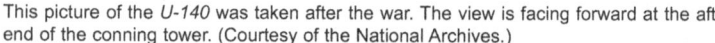

WAR CRUISE OF THE *U-140*

The *U-140* was a new class of U-boat whose construction commenced a year after the *Deutschland* and *Bremen* made their appearance as merchant submarines. It was officially commissioned into service on March 28, 1918, under the command of Kapitanleutnant Waldemar Kophamel.

At 311 feet in length, The *U-140* measured nearly half again longer than the *U-53* and the *Deutschland*-class U-boats. Its displacement tonnage was 1,930 tons on the surface, and 2,483 tons submerged.

The *U-140* was fitted with six torpedo tubes: four tubes forward and two tubes aft. It was armed with four guns topside: two 5.9-inch guns, and two 3.4-inch guns.

The *U-140* departed from Germany's Baltic coast on July 2, 1918. It took the northern route around Denmark, through the Skagerrak into the North Sea, north around the Shetlands, and west across the Atlantic Ocean. It was only two days into its voyage when it ran into rough seas and mountainous waves that demonstrated to Kophamel the U-boat's poor stability characteristics.

He wrote: "The stability is very bad. Boat does not roll but maintains 35° list and does not right herself for a long time, when turning into the sea. The boat's inclination to list is traceable to the masses of water that pour over the deck into the superstructure and cannot drain off fast enough. An estimated 50-70 tons of water remain on the weather side."

Kophamel compensated for this problem by shifting twenty tons of ballast to the starboard tanks, and by removing the ready ammunition from the deck and stowing it inside the pressure hull. These remedies helped somewhat, but the radio was put out of commission when the antenna supports were "destroyed by the high sea." Temporary antenna repairs were soon demolished.

The main ballast tank was put out of order by a leak in the bearing, causing the tank to flood whenever the U-boat was submerged.

Not until July 10 was the antenna repaired and the radio put back in order.

Continued rough seas allowed a convoy to escape. The periscope was either inundated by wave crests, or sunk too low in the troughs to enable Kophamel to see the horizon. "Use of weapons impossible."

Finally, after ten days at sea, the weather moderated to the point at which the hatches could be opened to air out the boat and recharge the batteries. "Drainage holes are cut into the upper deck." The use of weapons was still impossible, and remained so for several more days.

American records indicate that on July 18, the *U-140* fired on the *Joseph Cudahy*. The American tanker had fallen behind her convoy because she was unable to maintain speed. She escaped without suffering any damage. Kophamel's log mentions no such encounter.

According to U.S. Navy records, "On the 19th, she encountered and stopped a Danish ship, SS *Olaf Maersk*. After inspecting the ship's cargo and satisfying herself as to the propriety of the Dane's papers, which indicated that she was carrying petroleum and gasoline for the Swiss government, *U-140* allowed the neutral merchantman to proceed on toward her destination." Kophamel's log confirms this encounter.

On July 25, the *U-140* stopped the Swedish steamer *Uppland*. The neutral vessel had a safe conduct pass. She was allowed to proceed on her passage from Fernandina, Florida to Landskrona, Sweden with her cargo of phosphate.

On July 26, the U-boat lobbed shells at two British steamships: the *Melitia* and the *British Major*. Both

War Cruise of the *U-140*

steamers returned fire. The *Melitia* outran the U-boat. The *British Major* escaped under cover of darkness. Neither vessel was damaged.

On July 27, the U-boat encountered the Portuguese bark *Porto* in mid-ocean. The *Porto* was sailing from Savannah, Georgia to Oporto, Portugal with a cargo of barrel staves and 600 bales of cotton. She had been at sea for sixteen days, and had on board six months provisions for a crew of eighteen sailors.

The U-boat fired three shots across the bow of the *Porto*. Captain Jose Tude d'Oliveisa da Velha, master, gave the order to heave to. The U-boat tied off to the bark. When a German officer demanded the ship's papers, Captain da Velha gave him "the manifest, bill of lading, and everything."

The Portuguese crew was ordered to abandon ship. The men launched two lifeboats and divided themselves between them. As they drifted nearby, the Germans spent five hours relieving the bark of her provisions by the use of planks laid from the bark to the U-boat. They took flour, canned goods, salt port, three live hogs, three turkeys, and twenty-four chickens. They gave none of this food to the Portuguese sailors. No mention was made about the difficulty of forcing live hogs down the hatchway trunks, or about the mess they must have made inside the U-boat.

At 5:30 p.m., the Germans sank the *Porto* by means of "bombs and shell fire."

The lifeboats stayed together throughout the night. At 6 o'clock in the morning they were picked up by the British steamship *War Jackdaw* (also given as *Jackbow*) which transported the men to New York.

On the afternoon of July 29, the *U-140* intercepted an SOS from the *Osterley*. The message gave her position and stated that she was being chased by a U-boat. Kophamel deduced that the U-boat was the *U-156*. The position that the *Osterley* transmitted was 60 miles away from the *U-140*. Kophamel altered course to intercept the *Osterley*.

The next morning at seven o'clock he sighted a

steamer that was plying a zigzag course about three hundred miles east of the Virginia/North Carolina border. He gave pursuit. He submerged at 10:50 a.m. in preparation for an underwater attack from a distance of 1,000 feet. "The bubbles pass under the stern. No detonation. Reversed course at full speed for bow shot. No. 1 tube fired, distance 600 m[eters, or 2,000 feet]. Track angle 60°. Depth 3 m[eters]. Miss. Surfaced. So much sea has come up that the torpedo passed under the target, at least with the first shot which appeared to be absolutely sure. As for the second shot, I should no longer let myself get carried away. Also the boat was kept submerged only by cruising at low speed, and even then the conning tower was above the surface. Further pursuit had to be abandoned due to the sea state. Steamer sends contact report and gives her name *Kermanshah*."

The *Kermanshah* was en route from France to New York in ballast. "She carried three naval radio operators and an American armed guard crew of 21 men. . . . Her armament consisted of one 4-inch gun astern and a 2-pounder forward."

Captain Robert Smith, master of the American vessel, gave full particulars of the attack. Naval interrogators reported his words in the third person singular.

"The captain was standing in the chart-room doorway and sighted the wake of a torpedo headed toward the after part of the port side of the *Kermanshah*. He ran on deck, let the ship run off about four points to starboard, and the torpedo missed the stern by 10 or 15 feet. The helm was eased a trifle so that the ship would not be swinging too quickly to starboard in the event another torpedo was sighted. The ship had no sooner steadied a little when the wake of another torpedo was seen approaching amidships on the starboard side. The captain immediately put the helm hard to starboard with the idea of throwing the ship in a course parallel to that of the torpedo. In this he was successful, the torpedo passing the starboard bow about 5 feet away.

War Cruise of the *U-140*

"As soon as the second wake was sighted the commander of the armed guard fired one round from the 4-inch gun astern, the shot being directed at the spot the wake started from. The explosion that followed sounded like the bursting of the shell against a hard object, which gave the captain the impression that a hit had been made. After following a northerly course at full speed of 9.5 knots for about 15 or 20 minutes, the submarine was sighted on the horizon about 4 miles distant, the gun crew immediately opening fire. After a few rounds it was seen that the submarine was out of range and fire was stopped."

A periscope was spotted seven hours later. The gun crew fired at it and the steamer turned away from it. The periscope disappeared and was not sighted again. Captain Smith felt that one of his shots had struck the U-boat, but in this he was mistaken.

Kophamel saw no sign of the *Osterley*.

On August 1, the *U-140* fired a torpedo at the *Tokuyama Maru*. The Japanese passenger-freighter was bound from London, England to New York City with 1,300 tons of aluminum oxide. She transmitted an SOS: "*Tokuyama Maru* sinking now immediate assistance. Received answer for the call. The ship was hit on starboard side under bridge with one torpedo. But we could not see even a periscope of submarine."

The transmitted position, given in latitude and longitude, placed her about two hundred miles southeast of New York City. The log of the *U-140* recorded the position as 39° 03' north latitude, 70° 26' west longitude, or 104 nautical miles from the *Nantucket* lightship, on a bearing of 21°.

Captain Terada ordered abandon ship. Eighty-five (or eighty-seven) passengers and crew got away in lifeboats. The vessel settled by the bow but remained afloat.

The *U-140* lurked in the neighborhood throughout the night. At 5:00 a.m., Kophamel approached the lifeboats in order to obtain information, then hastened the sinking of the vessel by firing shells into her hull.

The survivors were rescued by the American schooner *Judge Boyce*, which transported them to Nova Scotia. It must have been crowded on board the schooner.

Two weeks later, on August 15, the Section Patrol yacht *Narada* picked up two of the *Tokuyama Maru's* lifeboats some 80 miles southeast of Block Island. "These two life boats were about 28 feet long by 9 feet beam and would contain about fifty to sixty men. Each boat had masts, sails, boat compasses, a few life preservers, nineteen oars, two cases of condensed milk and some canned goods, which the men on the *Narada* threw overboard. Both life boats were tied together. One was turned adrift and the other was taken on board the U.S.S. *Narada*. Lack of deck space prevented taking the other boat aboard. The boats showed that they had been occupied within twenty-four hours before being picked up."

The last sentence is curious in that the survivors had been landed in Nova Scotia on August 8 – a full week earlier.

The *O. B. Jennings* was the next victim to fall prey to the *U-140*. The tanker was armed with a 4-inch Vickers gun and one hundred twenty shells. She was in ballast, returning from England to Newport News, Virginia. On August 4, when she was less than a hundred miles from shore, the wake of a torpedo was sighted about one thousand yards off her port bow.

Captain George Nordstrom, master, swung his ship away from the charging torpedo. It passed less than five feet astern. The U-boat opened fire with its deck gun from a distance of eight miles. The *O. B. Jennings* broke out smoke boxes, made a smoke screen, and employed evasive maneuvers. The fighting flag was raised as the gunners took their places and fired retaliatory rounds. The airwaves were clogged with the tanker's bleating SOS.

For two hours the gun battle raged. The U-boat pursued the *O. B. Jennings* like a wolf nipping at the heels of a wounded lamb. The U-boat's gun was deadly accu-

War Cruise of the *U-140*

rate, landing shells so close to the tanker that shrapnel clattered continuously against her steel sides. It fired over one hundred fifty rounds. The *O. B. Jennings* fired at least sixty rounds, on two occasions exploding close enough to the U-boat to force it to submerge. But the U-boat was untouched, and fought back hard.

Captain Nordstrom stated, "A direct shot hit the engine room through the counter, smashing port engine and wrecking main steam line. Several men were wounded. At the same time another shell hit magazine and exploded, destroying all ammunition."

Lifeless on the deck lay James Scott, the second steward. Thomas McCarthy was seriously wounded.

With his vessel dead in the water and with no means of protection, Captain Nordstrom hauled down his colors and gave the order to abandon ship. Upon the tanker's surrender, the U-boat ceased firing.

While the lifeboats were being swung out, Captain Nordstrom exchanged clothes with the dead steward; he had no intention of being captured and interrogated. Then the lifeboats were launched, and the men rowed away from the sinking tanker.

When the *U-140* approached the three lifeboats that were bobbing in the slight swell, the following dialogue took place between the second officer of the U-boat and the men in the lifeboats:

Question: "We got you at last. I knew we would. What damage did the shell in the engine room do?"

Answer: "Put engine out of commission."

Question: "Where is the Captain?"

Answer: "He is dead."

Question: "Where is the Chief Wireless Operator?"

Answer: "Don't know. He must be dead too."

Satisfied with his inquiry, and not imagining that Captain Nordstrom was actually right in front of him disguised as a steward, Kophamel signaled for the boats to shove off. Now begins one of the strangest episodes of the East Coast U-boat war, an incident made stranger by conflicting testimony and apparent contradictions.

Rene Bastin, Second Officer of the *O. B. Jennings*, removed his life preserver, jumped to the hull of the *U-140*, and, according to the tanker's first officer, William Manning (and confirmed by others in the lifeboats), shook hands with the U-boat's officers and conversed with them in German. Bastin then climbed down into the U-boat and was not seen again by the men of the *O. B. Jennings*.

As the lifeboats pulled away, the U-boat approached close to the drifting hulk and resumed shelling. Even then, the *O. B. Jennings* proved to be a tough customer. It was another two hours before the tanker rolled onto her port side and slipped beneath the surface of the calm sea.

Captain Nordstrom reported, "Moving pictures were made of the *O. B. Jennings* and her lifeboats from the deck of the sub."

The lifeboats put on canvas and sailed west, managing to stay together despite the oncoming of night. At about 2 a.m., they sighted a U-boat "moving slowly along the surface. Submarine passed about 50 yards from First Officer's boat and about 300 yards from the Captain's boat."

U-boats sometimes followed lifeboats surreptitiously in the hope of using them as decoys. For that reason, when the U.S. destroyer *Hull* appeared on the scene a half hour later, and picked up two of the lifeboats, Captain Nordstrom refused to respond to her signals.

Thirty-four survivors were succored, and the wounds of the injured were treated.

The captain's lifeboat successfully evaded the rescue craft. After dawn, his lifeboat was picked up by the Italian steamer *Umbria*. The men were well fed and, at Captain Nordstrom's request, put back into the water off Currituck Beach, North Carolina. These fourteen men landed at Coast Guard Station 168, near Caffey's Inlet, on the morning of August 5.

Of the *O. B. Jennings'* crew of fifty, forty-eight were saved, one was dead, and one was unaccounted for: Rene Bastin. His voluntary desertion was suspicious in

War Cruise of the *U-140*

the extreme, so the Office of Naval Intelligence investigated what was known about him. Interviews with Captain Nordstrom and First Officer Manning sketched an unsatisfactory account of who Bastin was, or who he purported to be.

Manning: "I was acquainted with Bastin about one month before he signed on as Second Officer of the *O. B. Jennings*. Captain Nordstrom introduced him to me in the Southampton Hotel, Southampton, England, saying that he had persuaded Bastin to sign on as a Second Officer. At the time of this introduction Bastin was employed on one of the cross-Channel steamers of the Union Castle Line. . . . It was about July 6th that Bastin signed on as Second Mate . . . taking a six months' leave of absence . . . to do this. He was a good officer, did his work well, and never acted suspicious to me."

Bastin was a Belgian (or a Dane) who spoke fluent English, French, and German. "He was married to an English girl in Southampton, and has two children. His married life was apparently quite happy."

He was also a trouble maker. "After leaving Southampton, we called at Plymouth, awaiting convoy and sailing instructions. While at Plymouth, Bastin informed me that he had notified the principal Naval Transport Officer that the ship was in an unseaworthy condition. This was the cause of an examination of our boat being made at Plymouth, after which we were ordered to Davenport Dock Yards to have repairs made; but he should have notified either the Master or myself. The only explanation of this act that I can give is that he wanted the ship in as good condition as possible because I believe him a big coward at heart. . . .

"While we were awaiting repairs at Plymouth, Bastin made a request to the Captain to be paid off. This the Captain refused to do. He informed Bastin that he would have to live up to his contract. Bastin then told me that he did not like Capt. Nordstrom, and that he did not like the way things were run on board the ship."

Manning believed that Bastin "was always overstepping his authority."

A British officer appointed Bastin as the spotter for the gun. Because Captain Nordstrom no longer trusted him, once at sea, he appointed Manning as spotter and placed Bastin in charge of the ammunition passers. "During the fight with the submarine Bastin was naturally supposed to be in this position, but was nowhere to be seen. Just as I was using my last round of ammunition, Bastin was seen to come up out of the pump room. When questioned by the Captain as to where he had been, he said that I had sent him down to the pump room to see what damage had been done to the pump, but I had not given him any such instructions. This is just another instance of his cowardness [sic]."

Was Bastin a spy or a dastard?

Not until after the Armistice was signed did Bastin reappear in Allied territory, when he turned himself in to the Naval Flag Office in Brest, France. He filed an extensive report in which his evacuation from Germany reads halfway between release and escape. (At that time Germany was in a terrible state of disorganization and

The *U-140* at the Portsmouth Navy Yard, in New Hampshire, after the war. Boat stowage is behind the vertical plates under the raised deck. (Courtesy of the National Archives.)

War Cruise of the *U-140*

political upheaval.) He also described the three months that he spent aboard the *U-140*, what he learned about the U-boat and its crew, and which merchant vessel attacks and naval engagements he witnessed. The enigma of his character is accentuated by the differences between that report and an article that he later wrote for the Standard Oil Company magazine *The Lamp*.

In the report he claimed that he boarded the U-boat in order to receive treatment for his shrapnel wounds, then was not allowed to return to the lifeboat. In the article he claimed that he was captured against his will, taken prisoner as an officer of the *O. B. Jennings* in lieu of the captain, whereupon he received no medical attention even though a doctor was on board the U-boat.

Which to believe? And how serious could his wounds have been if they healed themselves without treatment?

Kophamel recorded in his log: "Upon his urgent request, the steamer's Second Officer was taken aboard as prisoner. The man seemed qualified to be able to make important statements. His statements are included in a Special Report."

Not having access to the Special Report, we can only surmise what it might contain. Kophamel's log does not reveal any hint that Bastin claimed to be a secret agent working for Germany. Nor did the British authorities ever uncover any evidence against him.

More than likely, he was afraid of being set adrift at sea in an open boat, and figured that his chances for survival were better within the hull of a U-boat. We will never really know. Once a person lies, his word is forever subject to doubt.

With that caveat, I now quote Bastin's description of the tanker's final moments. "Orders were given by the artillery officer for a continuous bombardment of the ship by the guns – two 6-inch and two 4-inch guns. At 4 p.m. the *Jennings* went down by the stern. At 4.30 she took a heavy list to port. At 4.45 she capsized, bottom up, and then would not sink. The submarine steamed at high speed around the *Jennings*, at a distance of 100 yards. At 5.15 she fired a stern torpedo amidships. At 5.30 she fired her bow torpedo which struck No. 2 tank. The *Jennings* disappeared. At 5.45 nothing was to be seen but a few planks and the wreckage of two lifeboats."

As a fillip to this strange tale, Manning claims to have seen the U-boat's second officer (the one who spoke English to the men in the lifeboats) in a New York saloon a week after the *O. B. Jennings* was sunk. According to his story, the two men recognized each other, whereupon the U-boat officer made his way through the elbow-benders and lost himself in the crowd outside the bar.

The U-boat's log makes no mention of putting men ashore, nor is there any corroborative evidence from German archival sources that U-boat missions involved dropping off spies.

Nonetheless, the *U-140* did in fact dock in one American pors – but not until after the war, when it was turned over to the U.S. government, was commissioned as a U.S. Navy vessel, and was dissected by naval engineers in a study of German submarine construction. For the circumstances of its sinking, read the chapter entitled "Victory Bond Cruise of ex-German U-boats." The *U-140* was scuttled not far from the site of the *O. B. Jennings* – a true case of poetic justice.

On August 2, 1918, the *Stanley M. Seaman* departed from Newport News, Virginia with 1,400 tons of coal that was consigned for delivery to Porto Plata, San Domingo. Three days later and about two hundred miles off the North Carolina coast, a German shell screamed across her bow. Captain W. T. McAlony, master, gave the order to lower the sails on all four masts and bring the schooner to a halt. The time was thirty minutes before meridian.

While the U-boat approached the schooner from a distance of several miles, the nine-man crew hurriedly abandoned ship in a motor lifeboat. The U-boat

War Cruise of the *U-140*

changed course from the schooner to the lifeboat. When the U-boat drew alongside, a German crewmember tossed a line to the lifeboat. This line was made fast to the U-boat.

A German officer questioned Captain McAlony about the nationality of the schooner, her cargo, and her ports of departure and destination.

Captain McAlony: "I suppose you are going to sink the schooner?"

German officer: "Nothing surer than that."

Captain McAlony: "We left the vessel in a hurry and we have not much food or water in the lifeboat; also there is some gasoline aboard which I would like to have. How about it, can I go back and get it?"

German officer: "We will let you go back."

The U-boat then dropped the lifeboat astern, and towed it back to the *Stanley M. Seaman*. According to the official report, "When they approached the schooner, they hauled the boat up alongside and the Officer and one man entered the lifeboat and were pulled to the schooner. Before they approached the schooner, the German Officer asked the Master if he had a good line aboard ship, and the Master answered 'Yes.' He then told the Master's mate to have the crew run a line from the stern of the schooner to the bow of the submarine, which was done. The line was about 100 fathoms. After making the line fast to the submarine, the boat returned to the schooner. The Master was aboard the schooner while the line was being run. While the Master's men were running the line, the crew of the submarine opened a door in a part of the superstructure forward of the conning tower, and pulled out a wooden boat, about 22 ft. over all; they lowered this boat and five or six men got in it and pulled to the schooner. They brought with them bombs, which they told the Master's mate they would use to destroy the vessel. They put the bombs on deck, but did not make any effort to place them while the Master was aboard. The Master told the boarding Officer that he would like to get his license and some personal belongings. The

Officer told him to go ahead but to work quick."

The American crew was given plenty of time to obtain provisions and gasoline for the lifeboat's engine. Captain McAlony asked permission to figure his position, "not having done so since the previous noon."

The boarding officer said, "When you leave the vessel, go alongside the submarine and they will give you the position." This was done. The Germans then ransacked the schooner for provisions.

The men started the lifeboat's engine and proceeded northwest toward Hatteras. They were out of sight of the schooner when they heard the bombs detonate. By this time it was one o'clock in the afternoon. The lifeboat droned toward shore for eleven hours. The engine conked out at midnight. The men were unable to work on the engine until there was sufficient daylight to enable them to see what they were doing. They repaired the engine, got it started, and proceeded once again toward land.

At eleven o'clock that morning, the British steamship *Maindy Court* hove into view, picked up the men, and transported them to Newport News, Virginia.

The afternoon of August 6 found the *Merak* proceeding southward around the Diamond Shoals of North Carolina. The freighter was transporting 4,000 tons of coal from Norfolk, Virginia to South America for the United States Shipping Board.

According to Second Mate Salvatano Monti, "We were traveling along smoothly at a speed of about eight miles an hour, the weather was fine and the sea calm. We were not far from the *Diamond Shoals* lightship, there were two ships in the distance and we were just about to change our course, when without warning a shot whizzed past the bridge. Several other reports followed but I was unable to make out a submarine, all I could see were flashes in the distance."

Enoch Payne Hardy, the *Merak's* third class radio technician, transmitted an SOS. He did not receive an acknowledgment.

War Cruise of the *U-140*

Although the U-boat was not visible from the bridge of the *Merak*, the crew of the *Diamond Shoals* lightship saw it clearly on the horizon when the first shot "attracted the attention of the First Mate of the *Diamond Shoals* lightship and the submarine was then discovered, between 3 and 4 miles East North-East of the Lightship and about 4 miles from the steamship."

The lightship radio operator sent a warning broadcast: "KMSL SOS. Unknown vessel being shelled off *Diamond Shoal* Light Vessel No. 71. Latitude 35-05, longitude 75-10." The position was that of the U-boat, not that of the lightship or *Merak*. Although the message was repeated three times, no acknowledgment was received.

Kophamel intercepted the messages. He wrote in his log, "She sends radio signals during shelling of the other steamer. In order for my operations to remain undisturbed, she must be captured quickly."

The Diamond Shoals consisted of a pair of submerged sandbars that extended southeast from Hatteras for ten miles or more. The *Merak* zigzagged frantically in an attempt to avoid shells that were landing uncomfortably close, and in the process ran aground on one of the shoals.

Seeing that the steamer lay helpless, Kophamel altered course for the lightship in order to silence her wireless transmitter. He fired shells that came close enough to inundate the lightship's deck and scare off the crew.

The *Diamond Shoals* was a defenseless vessel: ungunned, moored semipermanently, and with her boilers unfired so that she could not get underway. Her lights burned brightly at night, her bell clanged melodiously in wave-tossed seas, and her crew kept a diligent watch for ships that strayed too close to the shoals, so that she could issue warning signals to lookouts.

The lightship crew later issued the following statement: "At 3:25 PM submarine commenced shelling Lightship, firing six shots, none of which had effect. The period during which the six shots were fired was about five minutes. The crew of the Lightship, twelve in number, left the Lightship in one life boat just before the sixth shot was fired."

This last shell "exploded a few feet from the side of the Lightship and filled the upper deck with water from end to end. When the shells hit the water they threw the water up 75 or 100 ft. The sub was apparently using shrapnel."

The lightship crew departed in such haste that they left behind the Radio Code Book and the Merchants Ship Cipher – documents that could have been valuable to the German naval command. After rowing some ten to twelve miles, the men "landed one mile to the North of Cape Hatteras and proceeded to Coast Guard Station #183."

Upon observing the lightship crew rowing away from their vessel, and secure in the knowledge that the lightship's radio was silent, Kophamel returned his attention to the stranded freighter that was now a sitting duck.

Monti: "We had no guns to return the submarine's fire, and as a result, the submarine came steadily toward the ship, firing at intervals. After about 30 shots were fired, we decided to abandon ship . . . in two boats and started towards the shore."

According to Kophamel, he sank the *Merak* with a torpedo.

Monti thought differently: "We were some distance from the boat when the submarine went up to the ship and placed a bomb aboard which sunk the ship. . . . After this the submarine steamed towards the boat in which the Captain was and" interrogated him.

After ascertaining the name of the vessel, her nationality, cargo, tonnage, and ports of call, Kophamel said, "Have you a sail? You are about ten miles off shore and I don't think you will have any trouble in getting there. Thank you."

Monti: "The submarine then steamed away in the direction of the Lightship and opened fire on same. I did not see the Lightship sink."

War Cruise of the *U-140*

Kophamel's log entry was succinct: "Proceeded back to the lightship, which had already been abandoned by the crew. Sank her."

The report of the lightship's crew was more detailed: "The submarine then returned to the vicinity of the Lightship and fired seven more shots at the Lightship, commencing at a distance of about 2 miles from the Lightship and extending over a period of about ten minutes. The boat containing the crew of the Lightship was then five miles away from the Lightship. The submarine then stopped firing for about 45 minutes and then commenced again, firing about 25 shots up until 9 o'clock."

What the lightship crew could not see through the haze was that the *U-140* had already sunk the *Diamond Shoals* and had gone on to bigger game: it chased the British steamer *Bencleuch* and the American steamer *Mariners Harbor*. It lobbed shells at the *Bencleuch* but did no damage, and did not get within range of the *Mariners Harbor*.

The *Mariners Harbor* foiled Kophamel's plan to hold radio silence. She intercepted the lightship's warning and maintained wireless communication with nearby vessels. She alerted the passenger vessel *Cretan* of the U-boat activity. Both the *Mariners Harbor* and the *Cretan* crept northward in shallow water close to shore. The *Bencleuch* took a southeasterly course along the coast. All these vessels escaped destruction.

The *U-140* then turned away from shore, "as the water I was entering was too shallow."

Meanwhile, the men in the *Merak's* lifeboats raised sails and headed for land. By this time night had fallen.

Monti: "We lost sight of the boat containing the Captain and other members of the crew. When we landed on the beach, we built a fire, and thereby tried to attract the attention of the other boat. Not long afterwards men from Station 181 of the Coast Guard came to our rescue and took charge of the boat." These twenty men were taken to Elizabeth City, North Carolina.

Captain Charles Gerlach and the other twenty-two

men from the *Merak* spent the night at sea. The next day they were picked up by the steamship *Adonis*, which transported them to Norfolk, Virginia.

It is interesting to note that voluntary prisoner Rene Bastin claimed to have been brought onto the deck of the U-boat during the action, and to have observed the "*Diamond Shoal* Light Vessel at a distance of 150 yards. At the same time I saw three steamers on fire and the submarine was shelling the Light Vessel with her two 6-inch guns at 150 yards. I noticed the smoke of these shells was yellow and I think the shells fired on the *O. B. Jennings* were smokeless. I concluded, therefore, that the submarine was firing gas shells at the *Diamond Shoal*. I think she did that in order that none of the Light Vessel crew might escape. The Light Vessel blew up in a few minutes and the submarine could not go any further in as it was shallow water. That is how the Shoal Light boat escaped."

Bastin's account does not correspond to circumstances otherwise related and known to have occurred, thus throwing much doubt on either his powers of observation or honesty in reporting. I sincerely doubt that Kophamel would have permitted the prisoner on deck during a gun battle.

On the morning of August 10, the *U-140* attacked the Brazilian passenger-freighter *Uberaba*. She was southbound with cargo and 110 Navy personnel on board. The U-boat fired thirty-two shells in a running gun battle that lasted for an hour and forty-five minutes. These shells straddled the *Uberaba* but none struck her. She transmitted an SOS which brought the U.S. destroyer *Stringham* to the scene.

The warship spotted an oil slick that was created by fuel that was leaking from one of the U-boat's tanks. She followed the iridescent trail and dropped seventeen depth charges, of which one failed to explode. They were set to detonate at 120 feet. The explosions failed to sink the U-boat but allowed the *Uberaba* to escape unscathed.

War Cruise of the *U-140*

Down below, the U-boat was in serious trouble. The hull and fuel tanks suffered extensive damage from the close trouncing. Seawater flooded the pressure hull through broken pipes and valves. The conning tower hatch was unseated, allowing water to pour into the control room. Ruptured fuel lines worsened the leak of oil. The crew worked hard to make whatever repairs they could.

To escape from the depth charges, the *U-140* retreated to a depth of 250 feet. Kophamel: "As the compensating tanks are completely empty and the bilge cannot be dumped out with the destroyer still overhead, the situation becomes critical. The boat can continue to be held only by partially blowing the ballast tanks. A total of about 40-45 tons of water enters the boat. With the free water in the boat and the tanks, depth control becomes very difficult. In order to decrease the pressure of the penetrating water, rose to depth of 40 m[eters (135 feet)]."

The U-boat was leaking like a sieve. Kophamel wrote long passages about the location and severity of the leaks, at the end of which he speculated, "The overall leakages can be traced back to faulty workmanship at Germania Yard. Surfaced. Nothing in sight. The fact that the destroyer has let the boat get away can only be ascribed to her lack of experience."

The *Stringham's* action report provided a different perspective: "As this ship was detailed to escort the U.S.S. *Delaware* [a battleship that was then fifteen miles away] it was considered inadvisable to expend any more depth charges without a reasonable chance that they were not being wasted. After searching in the vicinity until 11:10 [an hour after the first depth charge was launched], both engines were stopped in order to listen more efficiently with the M.V. tube listening device but nothing could be heard. The ship then proceeded on duty assigned."

Kophamel: "Before there can be any further consideration of operations, the leakages – of water as well as of oil – must be eliminated. If a considerable improvement cannot be achieved, I must abandon this area and transfer my area of activity farther out to sea."

The crew worked for two days to repair the damage that the *Stringham* inflicted. Major leaks persisted. The outer doors of torpedo tubes one and two "have become loosened and partially battered. It is possible that they obstruct the opened bow-cap. Thus, both tubes are unusable."

The fuel was distributed among the tanks that leaked the least. Worse, it was unsafe to dive deeper than fifty feet without worsening the leaks of both oil and water. "An oil wake can be seen as far as the horizon. . . . The condition of the boat no longer permits operating near the coast. The boat could not escape a systematic pursuit. *Nantucket* lightship must be given up and a new area selected farther out to sea, where only isolated patrols will be encountered."

Kophamel ceased his near-shore operations, and proceeded offshore in a northeasterly direction.

On August 13, the *U-140* engaged the USS *Pastores* in a running gun battle. The U-boat commenced firing from a distance of six to seven miles. The first shot fell a mile and a half short of its target. This shot did not force the *Pastores* to heave to. The *Pastores* presented the profile of a common freighter because she was, in fact, a freighter. Prior to the war she was known as a "fruiter" or "banana boat" because she was in the trade of transporting tropical fruit from South American ports to New York City. After the U.S. declared war against the Central Powers, the U.S. Navy purchased the *Pastores* from the United Fruit Company and converted her to a troop transport.

The *Pastores* was now armed and dangerous. She returned fire with armor piercing shells from her 5-inch gun. Neither vessel was in range of the other. The U-boat fired about 15 shots, the closest of which fell nearly one mile short. The merchantman fired nine shots, never striking closer than two miles from the U-boat. The engagement broke off when the U-boat ceased fire

War Cruise of the *U-140*

and submerged.

By now it was obvious to Kophamel that the cruise had to be curtailed. More than thirty tons of diesel fuel was lost to leakage. Kophamel: "An indication of this large loss can be seen from the extent of the 'oily banner' the boat has unfurled."

The *U-140* headed for home.

Two fruitless weeks passed between the day on which the *U-140* sank the *Merak* and the *Diamond Shoals* lightship, and the day on which it made its final successful attack of the cruise.

The *Diomed* departed from Liverpool, England on August 12. On board were 106 officers, crewmembers, and naval gunners. The freighter was armed with a 4.7-inch gun that was mounted on the after deck. The *Diomed* was part of a convoy that consisted of nine freighters and troop transports, and which was escorted by eight destroyers.

In accordance with standard practice during World War One, the escorts did not accompany the convoy all the way across the ocean, but only until it was clear of home waters, where U-boats concentrated their attention. Then the destroyers returned to England and the merchant vessels dispersed and followed the routes and courses that were prescribed by their various sailing instructions, which were dependent upon their destination.

The speed of the *Diomed* was sixteen knots. Nine days after departure found her proceeding independently some three hundred miles east of Nantucket Island, Massachusetts, bound in ballast for New York. At 4:50 on the morning of August 21, Chief Officer Alfred Batt spotted a suspicious object about four miles off the starboard beam. He put his stern to the object and ordered the gun crew to stand by for action.

The U-boat opened fire before the *Diomed* steadied on her new course. The British gun crew returned fire. The Germans fired both shrapnel and high explosive rounds. The U-boat's fourth shot blew the starboard seaman's quarters to pieces, killing one man and injuring several others. Once the Germans got the range, their shelling became consistently accurate. The *Diomed* fired twelve shots without effect on the U-boat, and suffered five hits that killed another man, carried away the poop deck (making the ammunition locker inaccessible), and ruptured the steam pipe to the steering gear.

Now the *Diomed* was unable to defend herself and unable to steer. Dense volumes of scalding steam chased the men off the gun platform. Extra Second Officer J. G. Cocking tried to ignite the smoke boxes, but both refused to ignite.

Captain A. D. Baker, master, gave the order to stop the engine and abandon ship. Eight lifeboats were lowered: four from each side. Most of the survivors escaped further onslaught after they occupied the lifeboats. One boat was inundated with water that was thrown up by a nearby shell burst, forcing the men to abandon it and transfer to a different boat.

The men rowed away from the helpless transport. All the wounded men were transferred to one boat so that Surgeon Edward Clark could treat them.

The *U-140* closed to within three hundred yards of the *Diomed*, and positioned itself broadside. Using both guns, it fired three salvoes into the port hull. From his lifeboat, Second Engineer B. D. Wregg "took several pictures of the submarine, which was firing at the time." The transport slowly listed to port. The *Diomed* sank fifteen minutes after the first salvo.

The U-boat left the scene of destruction and proceeded back to Germany.

The lifeboats were tied together and rowed for six hours. The SS *Aungban* rescued the men at noon, and landed them at New York two days later.

On August 22, the *U-140* lobbed a shell at the American freighter *Pleiades*, which was en route from Havre, France to New York City. The *Pleiades* returned fire and turned away from the U-boat. During an

War Cruise of the *U-140*

engagement that lasted for fifteen minutes, the U-boat fired four rounds and the freighter fired thirteen rounds. Neither vessel was struck.

Kophamel launched a torpedo at an unidentified steamer on August 24. The torpedo missed and the steamer escaped.

Fuel was leaking from the tanks at an alarming rate. Kophamel reduced speed significantly in order to conserve fuel. He used the Gulf Stream as his primary means of propulsion.

On September 1, the *U-140* engaged in another running gun battle, this time with the American freighter *Frank H. Buck*. The U-boat opened fire from the extreme range of eight miles. According to Captain George McDonald, master of the *Frank H. Buck*, "We answered fire with forward 3-inch gun. We saw the shot fall about 400 yards short and immediately swung stern toward the submarine, using after gun of 6-inch caliber. Our shots were very close to submarine and the submarine's shrapnel was bursting very near to us, some of the pieces falling upon our deck amidships. We changed the course frequently in short swings, which seemed to upset the submarine's aim and range. As soon as submarine saw our range was equal to hers she hauled away from us."

American records credit the *U-155* with the attack on the *Frank H. Buck*. No such attack is noted in the log of the *U-155*, but the incident is clearly described in the log of the *U-140*, which intercepted the freighter's radio message in which she gave her name. Kophamel noted that the U-boat's poor shooting was due to rolling in strong seas.

The *U-140* made one more unsuccessful attack, this one occurring on the eastern side of the Atlantic Ocean on September 6. The vessel was unidentified.

On September 9, the *U-140* rendezvoused with the *U-117* (i.e.) at the request of the latter U-boat, which was low on fuel. The meeting took place off the Faeroe Islands (between Iceland and the Shetland Islands). The *U-140* transferred 20 tons of diesel fuel from its damaged bunkers to the bunkers of the *U-117*.

Both U-boats then proceeded through the North Sea Mine Barrage without incident. The *U-140* reached Kiel harbor safely on September 20, 1918.

This was the only war cruise of the *U-140*. It sat out the remainder of the war, then was turned over to the British at Harwich, England, on February 23, 1919. For information about its work for the American Victory Loan Campaign, and its ultimate disposition, see the chapter entitled "Victory Bond Cruise of ex-German U-boats."

Rene Bastin wrote a full account of his experiences aboard the *U-140*. His article in *The Lamp* might have satisfied readers of the magazine, but his names and dates were wrong, the incidents he recounted were unsupported by the evidence, and everything he wrote was grossly exaggerated.

For example, he wrote the name of the skipper of the *UK 140* [sic] as Kliphamel. He noted the speed of the U-boat as 25 knots (about double its rated speed). He stated that there were other prisoners on board. He wrote that the *U-140* did not reach Kiel until October 25 – more than a month after its actual arrival – explaining that the delay was caused by proceeding for five weeks at a speed of 3 knots.

Worst of all, he claimed to have witnessed the destruction of the *U-156*: "She must have struck a mine and was blown 500 feet into the air." Not until the invention of the atomic bomb did there exist a man-made explosion that was powerful enough to lift a submarine out of the water, to say nothing of blasting it to the height of a 50-story skyscraper.

The list of errors and embellishments goes on and on. None of Bastin's boasts could be corroborated. His repatriation must have been a relief to the beleaguered Germans who had to suffer his company for so long.

WAR CRUISE
OF THE
U-117

The *U-117* was newer than the *Deutschland*-class but older than the *U-140*. Despite the lack of the UC designation, it was designed as a minelaying U-boat – one that could operate at long range. This "in-betweener" measured 267 feet in length, displaced 1,164 tons on the surface, and displaced 1,512 tons submerged. Its could travel at a speed of 14.7 knots on the surface, and 7 knots submerged. The top speed was so uneconomical because of fuel consumption that the U-boat seldom drove so fast. The average cruising speed was 7 knots. The most fuel efficient speed was 5.5 knots.

The U-boat was fitted with two mine tubes, and could carry as many as forty-two mines. It was also fitted with four torpedo tubes. Deck guns included one 5.9-inch gun forward, and one 3.4-inch gun aft.

The *U-117* was commissioned into service on the same day as the *U-140*: March 28, 1918. It left Germany

Starboard torpedo tubes of the *U-117*. (Courtesy of the National Archives.)

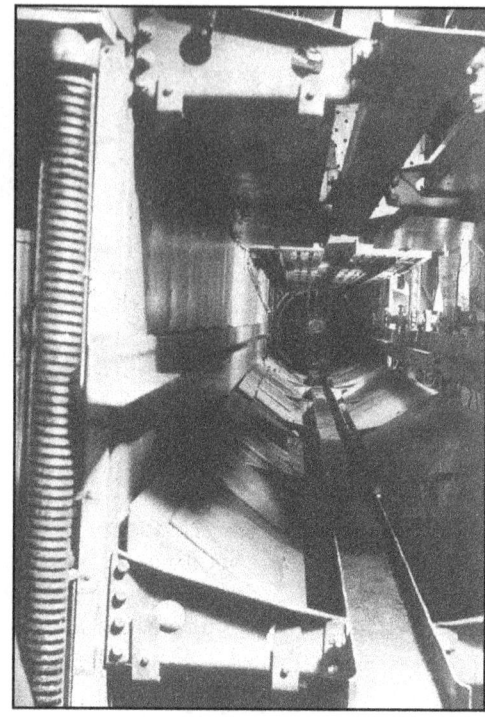

The passageway of a mine laying tube of the *U-117*. (Courtesy of the National Archives.)

for its first and only war cruise on July 11 – nine days after the *U-140* departed. In command was Kapitanleutnant Otto Droscher.

The *U-117* had an inauspicious beginning because of a number of malfunctions that plagued the U-boat throughout its cruise. A fuel oil leak was discovered on the day after departure, leaving a track that was visible on the surface. The starboard wheel bearings became overheated; they had to be removed and overhauled while underway. Both brand new diesel engines had to be overhauled, one after the other. The evaporators were defective, reducing the amount of drinking water that could be extracted from seawater.

The worst catastrophe – and one that was nearly fatal – was an uncontrolled descent that occurred while the U-boat was proceeding submerged. Droscher: "The boat suddenly sank to a depth of 60 m. [meters, equiv-

War Cruise of the *U-117*

alent to 200 feet] in spite of blowing in compressed air. It was ascertained later that the rapid air extractors of several of the auxiliary tanks were crushed."

On July 20, in mid-Atlantic, the U-boat was nearly run down while it was making a submerged approach on a westbound steamship. Instead of turning tail and taking off at high speed, the steamer suddenly turned toward the U-boat and attempted to ram. This novel and aggressive stance forced Droscher to make an emergency dive because he did not have time to veer out of the way of the charging steamship.

The steamer was out of torpedo range by the time the U-boat surfaced. Droscher pursued the steamer at full speed for a couple of hours, firing periodically. He lost sight of the target during intermittent rain squalls.

On July 26 he attacked the British steamer *Baron Napier* with gunfire. The *Baron Napier* returned fire, discharged a smoke screen, and turned into the waves. Although the steamer was not as fast as the U-boat, the tactic of heading into the sea put the smaller boat at a disadvantage. The *U-117* pitched so badly that zeroing in on the target was nearly impossible. The larger vessel was faster and more stable in a head sea than the narrow-beamed U-boat.

Droscher was falling behind in the uneven contest of maneuvering in increasing seas. He called for reserve speed. Although he was now able to maintain his distance from the steamer, the U-boat worked so hard in the heaving seas that gunnery control decreased dramatically. The U-boat's shots fell far to the side of their target.

The low-profile U-boat shipped volumes of water that cascaded down the hatch. Droscher finally broke off the attack.

On August 1, Droscher fired a torpedo from periscope depth at what he believed to be a small cruiser. He observed the torpedo running true, but then it submerged and no detonation followed. He could hardly have missed from a distance of less than half a mile. He assumed that the torpedo must have passed under the target. By the time he surfaced, the target was lost in the darkness.

Foul weather continued to put the U-boat at a disadvantage. Droscher sighted an eastbound convoy on August 2, but could not get into a favorable firing position because the seas ran too high to maintain periscope depth.

Droscher also learned that fuel consumption was greater than anticipated. Consumption conspired with leakage to reduce his ability to proceed at high speed. He reduced speed to a more conservative 7 knots.

Mechanical problems worsened. The friction couplings were undependable, sometimes engaging and sometimes not. When a friction coupling failed to connect the electric motor to the propeller shaft, the shaft would not turn. If only one coupling failed to engage, the U-boat could proceed under water but only at reduced speed on a single propeller. Otherwise, the U-boat had to surface, engage and disengage the diesel engines, then try again to connect both electric motors to the propeller shafts.

Droscher encountered another eastbound convoy on August 8. The convoy consisted of twenty-two merchant vessels, some of which were tankers whose tanks were gorged with petroleum product. Droscher advanced at high speed in order to obtain a favorable attack position. He was barely able to get within range of the last steamer in the convoy.

Once again his torpedo attack was thwarted, this time by a torpedo that stuck in the tube. It eventually worked itself free after the speed of the U-boat was reduced, but by that time the convoy was a smudge on the horizon. Droscher took the opportunity during calm seas to have the crew remove two spare torpedoes from their watertight containers that were located outside the pressure hull, and to reload the empty tubes.

The calm seas also enabled Droscher to observe that all the forward fuel tanks were leaking oil. He was concerned that the iridescent track would give away his presence, even if submerged, and that he might not have

War Cruise of the *U-117*

enough fuel to complete his mission.

August 10 found the *U-117* on the rich fishing grounds of Georges Bank, east of Cape Cod, Massachusetts. Droscher drove into a flock of sword-fishing vessels like a hungry fox darting into a henhouse. Not satisfied with one chicken, his appetite was not appeased until he had taken nine.

Although the U-boat lobbed warning shots at four fishing vessels, first struck was the *Aleda May*. She was drifting without power when the fishermen spotted the U-boat approaching at high speed. The skipper shouted for the engineer to start the engine. A shell screamed over the fishing vessel just as the engine opened wide. The second shell struck the mast and cut off the mainsail. Escape was out of the question, so the crew took to the dories.

A German officer demanded that the skipper and the two men in his dory come aboard the U-boat. They were ordered down below. An officer and two sailors then rowed the dory to the *Aleda May*.

In his official report to U.S. Navy investigators, engineer Fred Doucette said the German scavengers "took all our food. They took onions, candles, watermelon, bananas, and meat, and cleaned out all our provisions. They took a hose which I had there, also a can of gasoline and a can of cylinder oil. Took rubber boots and shoes. Also took the bow line and dumped it in the dory."

The Germans then lowered a bomb into the water next to the hull. The time delay fuse detonated seven minutes later, and the *Aleda May* duly sank.

Next to go was the *Progress*. Her crewmembers abandoned ship without a fight as soon as they saw the U-boat coming their way. The Germans looted the *Progress* as it had looted the *Aleda May* before setting scuttling charges that sank her.

The *Reliance* next came under attack. She tried to escape but two shells landed close aboard, so the vessel hove to and the fishermen launched three dories. They loaded food and water aboard the dories during the time it took for the U-boat to reach them. They also took some canvas so they could jury-rig a sail. The Germans then sank the fishing vessel with bombs.

William H. Starbuck was fourth fishing vessel to meet destruction. Shells landed so close to her that fragments fell on the deck. The men prepared three (or four) dories and abandoned ship. When the men tried to approach the U-boat in their dories, they were waved off. The *William H. Starbuck* was looted, then sunk by means of scuttling charges.

The attacks had started at ten o'clock in the morning. By two o'clock in the afternoon four fishing vessels had been sunk, three men had been captured and released, and twenty-seven men had been cast adrift in dories nearly two hundred miles from land.

A couple of hours later, the *U-117* found another cluster of swordfishing vessels to decimate. The fishermen tried to escape to the northwest, but the U-boat chased them with its guns blazing. The men took to the dories.

According to witnesses on the *Mary E. Sennett*, with quick dispatch the U-boat shelled and sank the *Old Time*, *Cruiser*, and *Mary E. Sennett*, all of which were within sight of each other. The *Gleaner* fled the scene "without molestation." The U-boat fired at the *Albert W. Black*, but she made good her escape while the Germans were pursuing the *Earl and Nettie*.

The crew of the *Earl and Nettie* abandoned ship in dories before the U-boat sank her with gunfire.

Now there were eight crews adrift in dories that were scattered all over the Georges Bank. None of the boats in this argosy was motorized. A few were equipped with makeshift sails; most had only oars and muscle for propulsion.

The men from the *Reliance* were sailing toward Provincetown, on Cape Cod, Massachusetts when they came upon the fishing vessel *Katie L. Palmer*. After James Nickerson, master of the *Reliance*, informed Edward Russell, master of the *Katie L. Palmer*, that a U-boat was bombing sword-fishing vessels in the

War Cruise of the *U-117*

neighborhood, Captain Russell immediately cranked up his engine and headed southwest.

The fishing vessel had been proceeding at her full speed of six knots for about three quarters of an hour when the men spotted the U-boat coming after them from the northeast. The *U-117* quickly overtook the fishing vessel. Captain Russell hove to, and the men took to their dories. For the men from the *Reliance* it was the second time that day that they had been forced to abandon ship.

Captain Russell and the three men in his dory were taken aboard the U-boat. The three men in the other dory were allowed to go free, as were the six men in the three dories from the *Reliance*.

The *Katie L. Palmer* was scuttled by placing bombs in the water next to her hull.

After being held on deck for half an hour, the four prisoners were told to go below. They climbed down through three hatchways and were led through the U-boat to the electric motor room, where they were offered small boxes on which to sit. The prisoners were given food and drink, including rum. The Germans interrogated the men, in particular about the locations of defensive minefields, about which the swordfishermen knew nothing.

After an hour or so, all seven prisoners – three from the *Aleda May* and four from the *Katie L. Palmer* – were led topside and released to their dories. By now it was ten o'clock at night. The U-boat motored east while the dories rowed west.

How all these fishermen found their way home is a multi-faceted story that rivals the peregrinations of Odysseus after the Trojan War.

Ironically, the last men to be set adrift were the first ones to be rescued. The swordfishing schooner *Helen E. Murley* picked up the seven released prisoners around midnight. She transported them to Bedford, Massachusetts, where they arrived on the afternoon of August 12.

The other three survivors of the *Katie L. Palmer* landed at Nantucket on the night of August 12, after rowing for more than 48 hours.

The men from the *Mary E. Sennett* rowed for twenty-four hours, until the trawler *Goodspeed* picked them up at 2 p.m. on August 11. Off Chatham, Massachusetts, the *Goodspeed* transferred the men to the *SC-223*. The sub chaser later transferred them to the SS *Rijndijk*, which took them to the immigration office at Highland Light, on Cape Cod.

The schooner *Corinthian* took aboard the men from the *Reliance* at noon on August 12.

The schooner *Acushla* picked up the crew of the *William H. Starbuck* and three crewmembers from the *Progress* around two o'clock on the afternoon of August 11. On August 13, she transferred all eleven men to a patrol boat at the Boston Harbor entrance. The patrol boat then landed them in Boston, Massachusetts.

The steam trawler *Surge* picked up the other four crewmembers from the *Progress*, and landed them in Boston on August 15.

The *SP-2840* rescued the survivors of the *Cruiser* on August 13.

An unnamed vessel picked up the men from the *Earl and Nettie* some one hundred miles off Nantucket.

Sub Chaser *SC-166* rescued four survivors.

All the other fishermen were "landed at ports within the 2nd Naval District."

There was great suffering but, at the end of the odyssey, there were no fatalities.

The newspapers had a field day with this latest spate of German depredations. Those who had been held prisoner aboard the U-boat agreed that during their interrogation, they were neither harmed nor humiliated but were treated with respect. As they were being released, a German officer told them to "tell the truth about the way they had been treated on the submarine."

These men told the truth to U.S. Navy investigators, but the newspapers told a different story: one that was geared to rouse the ire of the public, criticize the Huns, and sell copy – not necessarily in that order.

A *New York Times* article was especially imaginative.

War Cruise of the U-117

Unnamed fishermen from the *Earl and Nettie* supposedly reported, "they were subjected to many indignities by the U-boat's crew." This statement makes no sense, as these men rowed away of their own accord and were not taken prisoner.

The article continued in a worse demeanor: "An American flag, torn from the masthead of the little schooner *Lena May* [sic], one of the fishermen sunk by a German submarine off the New England coast Saturday, was taken aboard the enemy craft by a German officer, who wrapped it around his shoulders and gave a grotesque exhibition of dancing, while his men, each armed with a revolver, looked on and cheered.

"This was the story told here today by survivors of the vessel, who were forced to witness the performance. The fishermen had been ordered aboard the U-boat, where ten of them stood against the conning tower to be photographed. As they were being lined up for the picture they were jeered at by the U-boat crew, and knocked about when they failed to move as rapidly as the commander ordered. The mate of the *Lena May* [sic] declared:

" 'The Germans were half drunk at least. You would have thought that, too, had you seen the dance of the German officer, with the Starts and Stripes draped about his shoulders, and heard the cheering as the flag finally was flung down and stamped on, amid shrieks from our captors.' "

I have often said that the job of an historian is to report history the way it is recorded in contemporary documents, not to alter the record to suit his purpose. On the other hand, an historian is supposed to be an expert in his field – or, at the very least, is supposed to know more about the subject than his readers, because he has studied the field by reading a large quantity of contemporary documents. This supplementary knowledge enables an historian to weigh contradictory reports, and to render an expert opinion on the validity of the information they contain. To a certain extent, the reader must have faith in the expertise of the historian.

I would be remiss in my duty as an historian if I permitted the newspaper article to go unchallenged. I have examined all the official interrogations of survivors that exist in the files at the National Archives and at the Naval Historical Center (in the latter case, those that staff members permitted me to see). There is nothing to support the fabulous claims that are made in the *New York Times* article that is quoted above.

Either the survivors were getting even with the Boches for sinking their fishing vessels, or the reporter grossly exaggerated their accounts to make fascinating and rebel-rousing reading. I strongly suspect the latter. I seriously doubt that the men from the *Aleda May* did not know the correct name of their vessel.

While I am on the subject of historical inaccuracies, I need to draw attention to another aberration in the contemporary record: this with regard to the *Old Time*.

Every published account that I have read about the raid against the swordfishing fleet on August 10, 1918, lists nine vessels sunk and includes the *Old Time*. As best as I can determine, these modern authors relied up one of two sources for their information: *German Submarine Activities on the Atlantic Coast of the United States and Canada*, or *When the U-boats came to America*. The authors appear not to have looked any farther for corroboration.

As I noted in the first chapter of the present volume, Publication No. 1 is not without errors. I also noted that William Bell Clark relied primarily upon Publication No. 1 for source material for *When the U-boats Came to America*. Clark did not have the benefit of access to original archival documents except for those that were quoted in Publication No. 1.

Also noted above, I have taken a different tack in the preparation of *The Kaiser's U-boats in American Waters*: I relied entirely upon primary source materials, not publications that constitute secondary sources. Neither the National Archives nor the Naval Historical Center has a file folder for the *Old Time*. The only contemporary mention that I can find of the *Old Time* is in the interrogations of the men from the *Mary E. Sennett*.

These men landed on Cape Cod, then were transported to Boston for interrogation. The archival files contain affidavits of five of the seven crewmen. None of these men actually observed the sinking of their own vessel, having rowed out of sight in the patchy fog that was prevailing at the time.

Captain Manael Dias, Antoni Silva, and Tony P. Silva stated specifically that they saw the *Cruiser* and the *Old Time* sink. Joseph Suza spoke very little English; he stated that he saw two vessels sink but did not mention them by name. Juaa Maria spoke no English at all; he deposed that "I was with the Captain all the time and that my statement coincides with his."

Enemy soldiers and prisoners of war are isolated and interrogated individually, so there can be no opportunity for collusion with their fellows. The crewmen of the *Mary E. Sennett* were victims and innocent civilians. They had no need to fabricate a story. It is likely that they were all interrogated together in the same room at the same time. If the skipper or one of the other two men thought they recognized the *Old Time*, the others probably agreed with him.

The points that these men made were that they were swordfishing in close proximity to the *Cruiser* and the *Old Time*, that all three vessels "tried to run away toward the N.W. [northwest]," and that later they saw these vessels sink.

Captain Dias's statement was quoted in full in Publication No. 1. This statement differs from the archival statement in my possession only in that the spelling of *Rijndijk* was corrected without annotating that it was misspelled in the original statement (which was dated August 13, 1918). In the original document, *Rijndijk* was spelled *Ryndyke*. Because statements were given orally, either the interrogator or the typist must have spelled the name phonetically after hearing Captain Dias pronounce it.

Based on this statement, Publication No. 1 duly listed the *Old Time* in the statistical table in the back of the book as having been destroyed. Publication No. 1 also noted that all nine vessels were bombed, when according to the statements of survivors, the *Old Time*, *Cruiser*, *Mary E. Sennett*, and *Earl and Nettie* were shelled.

From these pieces of information I conclude that the real situation was this: the *Cruiser*, *Old Time*, and *Mary E. Sennett* were fishing together. According to his own statement, Captain Dias "was on mast looking for sword fish when two submarines were sighted E.S.E." In fact there was only one U-boat, so the captain was wrong in this regard. The harpooners were looking elsewhere during the flight from the U-boat. The proper identification of vessels was confused because of fog. The crewmen on the *Mary E. Sennett* observed the sinking of two vessels: the *Cruiser* and the *Katie L. Palmer* (which they mistook for the *Old Time*). The *Old Time* escaped.

There are multiple corroborations for this scenario. The weakest corroboration is that the *Old Time* does not appear in any of the contemporary newspaper articles that I have come across.

Much stronger is Senate Document No. 419, 66th Congress, 3d Session, which is dated March 2, 1921, and which is entitled "Claims of American Citizens Against Germany." This 32-page document sought reparations for damages, injuries, and loss of life that resulted primarily from enemy submarine warfare. Exhibit 11 (of 14) is a list of "American sailing vessels destroyed by submarine, raiders, or mines since the beginning of the war." This Senate Document was prepared in exhausting detail that was based on evidence that was available at the time.

All the vessels that were sunk on August 10, 1918 belonged to the swordfishing fleet of Gloucester, Massachusetts, and were privately owned by American citizens. Eight of the nine vessels that were supposed to have been sunk are tabulated. The *Old Time* is not listed.

Strongest of all is the deck log of the *U-117*. Under the entry for August 10, 1918, Droscher clearly wrote,

War Cruise of the *U-117*

"During the course of the day 8 sailing vessels were sunk. The sailing vessels were American fishing vessels with an average tonnage of about 75 tons each. The names are: *Aleda May, Progress, Reliance, William Starbuck, Earl and Nettie, Cruiser, Mary Sennett, Katie L. Palmer*. Signed: Droscher."

Droscher did not include the *Old Time* in his list. Furthermore, Droscher's war diary corroborates the names and number of fishing vessels that are given in the deck log. The *Old Time* is not mentioned.

I did not conduct this in-depth analysis in order to take 18 tons away from Droscher's credit score for the day. He is still left with 247 tons of fishing vessels sunk in one fell swoop. He still deprived 52 men of their property and means of livelihood. He did all this for the cause of world domination. I reconstructed events in order to set the record as straight as it can be set from the primary documentary evidence.

I have noticed in more than one recent account that the authors cited Droscher's log as the source of their information that he sank nine fishing vessels that day. I suspect that they used Publication No. 1 or *When the U-boats Came to America* as their source, but credited Droscher as a way of lending authenticity to their claim. Had they actually read Droscher's log, they would have noticed the same inconsistency in the records that I noticed.

But see below the statement made by Captain Alvor Quadras, the skipper of the *Rush*.

On August 12, while some of the men from the swordfishing vessels were still at sea in their dories, the *U-117* was cruising south of Long Island, New York when Droscher spotted a westbound freighter.

The *Sommerstad* was making a routine passage from Bergen, Norway to New York City. She crossed the North Atlantic along the great circle route, stopped briefly at Halifax, Nova Scotia, then continued south and west toward her intended destination, where she expected to fill her holds with corn, a commodity that was much needed by the people of Norway. Presently she was traveling in water ballast. This meant that she carried no cargo and that her deep tanks were filled with seawater in order to provide proper ballast.

The morning of August 12 found her twenty-five miles south of Fire Island. This location was in international waters, and well outside the "danger zone" or "blockade zone" that was proclaimed by Germany. The *Sommerstad's* neutrality and licit location meant that she was not fair game as a target for unrestricted submarine warfare.

Unknown to the thirty-one men aboard the Norwegian freighter, their vessel was being stalked. Droscher wrote in his log with characteristic military brevity: "Advanced to attack under water. The steamer had one gun in the stern. Torpedo launched – Hit. III tube. Depth adjustment 2 m. shooting distance 400 m. (G.6AV torp.) steamer sinks in a short while. Size estimated at 3000 t."

Droscher's annotation notwithstanding, the *Sommerstad* carried no armament of any kind. International law prohibited her from being armed because she was registered to a neutral nation. Norwegian vessels obeyed the law in order to protect their neutrality.

If the *Sommerstad* had gone down with all hands, Droscher's annotation would be the only account available to historians today. Fortunately, there were no fatalities on the Norwegian freighter, and the entire crew was interrogated after being landed in the States.

Captain George Hansen, master of the *Sommerstad*, gave the most complete description of the morning's events. (Ellipses denote the interrogator's questions). "A little after eight o'clock I came out on the bridge, where my chief officer and second officer were at that time. I went over to the port side of the bridge and looked out, and I thought I saw something in the water. I went and took the glasses, but I could not make out what it was. I stood for a few minutes looking through the glasses, and then saw a torpedo coming along a little aft from abeam of the ship. . . . As soon as I saw the torpedo I stopped the vessel, and ordered the engines reversed and full speed astern. The torpedo went under the ves-

War Cruise of the *U-117*

sel, barely missing it, a little on the fore part of the bridge, and came up on the other side. . . . I walked across to the other side [of the bridge] and I then gave orders for full speed ahead. . . . When I saw the torpedo start to swerve around I gave orders for full speed astern; and when it passed the bow it made two turns, making a complete circle, and then struck our vessel aft on the port side exactly between the third and fourth hold right at the bulkhead."

From Captain Hansen's testimony it appears that the torpedo was fired accurately but that it traveled too deep for the *Sommerstad's* draft – given as seven feet – then, perhaps having its gyroscope disturbed by the wash during the near miss, it made a complete circle counterclockwise around the bow of the ship and came back for another try at a shallower depth, this time being successful in its mission. The captain's account was corroborated by Chief Officer Johan Albert Haltlid, Second Officer Ludwig Nilson, Fireman Halden Helvorsen, Able Bodied Seaman Charles Nelson, and Mess Boy Sverre Svang.

Germany did not have guidance systems that could make a torpedo behave in the manner that was described. The torpedo malfunctioned and accidentally circled back and struck its target.

As soon as Able Bodied Seaman Eyvind Balstad Olsen spotted the torpedo pass under the hull, and before it began its errant curve, he warned the men below decks and shouted for them to make for the lifeboats. "I thought the submarine might appear and shell us."

Down below in the engine room, Chief Engineer Benedix Andersen ran around like a one-armed paperhanger trying to follow telegraph orders from the bridge. "The signal was turned to full speed astern, and I tried to get the engine to go full speed astern, but before I could do it, the signal was full speed ahead, and then it was changed to full speed astern again. I then got it to full speed astern, 4 or 5 revolutions, and then it was full speed ahead again. I got it working full speed ahead and immediately after that the explosion happened with the engine working full speed ahead. . . . The water came through the tunnel hatch, and when I saw the water come through I understood the ship had been torpedoed and was starting to sink. . . . The water came with great force through the tunnel hatch, and filled up the engine room. The water came up to my knees, and I was afraid to stop any longer. I tried to stop the engine and got it working dead slow ahead, but I didn't have time to stop it. I then went up the ladder and the water came down from the deck down into the engine room. When I came on deck the boat was ready to go away and I jumped right into it."

Captain Hansen: "Several of the watch on deck were knocked down by the force of the explosion, and the cook was blown clean out of the galley."

He quickly parroted the seaman's panicked proclamation and gave the official order to abandon ship. All hands who had not already done so went immediately to the lifeboats. It was fortunate that they did, for the *Sommerstad* went down by the stern only two to three minutes after the torpedo struck.

Charles Nelson described his experiences: "I then run to the boat deck, and cut the tackles that keeps the boats in. This permitted the boats to swing out; then I run to the forward boat fall, and lowered the boat half way out, and then I could not lower them any further because the ropes were fouled, and I made my end fast. . . . I then run down to the midship's deck; by this time the ship was sinking, and when it got close to the water, we cut both tackles; this permitted the small boats to leave the vessel, and I was left on board. . . . Then I run forward, and when I got down to the forward deck, the head of the ship was rising out of the water, and then I run up on top of the engine room skylight, and tried to get hold of the tackle to get down to the boats; then an explosion started while I was on top of the skylight of the engine room, and had to leave there and go to the midship's deck; then I jumped into the water, and swam to the boat."

As the men pulled at the oars they spotted a

War Cruise of the *U-117*

periscope cleaving the calm surface of the sea. It dipped beneath the ripples and did not reappear. The freighter's bow was still visible when last seen before being enveloped in fog. Then the men were alone in the broad, blue Atlantic, with nothing to comfort them but their thoughts.

Ludwig Nilson told his interrogator, "I have been torpedoed two times before." This was an extraordinary statement for a citizen of a neutral country to make. Nor was he the only crew member to have been torpedoed previously.

The *Sommerstad* was not equipped with wireless, and even if she had there had been no time to transmit an SOS. This meant that no one with any regard for the survival of the crew knew of their plight, and that their best prospect for rescue was to row toward land. They plied the oars for nine and a half hours.

Captain Hansen: "Toward sundown we heard Fire Island's siren, and made directly for the shore. Soon afterward we were sighted by the naval patrol vessel which brought us to this city [New York]. The men were tired with rowing all day, and were taken care of for the night on the patrol boat."

The rescue vessel was the USS *Aramis* (*SP-415*). The men were later taken to the Norwegian Sailor's Home in Brooklyn, where they received food and lodging and the kind care of people from their own country.

The Norwegian Minister was outraged. The *Sommerstad* was the twelfth Norwegian vessel to be sunk by U-boats off the American coast. And this figure does not count the number of Norwegian vessels that were deliberately sunk by U-boats in other parts of the world. Germany's continued disregard for neutral rights was intolerable, especially as it came on the heels of a proclamation from Berlin which guaranteed safe conduct for Norwegian vessels "running outside the blockade zone with imports to Norway."

Quoted one official document, "The Norwegian Minister, who has applied to the German department of foreign affairs on account of the sinking of the steamer

Sommerstad has been assured that the German government does not at all intend to prevent Norway's import of food supplies outside the stop-zone and that Norway will be righted as much as possible if the steamer, contrary to expectations, has been torpedoed without any warning."

German assurances were not worth the paper they were printed on, unless the assurances were hostile. U-boats continued to sink Norwegian vessels off the American coast and elsewhere.

Meanwhile, the *U-117* proceeded on the surface in a southwesterly direction in order to lay its first minefield. It drew close to the predetermined position shortly after meridian. Merchant vessel traffic hampered minelaying operations for several hours. While jockeying for position some five miles from shore, Droscher spotted a tanker that was too valuable a target to pass up, so he went after it. It was 5 o'clock when he launched a torpedo that struck the tanker abaft the wheelhouse.

The *Frederick R. Kellogg* was transporting a cargo of oil from Tampico, Mexico to Boston, Massachusetts when the torpedo slammed into the port hull adjacent to the engine room.

According to Captain C. H. White, master, the force of the explosion lifted "two steel decks and a wooden deck, and a life boat on the port quarter clean into the air. . . . I attempted to give the signal to clear the engine room, but communication had already been cut off, and stepping out on the flying bridge I pulled the whistle until the steam was out, and turning my head once more towards aft I saw the ship completely under water and sinking rapidly by the stern."

The tanker sank in less than fifteen seconds.

"There was one engineer, the 3rd assistant, one fireman, and one oiler on watch and all three were killed. Four others were killed or drowned. These men were in the vicinity of the engine room. They were the 2nd Engineer, one mess boy, and two cadets."

Chief Engineer Olaf Hanson was knocked off his chair by the blast. His office door, which faced the en-

War Cruise of the *U-117*

gine room, was blown off its hinges. He climbed to his feet, peered into the engine room, and "saw the water up to the main deck grating. . . . This means that within 10 seconds the engine room was filled up to the main deck with water."

The opposite door opened onto the poop deck. When he turned and looked outside, he saw the two cadets "heaving out life boat No. 3." By the time he picked up his life preserver the water was up to his neck. He swam out of the room onto the poop deck, where he was trapped under a canopy that provided shade for the deck. He was dragged under water. He managed to struggle to the edge of the canopy, where Second Assistant Engineer W. Johnston grabbed his hand and pulled him to the surface.

Hanson: "The two cadets were missing. On the after deck there was an awning about 30 feet long and it is presumed that when this submerged it carried all underneath it below the water, and there, Stillman and Cubberly died in this manner."

Cadet Alexander Hutchison pushed a life preserver toward Hanson, which saved him from drowning. Hutchison did not have a life preserver himself because he had dived off the rail of the bridge. The life preserver that he pushed to Hanson was one that he found afloat. Hutchison swam until both of them were picked up by a lifeboat.

That the survivors were able to launch two lifeboats despite the celerity of the sinking was due to the fact that the bow stayed afloat. The SS *Huron* picked up all thirty-four survivors three hours later.

The stern was resting on the bottom in 90 feet of water, but the bow was buoyed by its sealed tanks, and remained above the surface with a list to starboard. Local looters stripped the above-water compartments of nearly everything that was moveable.

The day after the sinking, a salvage outfit cleared New York City aboard the Merritt, Chapman Company tug *Resolute*. The U.S. torpedo boat *Shubrick* provided escort service. Two seaplanes circled the wreck to en-

The *Frederick R. Kellogg* resting on the bottom. (Courtesy of the National Archives.)

sure that no U-boats were lurking in the vicinity. Then began a protracted salvage operation that lasted for fourteen days.

After hard-hat divers examined the wreck, salvage engineers determined to decrease the list by pumping water into compartments on the side opposite the list, then to lighten the load by ejecting the oil.

Wearing diving dress, Lieutenant (jg) John Dahl "went down into the pump room to open the necessary valves for discharging cargo. At this time, a S.E. swell was sweeping across the decks of the vessel, making it necessary for another diver [Warrant Carpenter Olof Soderberg] to be stationed at the pump room door to tend Dahl's hose and life line. Attention is called to the fact that Mr. Dahl entered the pump room and opened the right valves in total darkness with only the knowledge he had gained from the plans of the ship to guide him."

Both of these men received a commendation for their heroic efforts.

More divers were dispatched aboard the salvage tug *Relief*, to assist in connecting air hoses. After two weeks of hard work under adverse conditions, the tanker was raised and towed to New York Harbor, where she was

War Cruise of the *U-117*

turned over to her owners. The *Frederick R. Kellogg* was then repaired and returned to service.

Several hours after torpedoing the tanker, the *U-117* deployed mines off the Barnegat Light Buoy, then proceeded south on the surface.

Minesweepers swept the area where the *Frederick R. Kellogg* was torpedoed. They did not locate any mines because they had been deployed some twelve miles to the south.

The following day (August 14), the U-boat fired a torpedo at a five-masted schooner off Cape May, New Jersey. The torpedo missed, so Droscher surfaced and lobbed a warning shot over the bow of the *Dorothy B. Barrett*. Captain William Merritt, master of the schooner, gave a detailed account of the action from his perspective:

"A submarine on the surface about 4 miles away ESE fired one shot. The *Dorothy Barrett* hove to and lowered her jib sail and abandoned ship. The submarine came within 2 miles and submerged. I started my [motor life] boat NW. to try to get some assistance. After getting within 1-1/2 miles of the submarine I stopped the boat for a while and then thought I had better try to secure some help."

The *Frederick R. Kellogg* resting on the bottom. (Courtesy of the National Archives.)

Droscher provided a different perspective. He submerged because he spotted a steamship in the distance. He was unable to obtain a favorable attack position, so he surfaced and commenced to shell the *Dorothy B. Barrett*. "As the sailing vessel is made of wood and the effect of the first shells was small, the vessel, on account of the close proximity to land is to be sunk by a torpedo. Projectile passed under the mark. . . . Emerged [surfaced]. Set fire to sailing vessel by artillery."

Merritt found the minesweeper *Kingfisher*. "He swung around as soon as I signaled him and I went aboard. I asked the captain what he had to fight with. He said he had three-inch guns, and I told him the submarine was too big for him to tackle with that kind of gun. I then went up on the bridge and asked him what he was going to do. He said he was going to run for shoal water. We had been running about west for only a short time when we sighted the oil tanker. I said to the captain, 'He is going to get that fellow, also, and to shift our course to warn the tanker.' The submarine was on our starboard quarter and we commenced firing."

Droscher: "The thunder of cannon is heard at the same time [as he fired upon the *Dorothy B. Barrett*]. 2 Volleys of a 15 cm gun apparently. Probably *U-140*."

Droscher did not know that the *U-140* was nowhere in the neighborhood. It was far offshore and on its way home. The guns he heard were being fired at him from the *Kingfisher*.

Merritt: "We were then heading about west and that submarine was about 2-1/2 miles on our stern, just so we could fire by the pilot house. I did not see the conning tower then, but the gunner said he saw it, and he fired a couple of shots."

Suddenly Droscher realized the truth of the situation: "During the firing two patrol vessels in sight which make towards the sailing vessel. Submerged and after a short time emerged again. The sailing vessel burns with a great deal of smoke."

Merritt: "When I saw the tanker she was headed SE. By this time she had also seen the submarine, I guess.

War Cruise of the U-117

We did not have but little time to go down toward him, and started to fire on the submarine, and then we had to watch the fellows. We kept right on down that way toward him and started to fire and put on all the steam we could; but, as I said before, we wanted to get in shoal water.

"Then the submarine came up and went right ahead of us and we fired about three shots. From the time we abandoned ship to the time these shots were fired, I judge it was about three-quarters of an hour.

"Some of them came pretty near. Just before we shot the last few times a big cloud of smoke came up out of the water. It was coming up just like steam. Then, about five minutes later, another big black cloud seemed to rise from the water from near the vicinity of the submarine and kept coming up for about 10 minutes."

The tanker that Captain Merritt mentioned was the *William Green*. While she was running for shoal water, she transmitted a wireless call for help. Although Captain Merritt did not know it, four prowling sub chasers intercepted the message, as did a seaplane and the U.S. submarine *N-7*. They all converged on the given position.

The radio operator on the *U-117* intercepted the SOS. He thought the *Five Fathom Bank* lightship had transmitted the call for the help. German lookouts spotted the *William Green*, "but seems to remain far inside the shallower water on our account."

The sub chasers fired shots, and the seaplane dropped depth charges.

Droscher: "Aviator alarm. Submerged. Bombed by aviator. The boat can apparently be accurately observed by the aviator. Depth of water about 25 m. [80 feet] 9 bombs fall within 50 minutes and each time nearer. What it is by which the boat can be discerned, is hard to determine. Either the oil track or compressed air bubbles or it is the gray paint on the outside of the boat washed light by the sea."

The *U-117* escaped without damage. What Droscher did not know what was that the seaplane dropped only one depth charge, on bubbles "presumably from the

The *Dorothy B. Barrett* afire. (From the author's collection.)

wake of the submarine." The sub chasers dropped the subsequent depth charges.

The sub chasers also witnessed the final moments of the *Dorothy B. Barrett*. The schooner burned, then slowly settled by the head with all canvas set – sailing for her final port of call. When the smoke cleared, she was gone. The black cloud that Captain Merritt observed was smoke from his own burning vessel, obscured by haze.

On August 13, the auxiliary schooner *Madrugada* cleared New York under charter to the American Fruit Company. This was to be her last voyage under the American flag. Upon arrival in Brazil with her cargo of cement, lubricating oil, and resin, she was to be sold to the Industrias Reunidas Motarozzo, of San Palo, and would then fly the Brazilian flag.

Two days later found her off the coast of Virginia. Droscher's first shot can hardly be called a warning shot, as it was followed immediately by another shot that splashed in the water barely twenty feet ahead of the wooden-hulled freighter. The third shot fell slightly over the port bow. The fourth shot entered the engine room, while the fifth tore through the hull at the waterline. Apparently the first four shots were duds, but the fifth did extensive damage.

War Cruise of the *U-117*

Those aboard the *Madrugada* did not sit idle through the fusillade. Captain Frederick Rouse, master, telegraphed the engine room to stop the engines, mustered the crew, and ordered the ship's boats swung out.

Wireless operator Frederick Cook "ran for the radio room to start up the motor. I asked for the position and the Captain said off Winter Quarter Light. Then I sent out SOS calls for help. After I got a hold of papers, code book and stuff, I wrapped them up and shot them out of the port hole. They were given to me the night before. I wrapped them up the best I could and put a weight on them."

Cook kept tapping away as shells exploded against the hull, until the second engineer charged breathlessly into the radio room, and said, "Wireless, they want you to leave."

It was too late. The lifeboat had already shoved off. The two men clambered down the rope falls and leaped for it. The *Madrugada* took a list to starboard.

Chief Mate Paul Hansen testified that the U-boat "fired two more shots, one striking the foremast top and the other hitting amidships on the starboard side, tearing a large hole in the side and deck."

The next shell struck the oil tank with a tremendous explosion of gas and flames.

Still dodging shot, the five men still on board got away in the yawl. The U-boat then came in close and fired four more shells at point blank range: two into the stern, and two into the bow.

According to Third Mate August Want, "When the submarine fired the last shots into the forecastle it caused the explosion of the kerosene stored in the forward hold and set the forecastle afire."

The whole vessel was smoking, the forecastle was ablaze, and the mast was a fiery brand. The U-boat took off without approaching the men in the boats or waiting to see the *Madrugada*'s final moments.

Hansen: "The *Madrugada* then turned over and sunk, only showing her bowsprit above the water, in about fifteen fathoms of water. . . . There were no lives lost and no one was injured."

Three hours later, the Norwegian steamship *Taunton*, which was en route from Port Antonia, Jamaica to New York City, picked up all twenty-two men. The survivors disembarked at the *Taunton's* port of call the following morning. The *Taunton* was experienced as a rescue vessel; she had picked one of the two lifeboats from the *Pinar del Rio*.

The *Madrugada* did not sink entirely. A thousand sacks of cement in the stern effectively anchored the vessel where she lay, but the oil amidships and 800 tons of resin in the forward hold kept her bow afloat. The U.S. destroyer *Hopkins* located the wreck on August 16. She radioed, "Found schooner *Drugada* [sic] burning and sinking thirteen miles 187 degrees from *Winter Quarter* lightship. Menace to navigation."

The wreck was spotted again on August 18, this time in a different location. The U.S. gunboat *Rush* found it on August 19 in yet another location. The partially buoyant hulk appeared to be dragging along the seabed. The sea was "strewn with wreckage" in the vicinity.

A coded telegram from the Commandant of the Fifth Naval District to the Office of Naval Intelligence noted, "Will be removed if practicable when weather permits."

The *Madrugada* disappeared without further notice.

At 2:45 on the afternoon of August 16, the *U-117* started to plant mines off Wimble Shoal, North Carolina. The operation was proceeding smoothly when Droscher spotted a pair of merchant vessels steaming northward. This was too good an opportunity to miss, so he broke off minelaying and got into position to make a torpedo attack on the vessel that appeared to be a large tanker.

Droscher noted that this vessel was "Fantastically painted. Of the two masts one was painted all in a light color, the other one all black. This kind of painting increases the difficulty of determining the vessel's course. It had already been observed several times but not been clearly recognized."

ONI would like to have learned that dazzle camouflage was so effective.

War Cruise of the *U-117*

Droscher launched a torpedo at a distance of a quarter mile from his chosen target. He noted in his log, "Steamer bursts into flames at once. The second steamer sighted is Dutch with neutrality flag. After the attack, went a short distance south. Continued laying mines in the direction of the [Wimble Shoal] buoy."

The stricken vessel was the *Mirlo*. The British tanker had departed from New Orleans, Louisiana on August 9. Her cargo tanks were filled to capacity with 9,250 tons of gasoline and refined oil. She planned to refuel in Norfolk, Virginia before making the Atlantic crossing for Thameshaven, England. Neither the lookouts nor the gun crew saw the track of the torpedo.

There was no warning as a tremendous explosion ripped through the *Mirlo's* No. 2 tank. A huge column of water spouted into the air, tearing up deck plates as if they were tissue paper. The concussion blew out the electrical system and plunged the vessel into darkness.

Down in the stokehold, Fireman John Griffiths said he "could not see anything but steam and dust." Bulkheads were twisted and jambs were warped. Griffiths called out to his companions but received no answers. When he tried to escape, he found that the engine room door was jammed. He crawled through blackness, located a hammer, and was beating against a door when a second explosion buckled the plates in the fire room and ignited the compartment. Fortunately for Griffiths, the door sprang open enough for him to squeeze through and make good his escape up the engine room ladder.

The second explosion occurred at the bulkhead between No. 1 tank and the stokehold. (The tanks were numbered from aft to fore.)

Captain W. R. Williams noted that the explosions caused "the dynamos to be put out of commission, also breaking engine and destroying telegraph, and putting wireless gear out of commission." Captain Williams noticed another steamship to the northwest (toward shore) and blew his steam whistle: his only way of calling for help.

The other steamer responded by taking off on a

zigzag course, her skipper undoubtedly thinking like Captain Williams, that the tanker had been torpedoed and that a hasty retreat was in order.

Flames and smoke rose high in the sky. The *Mirlo's* plight was observed by the lookout from Coast Guard Station No. 179. He saw "a great mass of water shoot up in the air which seemed to cover the after part of the steamer."

The *Mirlo* took an immediate starboard list that was quickly increasing. Flames licked out through cracked hull plates and decking aft. Captain Williams steered for shore and ordered abandon ship. While the boats were prepared for launching, Captain Williams threw overboard a weighted bag that contained the ship's confidential documents.

Williams: "The starboard lifeboat was lowered first, which got away from the ship. The port lifeboat was then lowered and entered the water all right, when it was noticed that the tiller fouled the after falls, causing the boat to shear off from the ship and capsize. All the men that were in her were thrown into the water. At the same time the boat capsized she cleared herself from the ship. The starboard boat tried to go to the rescue. Then the orders were given to clear the after boats and lower same."

According to another statement signed by First Officer F. J. Campbell and eight other crewmembers, "The men in the water grabbed the overturned boat and drifted clear of the ship. Two men climbed aboard over the falls. The Steward helped them aboard. The after boats could not be reached at first on account of the flames, but the Captain put the helm over and caused the flames to shift to the starboard side, making it possible to man the after boats."

Captain Williams stayed on the bridge until only one lifeboat remained onboard. "After ascertaining that all hands were off the ship we lowered away. During these operations the boat's falls caught fire, and it was with great difficulty that we succeeded in pulling away from the vessel. In a few minutes after leaving the ship, the ship exploded with terrific force fore and aft, at the same

War Cruise of the *U-117*

time catching fire fore and aft. It was with great difficulty that we managed to clear the fire and smoke that was floating on the water, caused by the ship bursting and all the cargo coming out."

The *Mirlo* came apart at the seams, and split in two.

The survivors pulled desperately at the oars as the oil and gasoline spread in a gigantic rainbow slick, with a raging conflagration not far behind. Ten of those who were dumped from the overturned lifeboat could not get away in time, and were either drowned or consumed by the blaze.

"Flames separated the two remaining boats. After pulling two hours, the port after lifeboat met the Life Saving Boat. The Captain, who was in the boat, told the officer in charge of the life saving boat that he better go out and see if he could pick up anyone from the other two boats."

By this time the *Mirlo* was completely submerged. The ocean was afire: a field of debris fed by the cargo of gasoline and oil that was rising from the vessel's ruptured tanks.

Coastguardsman John Midgett came to the rescue. "There were two great masses of flame about one hundred yards apart, with the sea for many hundreds of yards covered with burning gas and oil.

"At times, between the two great masses of flame when the smoke would clear away, could be seen a capsized life boat with six men clinging to it. The heavy swell was washing over the boat. With great difficulty I ran our boat through the smoke, floating wreckage and burning gas and oil and rescued the six men from the burning sea. All of them had burns, but none were serious; but it was not pleasant to hear them relate the story of how they had to dive under the water to save themselves from being burned to death. These six survivors informed me that they had seen some of the crew disappear in the burning sea, and they felt sure that none was afloat except those in the boats. However, I continued the search for some time, but no more men could be found at that time in the vicinity of the capsized boat.

The six survivors knew nothing of the other boats, they having been lost sight of in the smoke and fire.

"I headed my boat now before the wind and sea in hopes of finding the missing boat, and in a short time was rewarded by finding it with nineteen others of the crew of the *Mirlo*. It was overloaded and so much crowded, that the men could not row, and was drifting with the wind and sea.

"This boat, at the time it was found, was about nine miles south east of the station. I ran alongside, took her in tow, and proceeding in towards the land for the point I had directed the master's boat to await my return. Upon reaching the rendezvous, the master's boat was found to be in waiting, and taking her in tow also I proceeded towards the beach. There were thirty-six people in the two boats, as well as six extra persons in my surf boat. I headed for the station.

"Night was falling rapidly, the wind was increasing from the N. E. and the sea was breaking heavily upon the beach. When about two miles south of my station, I anchored the two ship's boats about 600 yards off shore, and proceeded to land the crew of the *Mirlo*, or at least the survivors. They were all landed in the station's surf boat, four round trips being made in the darkness. I was met at the beach by members of my crew who had been left on shore and by the crew of Coast Guard Station No. 180, who had come up to assist me in landing the boat.

"As fast as the survivors of the *Mirlo* were landed, they were taken to the station by our teams, given medical aid and their burns dressed. Each was given dry clothing by members of my crew, and from the stock on hand contributed by benevolent associations, after which they were given supper and allotted a place to sleep.

"The following morning, August 17, after breakfast at about 9 a.m., the S.P. [Section Patrol] U.S.S. *Legonia* arrived off the station, and the wind and sea having gone down, I transferred the survivors of the *Mirlo's* crew to her, and at 11:45 a.m., she sailed for Norfolk, Va. The master of the *Mirlo*, Captain Williams, however, left at

10:00 a.m. for Norfolk in the Seaplane A-765."

The day after the *Mirlo* was sunk, the U.S. destroyer *Taylor* radioed an urgent message to ONI: "Sighted floating mine one mile east of wreck. Due to shallow water vicinity of wreck probably mined with submerged anchored mine. Recommend that ships be warned and vicinity wreck swept by mine sweepers."

The minesweeper *Teal* spent the next two weeks combing the area around Wimble Shoal. She swept up two enemy mines on August 18, two on August 25, two on August 30, and three on September 5: nine mines in all.

ONI concluded that a mine had sunk the *Mirlo*. Publication No. 1 disseminated this conclusion. Modern day writers have copied from it.

Admiral Sims continued his intelligence operations after the end of the war. He obtained German charts that showed the locations of all minefields off the eastern seaboard, as well as the number of mines that were sown in each field. The German report indicated that nine mines were planted in the Wimble Shoal field.

Publication No. 1 duly noted the discrepancy that, working on the assumption that the *Mirlo* had struck a mine, there was one mine more than German records indicated had been placed in the field.

Today we have the advantage of Droscher's war diary, which not only states specifically that he sank the *Mirlo* with a torpedo, but also confirms that he deployed nine mines in the vicinity of Wimble Shoal. Thus the number of swept-up mines now tallies with the number of mines that were actually deployed.

While this new accounting has clarified an age-old contradiction, Droscher's log creates another one. After Droscher completed laying his mines, he rose to periscope depth, and made the following entry: "Steamer still burns giving off great quantities of smoke. At a distance of about 10 nautical miles another steamer is burning and giving off even much greater smoke. No detonation heard. A second tank steamer must have run upon a mine which had been laid before attack on the first ship. A number of smaller steamers in the vicinity."

No American records report any other merchant vessel casualties at that place at that time. So what did Droscher see? Because all the mines were accounted for, the only sustainable answer I can offer is that another steamer used smoke boxes in order to create a cloud of smoke to cover her retreat.

Another contradiction is found in Griffiths' statement, in which he mentions a second explosion that caused a fire in the compartment from which he was trying to escape. Without the intelligence report suggesting that all the mines were accounted for, one might speculate that the *Mirlo* drifted against a mine after she was torpedoed. Alternatively, it is a simple matter to infer that this other explosion was the ignition of part of the gasoline cargo, and that it was triggered by sparks from the torpedo blast. Secondary explosions were common in such cases.

All I can say in both of these regards is that, all too often, observations disagree with the confirmation of events – even in a case such as this in which there are firm observations from multiple points of view. Contradictory information is as frustrating for the historian as it is for the casual reader - perhaps more so.

Because of the continuing loss of diesel fuel through irreparable leaks in the tanks, Droscher made the decision to begin his homeward passage. "It is also impossible to foresee the final extent of the loss of fuel. Furthermore the diving tanks III and IV can no longer be blown out because of the crushed in evaporators. Thus the boat lies too deep in the water thereby causing the boat to lose speed."

At 6:30 on the morning of August 17, the *U-117* fired three shots over the rigging of the Norwegian bark *Nordhav*. The four-master had been at sea for two full months, since June 17. She was carrying 3,930 tons of flax seed in 69,000 bags from Buenos Aires, Argentina to New York City. She was moving slowly through calm seas when the shelling commenced. The U-boat drew alongside the bark and signaled for the skipper to bring

War Cruise of the *U-117*

the ship's documents.

Captain Sven Marsussen rowed to the submarine. After examining the cargo manifest, Droscher determined that flax seed constituted contraband because it was destined for New York, thus making the vessel liable to destruction. He ordered captain Marsussen to return to the bark and give the order to abandon ship.

The Norwegian crew launched two lifeboats. The lifeboat under the command of First Officer Torje Baakind was ordered to lie to next to the U-boat. The other lifeboat, occupied by twelve sailors under the command of Captain Marsussen, was ordered alongside. The captain and eight men were taken into the U-boat. Four men were assigned to rowing the lifeboat back and forth between the U-boat and the bark, so that the German boarding party could rifle the bark's provisions and everything else of value. This boat made six trips. The Germans took flour, butter, soap, manila, and some sixty bags of linseed.

The Norwegians onboard the U-boat were given German cigarettes and refreshments (pea soup, lime juice, lemonade, and cognac). A boarding party laid explosives alongside the hull of the *Nordhav*. She sank with all sails set. The men were released at noon.

Captain Marsussen: "Before setting us adrift we were given provisions and water, and I was shown our position on a chart, which was about 120 miles east-southeast of Cape Henry [Virginia]."

The lifeboats raised sail and headed toward shore. They managed to stay together despite the falling of darkness. A fresh breeze sprung up at midnight, accompanied by mounting seas. The men were obliged to bail the boats continuously in order to keep them afloat. Dawn found the lifeboats proceeding west-northwest "running under single foresail before a fresh easterly wind and rain squalls."

At 7 o'clock on the evening of August 18, after thirty-one hours of sailing and bailing, the lifeboats came across the U.S. battleship *Kearsarge*.

According to G. E. Gelm, commanding officer of the

Kearsarge, "There was a rough choppy sea at the time and a lee was formed bringing one boat along the port side forward and the other aft. The crew of both boats comprising 26 men were promptly taken on board, without accident or injury, together with their effects and the boats were cast adrift and this vessel proceeded en-route to Boston."

Both lifeboats washed up on Virginia beaches the following day: one at Virginia Beach, the other at Little Island.

On August 20 the *U-117* engaged in a running gun battle with an Italian steamship whose name is given as *Ansaldo the Third* in Publication No. 1, as *Ansaldo Primo* in the U-boat's deck log, and as *Ansaldo I* in Droscher's war diary. Droscher got the name by intercepting the vessel's SOS.

The *Ansaldo* was armed with three guns: one on the forecastle, one immediately abaft the bridge structure, and one on the fantail. Italian shots fell short of the U-boat by less than 400 feet.

Because of the problems that the *U-117* was experiencing with its diving tanks, the hull had a permanent list. Droscher: "This fault could only be removed for short periods by blowing out, flood and counterflooding. In addition the list often changed from one side to the other. This circumstance affected the shooting considerably, as had also been the case before. In consequence of the irregular twisting of the trunnions caused thereby the shots often fell wide of the mark and could not be taken into account by the observer."

The U-boat expended more than one hundred shells on the *Ansaldo*. A direct hit put the after gun out of commission and wounded three crewmembers. The *Ansaldo* fired as many shots in return, then ran out of ammunition. After three hours of this heated exchange, she was able to outdistance the *U-117*.

The next morning the U-boat fired a torpedo at the British steamer *Thespis*. Emergency maneuvers enabled the *Thespis* to avoid the torpedo by the narrow margin of twenty feet. The *U-117* then surfaced an engaged the

War Cruise of the *U-117*

steamer with its deck gun. The *Thespis* returned fire for half an hour, until she outran the U-boat and Droscher broke off the engagement.

On August 21, the *U-117* stopped the Swedish steamer *Algeria* with two shots that landed close to the hull. Captain Eric Risberg was ordered to come aboard the U-boat with the ship's papers. The *Algeria* was in ballast, en route from Gothenburg, Sweden to New York "for orders." Sweden was a neutral nation.

Droscher "took the *Algeria's* log and examined it, and when he found that she had been operating on the United States coast he said that was the 'end.' The captain replied, 'You should not be guided by what I have been doing in the past but by what I am doing in the present.' The chief officer of the submarine said to the captain of the submarine that the captain of the *Algeria* was correct; that they had nothing to do with what he had been doing before. At this point several of the officers of the submarine joined in the conversation, all of which was in German, and took the side of the chief officer, stating among other things that if they sank the *Algeria* the German Government would have to pay for it.

Examining papers on board the *U-117*. (Courtesy of the National Archives.)

"The discussion lasted about 45 minutes to an hour. The commander of the submarine then turned to the captain of the *Algeria* and stated he was sorry, but he would have to let him go; but the next time he caught him, he would sink him without warning. He asked the captain if he would give him his word of honor that the *Algeria* was not under charter to the United States Shipping Board, and the captain said 'Yes,' but added that all he knew was that he was under sailing directions to report to New York for orders."

The Swedish steamer was allowed to resume her voyage.

On August 23, the *U-117* encountered an empty lifeboat which, upon examination, proved to be from the SS *San Jose*. The *U-156* had sunk the Norwegian freighter six days earlier.

The next day the *U-117* encountered the three-masted schooner *Bianca* and halted her by gunfire. The Canadian schooner was transporting a cargo of tobacco from Bahia, Brazil to Halifax, Nova Scotia.

Captain Burke and his crew abandoned ship. "Her crew landed safely" in Canso, Nova Scotia.

The Germans set scuttling charges alongside the hull, then continued on their way. They should have hung around to ensure that the schooner sank. The tobacco swelled when it got wet, plugged the bomb holes, and kept the hull afloat. Three days later, a fishing vessel happened across the drifting hulk. There was a hole in the stern, but the hull was upright and in stable condition, so the fishing vessel towed her to Halifax.

Shortly after dawn on August 26, the *U-117* came across two dories that were occupied by fishermen. Droscher asked where they had come from. They indicated the direction in which their fishing vessel lay. Despite thick fog, Droscher soon located the auxiliary schooner *Rush*.

The *Rush* had a crew of twenty-one. Seventeen men were out fishing from their dories. Onboard were Captain Alvro P. Quadros (or Alvor Quadras, or Alvaro Quadros, or Manual Quadros – accounts differ), three

War Cruise of the *U-117*

seamen, and 90,000 pounds of codfish on ice. The men were ordered to row a dory to the U-boat.

According to seaman Joseph Golart, "When we got alongside, they took our boat and ordered us to go below, and we stayed below on the submarine for three hours and when we came on deck again we saw the wreckage of our vessel, but we did not hear any explosion.... We came on deck about 8.35 a.m. and they ordered us to shove off. Our captain told the captain of the submarine that we had no food, and they supplied us with two buckets of fresh water and some of our own crackers, which they had taken from our vessel. They took everything from our vessel, including stores, [1,200 gallons of] fuel oil and tools."

A couple of hours later, the fishing schooner *John J. Fallon* picked up all the men in their dories and landed them at Canso, Nova Scotia.

During their time spent inside the U-boat, Golart reported, "The Captain of the submarine showed our captain a list of the vessels he had sunk. I do not recall all of the names, but some of them are: *Progress*, *Old Time*, *Katy Palmer*, and *Mary Sennett*."

This statement begs the question: Why was the *Old Time* named on this list but was not named in the deck log? My exhaustive analysis notwithstanding, I have no personal bias in the matter – nor do I have a definitive answer. I am merely pointing out the idiosyncrasies and contradictory information that is found in historical documentation. For what it is worth, however, I can speculate that the list was not one of fishing vessels that the *U-117* actually sank, but that it was compiled from names that erstwhile prisoners told the Germans were known to have been fishing in the area.

The *Bergsdalen* was a Norwegian freighter that was under charter to the French government. She was bound in ballast from La Pallice, France to Baltimore, Maryland when she passed the crosshairs of the *U-117*'s periscope. Droscher prepared to launch a torpedo. The attack was hampered by heavy rain squalls that kept causing him to lose sight of the target.

He fired a single torpedo that struck the port side of the *Bergsdalen* with a tremendous blast that nearly tore the hull in two. The freighter sank in two minutes. So fast did she go down that there was not sufficient time to launch all the lifeboats. Some of the men had to leap overboard as the deck sank beneath them. One crewmember drowned in the process

The survivors were later rescued by a Swedish steamer which landed them at Cape Race, Newfoundland.

The *U-117* was far enough north by August 29 that Droscher spotted icebergs to port and starboard. He was careful to avoid them as he drove through the ice field.

On August 30, on the Le Havre Banks, the *U-117* stopped two Canadian fishing vessels by gunfire. First to go was the *Elsie Porter*. Droscher noted in his log that all of her crew spoke fluent German because they were German-Americans. The men were set adrift almost three hundred miles from the nearest land. The Germans robbed the *Elsie Porter* of provisions before scuttling her with bombs.

Next to go was the *Potentate* in similar fashion.

Because of the distance between them, neither of these vessels was aware of the scuttling of the other. Their plight seemed hopeless. They spent the night at sea in open boats, totally unprotected from the cold.

The next day the SS *Solberg* hove into view. At 1:15 p.m. she picked up the fishermen from the *Elsie Porter*. Later she picked up the men from the *Potentate*. Both crews were landed at St. Johns, Newfoundland. There were no fatalities only because of the chance encounter.

The *U-117* opened fire on the SS *Alleign* on September 2. The distance was too great for the shells to reach their target, and the U-boat was unable to get within torpedo range.

The *U-117* made one more unsuccessful attack, this one on September 5, when it launched a torpedo at SS *War Ranee*. Droscher watched the bubble track pass under the bridge but there was no detonation.

According to the Navy account, "The *War Ranee*

War Cruise of the *U-117*

sighted a periscope and then the track of a torpedo close alongside, which passed immediately under the engine room, but did not hit the ship. The ship had been stopped for minor engine repairs and when the submarine was sighted orders were given for 'full speed ahead.' After a delay of five minutes she steamed ahead, zigzagging, until the submarine was well astern. The submarine came to the surface and gave chase. Later the submarine opened fire. Two rounds were fired at three-minute intervals between shots. The last seen of the submarine, she was heading south and the *War Ranee* escaped."

Droscher noted the pursuit in his deck log, but made no mention of firing his gun.

He chased a couple of other steamers later that day, but could not catch up with them and had to break off the pursuits. He was afraid of long high-speed chases because of his precarious fuel situation.

Droscher made wireless contact with the *U-140* on September 8. He and Kophamel arranged a rendezvous for the following day. The U-boats met off the Faeroe Islands (between Iceland and the Shetland Islands). The weather was not conducive to transferring fuel: high swells were accompanied by rain. The two U-boats traveled in consort for the next two days, with the *U-117* trailing in the wake of the *U-140*.

The transfer of fuel commenced as soon as the weather turned fair, on September 11. Droscher described the laborious process in detail:

"On the *U 140* a great number of 15 cm [centimeter, or 5.9-inch] cartridge cases are filled with oil and fastened to a long hemp rope. At the same time a number of empty closed cartridge cases are also fastened to the hemp rope to serve as buoys. Then the hemp rope which had been lengthened to about 600 m[eters] by means of thinner ones, is passed over to and gradually pulled in by the *U 117* which is lying abreast at a distance of about 100 to 200 meters. The filled cartridge cases are removed and emptied into the oil tanks through funnels. Each time about 75 cases are transferred, with a total content of about 1 cbm [cubic meter]. By evening, in spite of a heavy swell about 7 cbm were taken on. Oil transfer stopped on account of darkness falling."

Twelve cubic meters of oil were transferred the next day, making a total of 19 cubic meters in all. This was equivalent to slightly more than 5,000 gallons, or a little more than 18 tons of fuel oil.

The U-boats continued their procession through the British blockage on September 14. This dangerous traverse took three days to complete. The *U-117* ran out of fuel on September 20. Droscher: "Sent out requests by wireless to be taken in tow. Steered slowly southward under electric power. Two German torpedo boats in sight. A Danish patrol vessel coming up abaft with war flag, passes at a distance of 30 m to port, salutes. Taken in tow by torpedo boat. Tow line broken. Steamed south under own power. . . . Voyage continued with escort. Transfer of oil alongside of S.M.S. *Hanover*."

The *U-117* docked safely at Kiel, Germany on September 22, 1918.

Although the war cruise of the *U-117* was over, its destruction of Allied shipping was not. The deadly mines that Droscher had sown along the American eastern seaboard were lying silently in wait to complete their nefarious mission for the Kaiser.

The *U-117* had been home for a week when the first of its sleeping explosive devices awoke. In the predawn hours of September 29, the U.S. battleship *Minnesota* was passing the Fenwick Island Shoal off the coast of Maryland when a heavy explosion occurred under the starboard bow. "Between frames 5 and 16, and from the lower edge of the armor belt to the keel, the ship's structure was practically obliterated."

The men on their watch below were tossed out of their bunks by the concussion, but no one was wounded or killed by the blast.

The massive influx of water caused the battleship to trim down by the bow and list to starboard. The collision alarm was sounded. Sailors rushed to examine the extent of the damage. Bulkheads adjacent to the damaged

War Cruise of the *U-117*

compartments were shored in order to curb the flooding. The *Minnesota* turned to port and headed westward for shoal water. Her condition soon stabilized.

Along with her escort, the U.S. destroyer *Israel*, the *Minnesota* shaped a new course for the Delaware Breakwater. After a pilot went aboard the *Minnesota*, the *Israel* resumed her assigned duties while the battleship limped up the Delaware River to her intended destination, the Philadelphia Navy Yard. As coincidence would have it, the *Minnesota* had been scheduled to undergo forty days of authorized repairs beginning on October 1.

The second victim of the *U-117's* mines was the American freighter *San Saba*. This was the same vessel that had performed valuable humanitarian service on June 3, 1918 by rescuing forty-one survivors from the depredations of the *U-151*. Unfortunately, the crew of the *San Saba* did not fare so well when she struck a mine on October 4 in almost the same spot where she made her selfless rescue.

At this time she was operating for the Mallory Line, under charter to the U.S. Railroad Administration. She departed from New York on October 3 with 2,500 tons of general cargo bound for Tampa, Florida and Mobile, Alabama. The night was dark and moonless. Shortly after midnight, Captain Bergen Birdsall noted Barnegat Light passing by his beam.

At 12:45 a.m., Second Officer Adolf Beer heard "a heavy noise knocking on the ship's side which followed with an explosion." This was a mine bumping along the iron hull. A few seconds later a thunderous detonation punched the aging freighter upward with such force that her keel was broken instantly. Because the explosion occurred in the vicinity of the engine room, which was located amidships, it was surmised afterward that many of the duty personnel were killed outright by the blast. The less fortunate – those who were injured and still conscious – were drowned by the massive flood of water that inundated the hull.

The ship buckled, tore apart, then went straight to the bottom. It was all over in less than five minutes. The

San Saba was not equipped with wireless, but even if she had been so equipped, it is doubtful that a Marconi man would have been able to transmit a call for help.

Beer "sustained himself by means of a life buoy." Four other survivors "sustained themselves on an improvised life raft made in the water from wreckage." Neither Beer nor the group of four was aware of the other's presence in the water. Separated from each other, they bobbed in the placid sea for the rest of the night, suffering miserably from the cold.

Around 6 a.m., the number of men on the makeshift raft was reduced by one when a survivor died from exposure. Another man died at noon. Seaman Edwardo Simona and coal passer Pedro Aceredo clung desperately to life throughout the long afternoon.

At 4:30 p.m., the Norwegian steamship *Briefond* hove into view and spotted the lone second officer in the water. Beer was hoisted aboard after spending fifteen hours in the water. Half an hour later, the *Briefond* – now maintaining a sharp lookout – came upon Simona and Aceredo on their raft, and picked them up.

Unknown to the men who were rescued by the *Briefond*, another group of five men clung to pieces of the pilot house throughout the night. One man died from exposure after nine hours. The remaining four, plus the dead body, were picked up by the American steamer *Lake Felicity* after twelve hours of suffering.

These seven men were the only survivors out of a crew of thirty-seven.

The water where the *San Saba* sank was 80 feet deep. Masts protruded above the surface of the sea. A week after her loss, "the Coast Guard cutter *Morrell* destroyed what remained of the *San Saba* as a menace to navigation."

During the course of two weeks subsequent to the sinking of the *San Saba*, the minesweeper *Teal* destroyed three more mines, and the minesweeper *Freehold* destroyed another one. Despite these extensive minesweeping operations, they did not get them all. The penultimate mine was found on October 27 by the un-

War Cruise of the *U-117*

suspecting *Chaparra*.

The Cuban freighter was carrying 14,000 bags of sugar from Cardenas, Cuba to New York. Captain Jose Vinslas (or Vinolas), master, testified that around 10 p.m. he "felt a heavy blow just forward of the bridge on the port side; there was a terrific explosion, and the vessel was fairly lifted out of the water. At the same time a column of water was thrown up which covered the bridge. The vessel listed to port and capsized, sinking within two and a half minutes."

The crew reacted with lightning-like speed and managed to launch two lifeboats before the ship slipped abruptly beneath the waves. Six men were missing, but the remaining twenty-three rowed toward shore. The boats became separated in the dark. The men were but lightly clad, "many being in their night clothes, and they suffered considerably in the cold, damp fog which enveloped the coast during the night."

The men rowed for twenty-two hours, until 8 o'clock the following night. "The captain and 11 men came in the inlet in one of their own boats and landed at Coast Guard Station 112. Another boat with 11 men landed on North Beach."

Mrs. Frank Thompson, wife of the assistant keeper of the Barnegat lighthouse, was acting as a volunteer lookout when she spotted a little yawl in the waves beyond the breakers. Through the thin mist she could see that the men were exhausted and were in danger of swamping. She yelled for help, jumped waist deep into the surf, grabbed the bow of the boat as a large comber swung it around, and dragged the boat to the beach. She helped the men out of the yawl, then half-carried two of them, who were too exhausted to walk, to the house.

Her cries alerted her husband and the Coast Guard relief, who arrived in time to assist Captain Vinslas and the survivors from the second lifeboat.

Not until November 9 did the *Saetia* have the misfortune to discover another of the *U-117's* delayed action devices. The position of the ship was then ten miles south-southeast of Fenwick Island Light, off the coast of

Maryland. The time was 8:30 a.m. The heavily armed freighter was returning in ballast to New York from Bordeaux, France, after delivering a valuable cargo of much-needed supplies to support the fighting "over there." She was under commission to the Naval Overseas Transportation Service.

Seaman G.A. Goldsborough was on lookout duty in the crow's nest: "I felt a shock and thought we had struck a rock. The mast bent forward and I almost fell. I looked aft and saw debris flying as high as the mast. I saw some hatch battens and dark sand [ballast] and chips of wood flying in the air. Some of this was higher than the mast."

Yeoman R.N. Ungemach: "The explosion felt like two freight cars bumping."

The detonation took place at No. 3 hatch, about fifty feet abaft of midships. By the time Fireman F.O. Wanamaker "got there the hatch was half full of water. The water was rushing in from the starboard side and judging from the volume of water I guess the hole must have been about eight feet. This was below the waterline."

Lieutenant Commander Lynch, in command, thought that they must have been torpedoed. "Knowing the usual practice of these submarines, and being afraid of being boarded, I immediately put everything of a confidential and secret nature in a weighted bag and threw it overboard." He also ordered abandon ship.

Within five minutes they made good their escape: sixty-six men distributed among four lifeboats, and nineteen men on two rafts. There were no fatalities. Boatswain's Mate B.A. Swarr stated, "I was in the last catamaran which left the ship. We passed close to the spot where the explosion took place on the starboard side. I could clearly see that there was a slit up the side of the boat about two feet wide. It appeared to be cracked at the seam. This extended from the waterline to the deck."

The *Saetia's* stern soon settled to the bottom, but not until forty minutes after the explosion did the foremast disappear.

War Cruise of the *U-117*

The four lifeboats landed at Coast Guard Station No. 146, in Ocean City, Maryland. Three injured men were hospitalized. The SS *Kennebec* picked up the men on the two rafts. They were transferred to the Navy patrol boat *S.P. 371*, and were taken to the section base of the Fourth Naval District at Cape May, New Jersey.

After the Armistice was signed, the U.S. Naval Aide to Britain, Admiral William Sims, obtained the German records for the placement of all mines off the American coast. Even so, it was not until January 1919 that the rest of the mines-in-waiting in the Fenwick Shoal field were swept up and destroyed by the *Teal*.

Thus finally ended the war cruise of the *U-117* – not with a whimper but a bang.

This picture of the deck gun on the *U-117* was taken after the war. (Courtesy of the National Archives.)

War Cruise
of the
U-155

The *U-155* made more trips to American waters than any other U-boat in history, including those in World War Two. It made two merchant cruises when it was named *Deutschland*. Now it was returning for its third cruise, this time as an armed warship.

The *Deutschland* was converted from a merchant vessel to a warship by the installation of six torpedo tubes in the bow, and the mounting of two 5.9-inch deck guns that were removed from the SMS *Zahringen* when that obsolete battleship was deactivated and reduced to a target vessel.

Under the command of Korvettenkapitan Ferdinand Studt, the *U-155* departed from Kiel on August 11, 1918. The cruise was underway for barely twenty-five minutes when the fuel pump for the port engine ceased to function. The U-boat proceeded at five knots on the starboard engine until the problem was fixed some nine hours later. The fuel pump broke down again three days afterward, and had to be repaired while the U-boat proceeded slowly on one engine.

The *U-155* passed safely through the barrage zone, then headed for the passage between the Shetland and Orkney islands.

On August 18, Studt opened fire on the Norwegian steam whaler *Svarsard*, which he mistook for an armed British merchantman. The crew hoisted the Norwegian flag, manned the lifeboats, and abandoned ship. The lifeboats drew alongside the U-boat.

Studt: "I interrogate the captain and advise him to avoid cruising near the Barrage Zone in the future. Made sure the ship is not damaged and the crew unhurt."

War Cruise of the *U-155*

He allowed the *Svarsard* to proceed after establishing her neutrality and the peacefulness of her voyage.

The following day he fired a warning shot at a steamer whose hull had white markings. This was the Norwegian steamer *Tungus*, which was operating in the service of the Belgian Relief Commission. He permitted her to proceed unmolested.

According to some contemporary American records, the *U-155* attacked a three-vessel convoy on August 27.

The American freighter *Montoso* was eastbound in consort with the animal transport *Ticonderoga* and the freighter *Rondo*. When a lookout spotted a suspicious-looking wake off the port beam, Captain A. O. Forsyth, master of the *Montoso*, suggested that the convoy make a radical course change away from the unidentified vessel. All three vessels turned 20° to starboard.

Three hours later, under the cover of darkness, the stalking U-boat got within range of the *Montoso's* guns. She opened fire with both her forward and after guns. The *Ticonderoga* also opened fire. The *Rondo* was unarmed.

The U-boat replied immediately. Two shells landed several yards astern of the *Montoso*. The three vessels then scattered at high speed, and the U-boat broke off the attack.

The deck log of the *U-155* records no such attack. In fact, Studt recorded that he did not even spot any enemy vessels for nearly two weeks after the *Tungus* incident. The U-boat that attacked the convoy must have been some other U-boat that was on local patrol, and not on its way to American waters.

The *U-155* was still in mid-Atlantic when it made its first destructive attack of the cruise. On August 31, Studt stopped the unarmed Portuguese fishing vessel *Gamo*, which was bound from St. John's, Newfoundland to Lisbon, Portugal. He set her crew adrift in lifeboats, and sent the bark and her cargo of fish to the bottom by means of scuttling charges.

On September 2, the *U-155* stopped the Norwegian freighter *Stortind*. She was en route from Norfolk, Virginia to La Pallice, France with a cargo of piece goods and wire. The state of the sea was so bad that it was impossible for the U-boat to go alongside the freighter.

Studt: "Ship is sunk by gunfire. Advised crew in the lifeboats to head for the Azores, 350 miles away."

The *U-155* continued westward while the survivors of the *Stortind* were left to their fate.

Studt tried to shell big game on September 7, but the vessel opened fire, deployed a smoke screen, and outran him. Once again he had to settle for stopping a two-masted sailing vessel that could not muster the speed to get away from him. This was the Portuguese fishing vessel *Sophia*. She was loaded with fish from the Newfoundland Banks. The crew was permitted to escape. "She is scuttled with demolition charges."

Studt attacked a steamer on September 10, but when he determined that she had been chartered by the Belgian Relief Commission he broke off the attack.

Portugal continued to take a beating from the *U-155*. September 13 found the armed Portuguese freighter *Leixoes* bound in ballast from Hull, England to Boston, Massachusetts. Her end came shortly after 5 o'clock in the morning.

According to Captain Joaquim Ferreira Sucena, master, "The torpedo struck on the starboard side of No. 4 hatch; submarine was not visible.. As soon as the ship was hit, I saw she was going to sink, and I ordered all hands to take to the life boats and all of my confidential books were sunk. . . . . Fifteen minutes after the ship was struck the submarine appeared on the starboard beam about one-quarter-mile distant. Our vessel sank in about fifteen minutes. . . . One man lost his life on the ship. He was probably asleep when the ship was struck and did not wake up."

The nearest points of land were hundreds of miles away: Newfoundland to the north, Sable Island to the west. The four lifeboats drifted apart. Records are sparse with regard to survivors. The men spent five days at sea in open boats.

A telegram dated September 16 stated, "Survivors

landing somewhere in Canada, comprising the Captain and sixteen members of the crew. . . . So far, there are thirty-five members of the crew missing."

A telegram dated September 17 stated: "One boat with ten men landed Canso."

A telegram dated September 18 stated: "Canadian trawler picked up last boat of *Leixoes*, with eleven men." This implies that another boatload of survivors were either picked up or made land on their own.

Yet according to an ONI summary dated September 20, "Three men lost their lives; one man was lost when the ship went down, and the other two lost their lives from exposure and cold. . . . One life boat with the third officer and eight men is still missing."

The last report contradicts the earlier tabulation. The number of dead and missing does not tally. Three men definitely lost their lives, and there may have been as many as twelve fatalities.

Later in the morning of September 13, the *U-155* attacked the British steamer *Newby Hall*. According to Captain F. O. Seaborne, the merchant marine master, "We sighted a torpedo coming toward us from three points on the port bow. We immediately put helm hard starboard. The torpedo missed by about 6 feet, passing our bows from an angle over to the starboard side. I then steered parallel to the track of the torpedo, and at 9.56 a. m. (approximate) I altered to SSW, thereby bringing position of the submarine astern and instructing engineers to give all speed possible.

"At 10 a. m. we sight submarine coming to surface bearing north; I then kept him astern steering an irregular zigzag course (about 3,000 yards).

"We saw their gun crews coming out of the conning tower and manning the two guns. They commenced firing immediately and we replied with our gun. He was then steering in a westerly direction and going at a moderate speed, and to keep him astern we had to gradually alter course to the eastward.

"The enemy was firing rapidly with both guns. The forward one appeared to be of larger caliber than the other. After about 50 rounds with our gun a direct hit, smoke, flash, explosion put his forward and largest gun out of action. When the smoke cleared we found this gun had tilted over to an angle of about 30° and no gun crew was to be seen. Soon after we scored another hit on his forward end, the fore part of the forward gun causing an explosion and a volume of smoke. After that we scored another hit on his after end, about 20 feet aft the after gun. He then reduced his speed and seemed to be under difficulties, but continued firing with his after and smaller gun.

"At about 13,000 yards we outranged him and he ceased firing. He headed toward us and appeared as if he was chasing us, but in a few minutes he was broadside on to us again and stopped and suddenly disappeared. Action lasted from 10 a. m. to 11.20 a. m., when firing ceased. Enemy commenced and ceased firing first.

"During the action the enemy used shrapnel and high explosive shells, but none hit the ship except shrapnel. None of the crew was injured. Two boats on the port side were riddled and one plate amidship on the port side dented and badly cut in numerous places by shrapnel or burst shell."

Studt described the damage that was done by the enemy shell: "During the action, *U-155* was hit by a 14-cm [centimeter] shell from a range of about 100 hc [hectometers; one hectometer equals 100 meters; 100 hectometers equals about 6 miles]. The shell struck the foredeck in the immediate vicinity of the hatchway, making a slight dent in the pressure hull. The plates are depressed to a diameter of about 60 cm [almost two feet]. A number of rivets have been sprung, and the forward minelaying gear is damaged. Despite the damage, the mines can be moved. . . . Further investigation of the damage shows that the port exhaust system is damaged (in particular: exhaust pipes 4, 5, and 6)."

For the next several days, foul weather hampered the U-boat's ability to chase enemy vessels or utilize its weapons. Studt: "Boat resumed heading with the wind to continue pressure hull repairs. We were unsuccessful in welding the sprung rivets with the torch, since the sea is washing over the damaged side of the hull. The job has to be accomplished with screw bolts."

The *U-155* made a successful test dive on September 17. That afternoon, Studt sighted Halifax, Nova Scotia. The following day, he commenced minelaying operations outside the harbor. His original orders called for him to sow his waiting weapons off St. John's, Newfoundland. His conversation with the survivors of the *Gamo* convinced him that the harbor was too small to accommodate large vessels. He decided instead to sow his mines off Halifax, where shipping traffic was busy. This phase of his operation was completed in the wee hours of the morning of September 18.

Minesweepers eventually found and swept up three of these mines. The undiscovered mines damaged no vessels; they either flooded and sank, or broke free of their moorings and drifted out to sea.

While at first blush it might seem that planting mines was a wasted effort, a look at the larger picture reveals a different viewpoint. The presence of mines off harbor entrances kept minesweepers busy. Sweeping operations were constantly ongoing. In the U.S. alone, this tied up the service of fifty-nine vessels that could otherwise have been employed in coastal patrol and escort duty.

The next mission of the *U-155* was to cut communication cables in the area between Halifax and Sable Island. This proved difficult to accomplish due to the constant presence of enemy warships, forcing the U-boat to crash dive time and time again in order to avoid detection.

Then the cable-cutting mechanism broke down, "As a result a set of cable claws and both cutters are lost. The failure was not noticed until the indicator needle suddenly jumped to the 5-ton cutting-pressure point. Since the missing parts cannot be found on the bottom, they were replaced and a second attempt of cutting the cable commenced. As previously mentioned, it is possible the bottom in this area may contain many rocks, which endangers the procedure. We did not succeed until the third attempt. Deflections of the indicator needle alternately showed that objects were cut with force units of 1.8 tons; 2.2 tons; 2.6 tons. We may assume that we were actually cutting cables. I myself am quite sure that the cables were successfully severed. The success of this operation is generally verified by the mentioned movement of the indicator pointer: first to the dial setting (force unit) and then return of the pointer to zero. Both of these indications demonstrate a cable was cut. . . . After surfacing, many parts of the complicated cable-cutting mechanism were found to be scattered or damaged. In summarizing this operation, it must be said that the design of a fully serviceable cable-cutter – regardless of the nature of the bottom – needs much improvement."

Archival records do not indicate that any communication cables were severed.

On September 20, the *U-155* fired a shot across the stern of the steam trawler *Kingfisher*. Captain John Boyle O'Reilly ordered the engine stopped and all hands on deck. "We did not send out any SOS signals as the dynamo was not running." Four minutes later the U-boat fired a second shot, which passed over the smokestack. The crew took to a pair of metallic lifeboats "as quickly as possible."

There were thirteen men in each lifeboat: one under the command of the skipper, the other under the command of the mate, T. F. Fleming.

The U-boat drew alongside the lifeboats, made inquiries, and dismissed the crew. A German boarding party ransacked the galley, took whatever provisions were left behind, then set scuttling charges that sank the vessel.

The survivors were stranded some 85 miles from land. They started rowing toward Halifax, but an adverse tide carried them off course. Favorable weather enabled the boats to stay together. After spending the night

War Cruise of the *U-155*

at sea, they steered toward Beaver Island and from there proceeded to West Quoddy, Nova Scotia. They landed safely after twenty-four hours bent over the oars.

Farmers drove the men to Port Dufferin where they caught a steamer to Halifax, Nova Scotia. After arriving in Halifax on September 24, a U.S. Navy representative interrogated the men and took photographs of them. He forwarded his report to ONI in Washington, DC. The men were then sent by rail to Boston, Massachusetts, where the skipper and presumably the bulk of the crew made their residence.

Ordinarily the *Kingfisher* incident would have ended at this point. Special circumstances dictated otherwise. One salient feature that emerged during interrogation concerned confidential codes. Standard protocol called for all documents of a confidential nature to be thrown overboard in a weighted bag. According to Captain O'Reilly, "In the excitement incident to abandoning the vessel the code was left on board."

It also developed that the crewmembers did not actually witness the sinking of their vessel. They were several miles away when they heard three detonations that they presumed were bombs that they had seen the boarding party take to the *Kingfisher* in a small boat that they removed from a compartment abaft the conning tower.

This left ONI with several unanswered questions. Were the explosions a ruse to trick the *Kingfisher's* crewmen to believing that the vessel had been scuttled, when in fact the Germans intended to use it as a decoy, as the *U-156* had done with the *Triumph*? Had the Germans taken the time to examine the *Kingfisher* and discover the radio codes? Or had O'Reilly intentionally left the codes on board because he was in league with Germany? This latter scenario was not as farfetched as it might seem to modern readers.

Although O'Reilly was of Irish descent, only he and seven other crewmembers were American citizens. The other eighteen fishermen were foreign nationals whose allegiance could be considered questionable. In fact, ONI and the U.S. Department of Justice were suspicious of the entire crew.

O'Reilly filed a deposition with the American Consulate-General in Halifax, in which he swore, "A confidential publication in my possession was left on board the ship. I do not know the number of this publication and never opened it. It was placed underneath my mattress. The radio operator left this publication on my desk, and I do not know where it came from whether by mail or messenger, and it had been on board the ship about two months. The radio operator, Walter C. Bay, who is now in Portland, Maine and is going on the *Fish Hawk*, handed me this confidential publication and told me to burn the old Merchant Ship Cipher, which I did, and that this publication was a new one."

What O'Reilly did not know was that Bay's replacement, Thomas McQuade, was spying for the Office of Naval Intelligence.

The Department of Justice started its investigation of the *Kingfisher* incident on September 27. A review of the statements that were filed by O'Reilly and several of his crewmembers revealed "nothing out of the ordinary."

ONI was not satisfied because, according to an intelligence summary that was compiled on October 2, 1918, "The East Coast Fisheries Company has been under investigation by this office and the Department of Justice for some time as it has been suspected that this company was organized for the purpose of aiding the enemy. The stock of the company is owned mainly by Germans and German Americans and the brokerage house which is floating the stock has a sales force consisting mainly of alien enemies.

"This office has reason to believe that an attempt might be made in some way to communicate with submarines from the trawler *Kingfisher* which was the first trawler put in operation by the East Coast Fisheries Company, and the Boston office was advised of these suspicions and arranged for a wireless operator on board. Among other things, this office had information that the Captain of the *Kingfisher* had papers showing

War Cruise of the *U-155*

the German ownership of the stock of the East Coast Fisheries Company and the history of Prussian officers who were very active in its affairs. This office has also received information that when the *Kingfisher* was captured the confidential code book was left on board and that no effort was made to destroy it.

"In spite of the foregoing suspicious circumstances it is apparent from examination of the annexed report that very little effort was made to obtain information from the crew of the vessel as to the facts and circumstances which would aid this office in this investigation, either in giving the East Coast Fisheries Company a clean bill of health or in strengthening the suspicions of this office as to the activities of that company.

"Apparently the Captain and possibly one or two of the crew were asked to make a statement, but it is apparent that they were not put through such an examination as a case of this character and involving such serious consequences demanded. It is the opinion of this office that in a case of this character effort should have been made to cross examine the entire personnel of the crew in question and that the examination should be conducted by a person who has had experience in such matters. Only by such an examination is it possible to obtain truth as to the action and motives of the different members of the crew. Unless such examination is conducted it may well happen that the guilty parties might escape and that this office might be hampered in its work of investigation."

The Canadian Naval Staff in Halifax advised the Admiralty via telegram that the U.S. radio cipher code was "probably captured by the enemy." Upon reflection from this remove, however, it seems likely that ONI would have hedged its suspicions by having its spy plant a fake or out-of-date cipher code on the *Kingfisher*.

Considering the vast amount of money that Germany was spending on the war, it is certainly within reason to deduce that the German high command was willing to sacrifice its investment in the *Kingfisher* in order to obtain a current radio cipher code. Notwithstanding this premise, the East Coast Fisheries Company avoided any monetary loss by over-insuring the vessel.

According to a news report, "I. M. Taylor, president of the East Coast Company, said to-night that the vessel was valued at $175,000 and was insured against submarines for $250,000, covering the value of the vessel and the cost of operations. He said that the sinking of the *Kingfisher* would not deter the company from further operations, and that another trawler which has just been completed would be sent out next week. Several additional vessels are under construction for the company."

It seems that not only was the East Coast Fisheries Company well capitalized, but it could expect its underwriters to reimburse it for the loss of the *Kingfisher*.

Navy records do not indicate that the company was ever indicted for conspiracy, but it must be remembered that the end of the war was less than two months away. Perhaps ONI did not possess enough proof to prosecute its case before the situation became irrelevant.

An interesting follow-up was published in the January 1921 issue of *The World's Work*. The monthly magazine's anonymous investment editor chronicled the beginning and the end of the East Coast Fisheries Company. I. M. Taylor organized the company in 1917. He promoted the sale of stock by distributing a fictitious financial publication that gave the company a favorable write-up. The investment editor's investigation established that the "property and property rights" that the company claimed to possess did not exist, that its actual assets were meager, and that a so-called affiliated company was bogus. After the war, the East Coast Fisheries Company went into receivership, and the stockholders were bilked of their investments.

Was the East Coast Fisheries Company a German scheme to get Americans to pay for collusion with the Fatherland? Or was it a stock scam to enrich a single individual? I doubt that anyone will ever know.

In any event, Studt did not mention the recovery of

War Cruise of the *U-155*

radio codes in his deck log. In hindsight, it appears that the German boarding party overlooked them.

Studt experienced two weeks of frustration after the *Kingfisher* sinking. For most of that time there were no targets in sight. For the rest of the time, bad weather made it impossible for the *U-155* to catch its targets or use its weapons. One intended victim spotted the U-boat and turned to ram. Studt submerged to avert collision. When he surfaced, "The attack angle is too great, even at a range of 25 hc [hectometers]."

By this stage in the war, American coastal waters were heavily patrolled. Time and again the *U-155* was forced to submerge by the presence of warships.

Studt fired thirty rounds at the British steamer *Reginolite* on September 29. The *Reginolite* fired seventeen rounds in return, zigzagged, and outran the U-boat. At the same time, an escorting destroyer forced Studt to crash dive. By the time he surfaced the chase was hopeless.

To make matters worse, the starboard diesel would not restart. The U-boat drifted throughout the night and used the port engine to recharge its batteries while the crew effected repairs.

Studt spotted other vessels, but they were either too far away or were traveling too fast for him to intercept.

The sole vessel to steam into range got away because the torpedo malfunctioned. Studt: "It changed course immediately after leaving the starboard torpedo tube, and passed far ahead of the steamer's bow."

Although there is no such thing as fate, it almost seems as if the *Alberto Treves* was fated to be torpedoed by a U-boat. On May 5, 1918, she was part of a westbound convoy when the *U-38* fired a torpedo into her port side. The USS *Yankton*, a converted yacht that was one of the escorts, dropped depth charges on the U-boat and kept it submerged until the convoy steamed out of its range.

The *Alberto Treves* was severely damaged, but she

turned around and managed to reach Cartagena, Spain on her own power. Her cargo of general merchandise was discharged. After three months of repair work, the cargo was reloaded and the freighter made another attempt to deliver it to New York. This time she traveled independently.

The Italian freighter was not as fortunate with her next encounter, on October 3. Captain Giacomo Profumo gave the following account: "I saw the torpedo 65° on the starboard bow close aboard. Put the helm hard aport, but the torpedo struck a few seconds later abaft the engine room in #4 hold. The explosion was terrific, lifting hatches and main deck clear away. Pieces of metal flew over the bridge and particles landed all over the ship. One member of the gun's crew, Posino Dominico, was struck on the foot by a splinter of steel, but was not badly injured. I stopped the engines and examined the ship. Found #4 hold full of water and engine room bulkhead partly carried away. Bulkhead to No. 5 hold was also damaged beyond repair. I at once gave the order to abandon ship, and by 8.00 a.m. the three boats shoved off, leaving no one on board. The reason for such haste was that we had all had experience with submarines and believed that they would be shelling the ship in a few minutes. The submarine came to the surface . . . and at about 9.30 a.m., she fired about forty shells at the ship before the ship went down at noon."

Left adrift were thirty-four men: thirteen in the captain's boat, five in #2 boat, and sixteen in #4 boat. The closest point of land was Nantucket Island, which was several hundred miles away. The lifeboats were well stocked with biscuits, canned beef, and water – enough to last for several days. Each boat was equipped with a compass, sextant, chronometer, chart, and navigation book.

The men raised sail and bent over their oars.

The boats got separated under the cloak of darkness during their first night at sea. All had instructions to steer north-northwest. Captain Profumo's boat was "obliged to go south on account of heavy weather." At

War Cruise of the *U-155*

nine o'clock on the morning of October 4, the skipper's boat was able to resume its course toward Nantucket. This boat spent the next three days on a heading of north-northwest.

On the morning of October 7, the U.S. troop transport *Orizaba* loomed out of the fog. She was part of a four-vessel convoy on its way back from France. The U.S. destroyer *Taylor* and the French cruiser *Lutetia* were escorting her and the troop transport *Siboney*. Visibility was variable between one and three miles. Her position at that time was approximately 300 miles from Nantucket Island.

The *Orizaba* lost sight of the other vessels in the thickening fog. She veered out of formation to take a look at the boat, saw that it was filled with men, and hove to. She picked up the occupants but did not take time to retrieve the lifeboat. A doctor treated the men for exhaustion, but they were otherwise in good health. The *Orizaba* then relocated the convoy and explained her absence to the convoy leader.

Commander Richard White, in command of the *Orizaba*, was severely criticized for rescuing survivors. The convoy leader onboard the *Siboney* commented, "It is not the mission of a loaded transport to dally with drifting boats, particularly when an escort vessel is present. Think the *Talbot* could have been got back in time."

Commander White felt compelled to explain his actions. "I regret that my judgment in deviating from the well-established mission of loaded transports should be called into question, under the weather and other conditions surrounding my action. I attempted, by the only safe means I had, to communicate with the escorting destroyer. Available time was exceedingly brief on account of the fog, and communication via the *Siboney* would have caused excessive delay. The small boat was sighted in such a position that, with small left rudder, an opportunity was at once afforded for the boat to intercept the *Orizaba* under her own sail power, which was being assisted by oars. By the time it was found impossible to reach the *Talbot*, it was likewise impossible to reach the

Siboney by visual signal. There was no assurance that the *Talbot* or *Siboney* had sighted the boat, and certainly no evidence that the former had, although the boat was almost, if not quite, as close to it as to this vessel. The fog was visibly increasing in the area in which the ship found herself and it was possible that the weather might have become definitely thick, with all the attendant difficulty that would imply in attempting to direct a destroyer from a zigzagging convoy to a shifting point astern (the small boat was moving with fair speed). The visibility was so low that it is considered very probable that a submarine would have been on the surface to within a very short distance of this ship, with consequent possibility of discovery. If not, then the probability of a submarine discovering in sufficient time for well directed attack that the ship was stopped, from periscope observations alone, is believed to be remote. In any case, the ship was at no time involved in such a way that she could not maneuver freely. There was a chance taken certainly, but it is not considered to have been so great as the chance of the boat having been missed entirely, with the consequent stigma to the Navy attached, especially if fog had shut in close enough to render impossible the sending of a visual signal of information. Coding and decoding a radio signal would have resulted in fatal loss of time. In addition to the existing weather conditions, there was another attendant feature that merits consideration. The convoy was moving at two-thirds speed. The small boat was in such a position as to make it possible to pick her up with a minimum of maneuvering. Had the survivors been otherwise than approaching exhaustion, the whole boat crew could have been picked up practically in passing. As it was, the delay was small and the ship only about eleven degrees off the base course when the small boat was cast adrift. There was at no time any doubt in my mind as to the procedure I would have followed in case of clear weather, but the allos [sic] received indicated no submarine activity nearby, although several vessels had been sighted, and I consider a definite possibility existed that the escorting

War Cruise of the *U-155*

destroyer might readily have missed the small boat under the conditions of visibility existing in the locality. The situation called for a rapid estimate. I immediately decided to inform the *Talbot*, a choice presented itself between accepting an almost ideal set of conditions for a flying pick-up of a boat load of men and a chase into the fog after a destroyer that had already failed to answer signals, with the possibility of losing the men. The traditions of the Service indicated the choice to be made."

No attempt was made to search for the other lifeboats. They were never found.

Meanwhile, as the *Alberto Treves* was sinking, the *U-155* was damaged when a shell exploded "while still in the gun barrel, causing some damage to the foredeck. Gun is now canted at an angle of 310°. As far as we can determine, there is some damage to the port fuel tank, which will require emptying and inspecting the tank."

On October 4, the *U-155* stopped the British schooner *Industrial*. She was en route from Nova Scotia to New Haven, Connecticut with a cargo of salt herring. The vessel was sunk by means of demolition charges. I found no records with regard to the life or death of the crew.

The reported position was a couple of hundred miles southeast of Nantucket. This was the closest approach that the *U-155* made to the coast of the United States.

Storms continued to plague the U-boat's operations, rendering it impossible to use its weapons, and forcing it to heave to for a couple of days. The deck log records temperatures as high as 86° in the cabins, and 122° in the engine room. "The ventilation and air conditioning systems designed for this boat are rather insufficient. This fact becomes much more apparent when cruising with all hatches closed."

On October 11, Studt noted in his log, "For the first time in 14 days, weather permits the use of weapons." That same day he received a radio message from U-boat command: "Exit immediately American waters. Continue cruiser warfare in areas around the Azores." The U-boat headed eastward.

On October 12, the *U-155* was once again bested in a gunfight. It opened fire on the American steamer *Amphion*, in ballast from Bordeaux, France to New York. The U-boat's second shot carried away the wireless antenna and radio shack.

According to the Navy report, "A battle lasting over an hour ensued during which time the *Amphion* gradually drew away from her pursuer. The submarine fired almost 200 shots, a number of which took effect. Two men were mortally wounded and a number of others were seriously injured by shrapnel; five of the steamer's lifeboats were riddled and her superstructure was badly damaged. The *Amphion* fired 72 shots in return, the last of which appeared to be a hit. Immediately after this the submarine, by this time well astern, abandoned the chase and submerged."

The *U-155* was not struck by any of the *Amphion's* shells.

The final action of the *U-155* took place in mid-Atlantic against the U.S. Army transport *Lucia*. She was one of a four-vessel convoy that was traveling from New York to Marseilles, France. Accompanying the *Lucia* were the *Hawaiian*, *West Durfee*, and *Pastores*. No warships escorted the convoy, but the vessels were armed and extra lookouts were posted.

The *Lucia* sported two 3-inch guns and an armed guard consisting of twenty-four men. There were two men with binoculars in the forward crow's nest, two men on the forward gun platform with one pair of binoculars, three men in the after gun platform with one pair of binoculars, and one man in the after crow's nest with binoculars.

In addition to the gunners there was a crew of sixty-six officers and men.

The *Lucia* was loaded all the way to the hatch covers with 1,500 tons of steel, 1,500 tons of shrapnel, 1,000 tons of copper, 1,000 tons of hay (for the cavalry), and

War Cruise of the *U-155*

miscellaneous canned goods. Dodge cars and Pierce-Arrow trucks were parked on the weather deck.

On October 17, chief gunner William O'Brien spotted a white wake at the same moment that the torpedo struck the port side amidships. The warhead detonated against the engine room hull, instantly killing four duty personnel, flooding the fire room, knocking out the dynamo, destroying one of the lifeboats, and lifting the gunners on the after platform off their feet. A shower of dust and debris engulfed the after gun platform and crow's nest. O'Brien ordered both guns trained to port, but no one was able to spot a target.

Without an operable dynamo there was no electricity to power the wireless set. Captain Charles Leary, master, sent a semaphore signal to the *Hawaiian*. The *Hawaiian* transmitted an SOS. The other three vessels in the convoy scattered northward, leaving the *Lucia* to face the U-boat on her own.

Although the *Lucia* was not in imminent danger of sinking, she was a sitting duck. Captain Leary expected the U-boat to surface and shell the helpless transport. He ordered abandon ship. The captain, six crewmembers, and the entire gun crew remained on board. The rest got away in three lifeboats. These lifeboats remained tied to the stern of the *Lucia* throughout the night.

The radio operator connected the emergency battery to the radio. He periodically transmitted the *Lucia's* position.

In the morning, Captain Leary had the men in the lifeboats return to the ship for breakfast. By this time the transport had settled so much that her after decks were awash. The engine room, fire room, hold No. 3, and hold No. 4 were filled with water. Hold No. 5 was half full and was gradually filling. The men returned to their lifeboats to await the inevitable.

One reason that the *Lucia* remained afloat so long may have been due to "special buoyancy boxes." These experimental flotation devices had been installed as a measure to offset flooding in the event of a catastrophe such that the transport was undergoing.

The *Lucia* low in the water. (Courtesy of the Naval Photographic Center.)

The day dragged on with the *Lucia* settling slowly but continuously by the stern. The gun crew maintained a constant vigil. The men in the lifeboats went aboard for lunch. By two o'clock in the afternoon the after gun platform was awash, and heavy swells were breaking over the taffrail. O'Brien ordered the gunners to take to the lifeboats.

The weather was worsening. The lifeboats deployed sea anchors in order to stay in the vicinity of the transport. Several gunners were seasick. The *Lucia* finally sank at 3:20 in the afternoon of October 18 – some twenty-two hours after the torpedo struck.

Five lifeboats bobbed on seas that rose so high that "it took the utmost precautions to prevent the boats from capsizing." Only by bailing continuously were the lifeboats kept afloat. Darkness fell. Eighty-six survivors were in dire straits.

Meanwhile, Troop Convoy Group No. 74 had intercepted the calls for help. The U.S. destroyer *Fairfax* was directed to leave the convoy at dark and rescue survivors. She arrived on site at around 9:30 p.m. The survivors "shot up blue lights" to denote their locations. Because of rough seas, three hours of hard work and deft seamanship were required to effect the rescue of all the men.

The *Fairfax* returned to her convoy. The *Lucia* survivors were transferred to the U.S. armored cruiser

War Cruise of the U-155

Huntington. They were fed and issued clothing. The survivors were disembarked at Hampton Roads, Virginia.

The *U-155* took the southern route past the Azores. It continued to be plagued by foul weather and mechanical problems. "Boat can be steered while submerged only if heading diagonally to the direction of the sea. We cannot hold a steady course at periscope depth. Boat is bow heavy."

During one test dive, the stern diving planes failed to operate, necessitating emergency repairs.

There were occasional ship sightings, but no vessels were attacked because of bad weather, exceptional speed of the targets, or aggressive escort activity.

On October 21, the *U-155* received another message from U-boat command, this one putting a severe cramp in offensive operations: "Return immediately to the base because of the current negotiations. All manner of merchant warfare must be stopped. Attack warships only in daylight."

The condition of the engines was so bad that both needed to be overhauled. The *U-155* proceeded on one engine while the crew worked on the other.

On October 23, Studt spotted "a very large steamer." He noted wryly in his log, "*U-155* turned away in compliance with recently received orders. The sinking of this large steamer would have been the crowning achievement of the present mission."

The vessel was the *Oxfordshire*, 8,623 tons. While the U-boat was under orders to cease attacks against merchant vessels, British merchant vessels operated under no such constraints. The *Oxfordshire* turned away and opened fire on the U-boat. Two shells from the after deck gun fell short.

Studt transmitted a wireless message: "Why do you shoot?" The *Oxfordshire* sent signals. Studt transmitted another message: "Use your wireless radio to reply." Apparently, Captain F. W. Midgely, master of the *Oxfordshire*, did not wish to communicate with the U-boat, as his radio remained silent.

Subsequent vessel sightings were meager. The main steering gear had to be repaired on October 24. One of the diesel engines was overhauled on October 28. A cable leading to the radio apparatus melted on October 29. The log entry for October 30 read: "Port engine is reported to be operational. Now we have to switch to it, and commence an overhaul on the starboard engine."

Except for constant repairs, the only break in the routine of proceeding homeward was the occasional test dive.

On October 31, the *U-155* received another message from U-boat command: "To all submarines. Return immediately."

The stern diving plane ceased to function on November 3. Despite continuing inclement weather, the U-boat was forced to proceed on the surface for twenty-four hours, during which time the starboard diesel engine was put out of order: "The exhaust pipe to piston III caused the trouble, requiring further detailed inspection of these parts of the engine."

The U-boat drifted idly for hours while the functioning engine was used to recharge the batteries.

The diving plane was repaired on November 24, and a test dive was conducted successfully. Engine overhauls were completed. "Continued with both engines full speed ahead. Plotted course to the channel between Faeroes and Shetlands."

The *U-155* stopped north of the British minefield on November 7. Seas were so heavy that they washed over the deck, forcing the U-boat to heave to until the following day. The diesel engines could propel the U-boat no faster than 9.5 knots. "Therefore, we cannot pass completely through the barrage zone before dusk." Mines were spotted on the surface, and avoided. The *U-155* emerged from the minefield on November 9.

According to wireless intercepts, the situation in Germany was dire. Studt offered insights about the chaotic situation in Germany by noting at length in his log entry for November 10: "The most recent radio messages indicate the Soviet Revolution in Germany is rising

War Cruise of the *U-155*

and spreading. This movement now appears to threaten the while Imperial State, including her Navy. Some of the radio messages and orders contain facts that indicate these wireless stations have been taken over by councils of soldiers and workers. Berlin and the surrounding counties have apparently joined the revolutionary movement, as have the army units garrisoned there. Nauen Station, which transmitted the radio messages while the boat was cruising in the Atlantic, has been quiet since 8 Nov. However, Rugia Station continues to transmit orders, etc., given by the B.d.U. [Befehlshaber der Unterseeboote, or U-boat command], and makes it possible for boats to contact each other (for example: *UB-64* and *U-53*). I really think this station is still in our hands, even after receiving a radio message from the 'Soldier Council'. The message, itself, contained orders on how the returning submarines should deal with warships flying the red flag. It was advised to negotiate with these ships. It seems to me that some of the U-boats have changed sides. However, we can rely on the personal deportment of the crews of many boats in the Baltic Sea and Kiel. This information was contained in a message from B.d.U. on 7 Nov. I do not trust the messages received last night. They were repeatedly transmitted by an anonymous naval station, stating that the armistice has been signed. . . . I shall next find out who gives the orders at the present time. B.d.U. might have been taken over. I became suspicious of the radio messages on 6 Nov. (1755j10); it orders all submarines to return to their bases."

Later that day, Studt noted: "Nauen Station has been taken over by the Worker and Soldier Councils."

And on November 11: "All the wireless stations are now taken over by the Councils of Workers and Soldiers. . . . It is difficult to decide which orders are to be executed. The trouble is that the decoding key to the last message is not on the boat. For this reason, we cannot read the orders given to all units of the Navy. After entering the harbor, I will have to obtain that key. . . . It is unclear who is giving orders to the submarines now. I do not understand the order I received on 10 November (0 202), which is identical to the B.d.U. message of November 5. It contains strict orders to fire on ships flying the red flag. Accompanying this order from Rugia was an order to enter the harbor, signed by the Soldier and Worker Council and Chief of the Flotilla. Another radiogram received on November 10, gives contrary orders to the signal No. 1735j2, received on Nov. 6. It states that submarines east of Gjedser are not permitted to proceed to Kiel. They are ordered to report their positions. I believe, and so does the crew, that we still are obliged to keep the oath. If the Kaiser abdicates and ceases to be a warlord, I will serve a new government until the end of the war."

Later that evening: "Received FT message, reporting the signed armistice. The message is signed, 'Admiralty Staff.' This message was transmitted from Nauen. It contains only superficial facts of the armistice. . . . All men of the crew are ordered to the control room. I inform the crew about the recent developments in Germany, and my personal opinion and intentions. Since the last messages have not yet been confirmed, we cannot make any decisions at this time."

November 12: "Sailing on a zigzag course at dawn. Guns are manned. Passed the Ose-Sound flying the German Battle Ensign and pennants. . . . Boat runs aground for a short time, due to a movement of some buoys marking the Sjotten Flats near Malmo, but floats free without help. The Danish Barrage is reached by dusk, and we run afoul of the chain. We succeed in freeing the boat without sustaining damage. . . . I am still without definite orders. . . . Boat is ordered to head for base. Received FT message from *U-139* (Commander: V. Arnauld de la Perriere), Base Sassnitz.

November 13: "Boat entered Sassnitz, moored alongside submarine tender. *U-139*, *U-151*, *U-153*, and 4 patrol boats are berthed in the port. Attempted to get some news of latest political events and the armistice. Conference of the submarine commanding officers berthed in port. Information of recent orders and decrees. I assume

War Cruise of the *U-155*

duties of senior officer present. Wireless message to U-boat pen Kiel: Exit of all submarines is scheduled for November 14. Received message from B.d.U.: *U-151*, *U-153*, *U-139* return to Kiel immediately. I assume this order also includes my boat. Issue order to make the boat ready for the cruise to Kiel. Sent FT message to B.d.U.: *U-155* arriving at *Rutt* lightship, Nov. 14 8:00 A.M."

November 14: "Passed through Barrage area. We do not see any warships. Sighted some red flags flying from masts of berthed ships and shore stations. Ordered to strike the Battle Ensign. Crew cheers (three hurrahs) for the old flag. Berthed alongside *Prinz Heinrich*. Following the example of the other boats, hoisted merchant flag at the stern and a red flag on the periscope. Boat is ordered (according to the conditions of the armistice) to be ready on Nov. 17, to sail for a harbor determined by the allies."

The first merchant cruise of this submarine as the *Deutschland* ended triumphantly. The war cruise as the *U-155* ended anticlimactically.

The *U-155* in England after the war. (Courtesy of the Navy Department Library.)

War Cruise
of the
U-152

The *U-152* was a *Deutschland*-class U-boat under the command of Kapitanleutnant Adolf Franz. The U-boat departed from Germany on September 5, 1918. Franz took the northern route around the Shetland Islands.

The steering gear broke only six days into the cruise, forcing Franz to steer manually until the crew could fix the problem.

The Danish schooner *Constance* was steering northward some 100 miles north-northwest of the Shetlands. Despite heavy seas only a light breeze was blowing, propelling the schooner at about 2 knots. She was carrying 118 standards of planks from Goteborg, Sweden to Lisbon, Portugal. (A "standard" is taken to be short for "standard cord," which is equivalent to a stack of wood that measures 4 feet by 4 feet by 8 feet.)

At two o'clock on the afternoon of September 11, Franz opened fire on the *Constance* from a distance of two and a half miles. Captain Hans Kristensen, master, "Stopped the ship by turning the yards and pull [sic] down some of the sails. With the crew I then went into the lifeboat and pulled away from the ship."

Franz was cautious. Although the *Constance* appeared to be unarmed, he suspected that she was a Q ship: a disguised merchantman that hid guns behind false bulwarks. He kept his distance from the schooner, then approached the lifeboat after her occupants distanced themselves from their vessel.

Captain Kristensen and his men tied up alongside the sleek black hull, and climbed aboard. The captain protested the attack on his vessel by showing Franz his ship's papers, exclaiming that Denmark was a neutral

War Cruise of the *U-152*

nation in the global conflict, and that the *Constance* was transporting a neutral cargo from one neutral port to another.

Franz turned a deaf ear to the skipper's entreaties, claiming first that the *Constance* was inside the German barred zone, and second, "Your cargo is contraband. I am bound to sink your ship." Franz did not take into account the fact that the only way a vessel could travel from Denmark to the open ocean was through the German barred zone. He commenced to shell the schooner.

Kristensen: "The damage was mostly in the middle of the ship between the fore mast and the mizzen mast. The port side of the ship was all broken up and the rigging was shot overboard. Four men from the submarine afterwards went in our lifeboat to the *Constance* and placed 2 bombs on board, which exploded about fifteen minutes afterward. There were two big holes in the bottom of the ship which I think were made by the explosion of these bombs."

The Germans ransacked the *Constance*, taking all her provisions and the spare clothing of the crew.

Kristensen: "After the submarine had finished with the *Constance* it towed our lifeboat about forty miles toward the Faroe Islands, when the rope broke, and the submarine left us steering about west."

The seven Danes were left to fend for themselves. It took them forty-six hours of steady rowing to reach Norswick, a small island that was one of the Shetland Islands. The men were soaked and suffering from the cold, "but were well taken care of by the people of the island."

The 199-ton schooner proved to be a tough customer. The *Constance* was not only constructed of wood, but she was carrying wood as her cargo. Wood floats, and so did the *Constance*. When Franz saw that the three demolition charges failed to sink her, he expended fifty rounds of ammunition which did not sink the vessel, but certainly demolished her upperworks. "Bombardment served as practice for gunners, which is very useful for them."

Franz decided against pouring oil on the schooner

and igniting it "because of smoke and the glow of fire." He did not want to give away his position.

On September 14, the Danish patrol boat *Beskytteren* found the *Constance* drifting idly on the surface of the sea. She was a shambles. Her bulwarks, bowsprit, and two of her three masts were practically destroyed. It took two days for the patrol boat to tow the half-sunken schooner to Bergen, Norway. Most of the cargo was salvaged.

Kristensen: "The ship itself is a wreck and I do not believe it can be repaired."

The hulk was later sold.

On September 13, an engine breakdown forced the *U-152* to proceed on one engine until the crew replaced an exhaust valve. Repairs took all day. Then an oil-level meter was found to be full of water. The U-boat heaved to during rain and snow squalls.

The following afternoon, Franz fired warning shots to stop a steamship. Captain Alek Juel, master of the Norwegian freighter *Bjornstjerne Bjornson* rowed to the U-boat with his ship's papers in hand. The paperwork was in order: the freighter was operating for the Belgian Relief Commission.

Franz noted in his deck log: "Papers are unobjectionable. Ship is released with freedom of passage."

Two hours later, after dark, Franz stopped a three-masted schooner that was traveling with no navigation lights illuminated. She proved to be the *Ellen Benja*, with a Danish registry. The windjammer's first mate rowed to the U-boat with the ship's papers. He explained that she was "cruising without lights due to gasoline shortage."

Denmark was neutral and so was the cargo of salt, so the vessel was released.

Afterward, the U-boat's port engine needed to be overhauled. Then the exhaust valve on the starboard engine had to be replaced.

Franz noted the great difficulty he had in maintaining a periscope depth of 40 feet. The U-boat kept settling down to depths of 70 to 100 feet. "Upon holding at 13

War Cruise of the *U-152*

m[eters], the trimmer and quick-diving tank had to be flooded immediately to prevent the boat from being thrown up out of the sea. Changes of course from the diving course are scarcely possible at attack depth; changes of speed under the prevailing weather conditions entail each time a return to 20-25 m. depth. In other words, not even a systematic overtaking of the enemy for attack was possible."

These problems proved the point that World War One submarines were more like warships that could escape under water than true submersibles.

After failing to close with a convoy in a difficult sea, Franz expressed his frustrations in his log: "The helplessness of the old submarine under today's circumstances was vividly demonstrated to me. Limited speed both surfaced and submerged, bad diving qualities with the sea state (boat can only be forced under water diagonal to the sea and even then only slowly and with effort, it hovers at the surface for minutes on end) together with bad qualities of maintaining depth have not allowed the boat to approach sufficiently near and to hold contact for a longer time. A newer submarine would not have missed this convoy."

The swells were so large that when the U-boat slid down to the bottom of a trough, the periscope did not extend above the crest.

Franz spotted the tops of four funnels of a large ocean liner. He kept losing the target in the swells. He had two forward tubes loaded with torpedoes. He spent hours chasing the zigzagging steamer, but was unable to get within torpedo range before she disappeared over the horizon. In the vicious game of cat and mouse, the mouse had all the advantages of speed and stability.

The U-boat suffered more engine troubles for the next two weeks. The crew was constantly employed in replacing crank bearings and sprayers, cleaning piston rings, stopping leaks in the lubricating systems, and so on.

On September 24, the *U-152* lobbed 44 shells at the

British steamer *Alban*, but did not strike her once. She returned fire, laid a smoke screen, zigzagged, and escaped by means of her superior speed.

The *U-152* was now attended by additional mechanical problems. The steering gear malfunctioned and required immediate repair while the helmsman steered by hand. A leak in one of the fuel tanks resulted in the loss of more than 10,000 gallons of oil.

On September 29, the U-boat engaged the U.S. tanker *George G. Henry* in a running gun battle that lasted for nearly two hours. The tanker fired the first shot of the engagement as soon as the U-boat was spotted off her port beam at a distance of three miles. The U-boat returned fire as the tanker sped away. Despite radical course changes, the U-boat managed to strike the tanker's after magazine. Exploding shells ignited a fire that engulfed the after deck.

The skipper turned the vessel in order to enable the forward gun to bear on the enemy submarine. Smoke boxes created a black pall that effectively hid the tanker for twenty minutes, until Franz maneuvered into clear air and resumed firing. Shrapnel shells struck the tanker, "inflicting minor injuries on 14 men."

The *George G. Henry* then got out of range of the U-boat's guns, and Franz broke off the action after expending 116 rounds of ammunition. This incident occurred northwest of the Azores on the latitude of Nova Scotia.

September 30 found the U.S. animal transport *Ticonderoga* eastbound in mid ocean. On board were 237 crewmembers, soldiers, and sailors. On previous passages she had delivered horses to the fighting front in France. On this passage she carried no animals, but was loaded with 140 tons of hay, 21 Cadillac touring cars, 3 reconnaissance trucks, 2 light repair trucks, 200 boxcars, 4 observation cars, 6 packages of ambulance trailer parts, and 1,557 tons of steel billets (bars of steel). The transport was armed with a 3-inch gun forward and a 6-inch gun aft.

The freight was loaded at Norfolk, Virginia. The

War Cruise of the *U-152*

Ticonderoga then proceeded north to New York, where she joined Convoy HN 85 for the transatlantic crossing. The 19-vessel convoy was protected by a single escort: the U.S. cruiser *Galveston*.

During the night of September 28, the *Ticonderoga* found herself unable to maintain the speed of the convoy. The engineer explained that "he had struck a streak of bad coal which would hardly burn." The transport limped along and steadily fell behind the convoy. By 2:30 a.m. on September 29, the convoy was no longer visible ahead in the misty darkness.

As a precaution, Lieutenant Commander James Madison, in command of the *Ticonderoga*, ordered the wireless operator to transmit position data every half hour.

According to Madison, "At 5:45 A.M. while trying to see the convoy, I sighted a submarine – almost dead ahead, lying broadside to ship's course, distance about 200 yards. I gave the order to fire, stated the range, and sounded the battle quarters, also put more speed on the engine and headed right for the submarine."

Prior to being spotted, the *U-152* was stalking the lone transport from a parallel course. Franz noted in his log that the camouflage paint confused him: "The bow, stern, and course are difficult to distinguish under the conditions. For a short time I mistook the bow of the steamer for her stern and by turning further to port, wanted to bring to her stern on the starboard side and follow astern of her. When the error was appreciated, it was no longer possible to stop the turn to port. About the same time the steamer turned to port toward *U-152*, after the former had sighted the submarine cruiser, in order to avoid presenting her broadside to a torpedo shot or to ram."

Madison: "At about this time the submarine apparently had seen us, for the wash from his propeller – as if he had suddenly started full speed – could be plainly seen, and he tried to get over my bow, from port to starboard, but I put my wheel hard-to-right, and headed him off."

The U-boat surged ahead "with full power." It passed directly across the bow of the *Ticonderoga*. It also opened fire with both guns at point blank range.

One shot struck the transport's forward gun platform, killing nearly all the gunners and wounding those who had not been killed outright. The other shot struck the wheelhouse with the same effect, and knocked out the wireless equipment. Only Madison and Ensign Gustav Ringelman escaped death. Madison was struck by a shell fragment that knocked him down to the deck.

Ensign Clifford Sanghove was on his watch below, in his cabin, when a shell crashed through the room and jarred him out of his slumber.

The two vessels danced a slow but deadly pirouette. Franz noted, "The submarine turns harder than a battleship."

The *Ticonderoga's* after gun entered the action.

The U-boat "put his wheel hard-to-starboard, and tried to cross her over on the other side. I did the same, and this time missed him by about twenty feet."

Franz: "Steamer continued turning to port. *U-152* draws away by likewise turning slowly to port, while continuing to keep the opponent under fire and scoring hits. Steamer opens fire again; shots fall over and short, deflection good."

The transport's wheelhouse was ablaze. Officers and men, awakened by the alarm for battle stations, swarmed into the wheelhouse. They found their skipper barely conscious and the steering gear knocked out of commission. They carried Madison to the after upper deck and connected the emergency steering gear.

Some men stayed behind and fought the bridge fire, extinguishing the flames after a twenty-minute battle. Sanghove "organized gangs to fight the fire. Some of the men would be shot away and I would have to organize a new gang."

As the *Ticonderoga* swung around, the after gun got the U-boat in its sights, but after firing a single round it was silenced by a perfect shot that killed the entire gun crew. Shrapnel from the transport's single shot injured

War Cruise of the *U-152*

a gunner on the U-boat but did not put the gun out of commission.

The U-boat submerged when Franz spotted flashes of gunfire in the distance, and saw the approach of the convoy escort, which he identified by her two stacks as a large cruiser that could easily outgun him.

The *Galveston* observed the muzzle flashes of the U-boat and transport. She opened fire from a distance of six miles, but ceased firing after several shots for two reasons: the flashes from the two vessels were so close to each other that she could not distinguish friend from foe. Then, when the U-boat submerged, all firing ceased, the bridge fire was extinguished, and Commander C. C. Fewel presumed that the action had ended. The *Galveston* returned to her position in the convoy.

The U-boat had fired thirty-five rounds at the *Ticonderoga*. A large number of her men were dead and dying, and the damage to the hull and superstructure was telling. Number 2 hold had eighteen feet of water. The hull was riddled with holes at the waterline, "many of the shots entering one side and passing out through the other." Some of the lifeboats were shot to pieces; others were pierced by shell fragments.

Madison called Executive Officer Frank Muller to his side. He ordered the engine reversed and abandon ship. Then he passed out from loss of blood.

Franz was having difficulty in maintaining periscope depth because the condition of the sea was worsening and the speed of the wind was increasing. He gave up the attempt to approach the transport submerged for a torpedo attack. After sunrise, he observed that the burning transport was the only vessel in sight. He surfaced in the morning light and recommenced shelling the *Ticonderoga*. This time he expended 48 shells on the hapless transport. None of the Americans escaped injury from the intense German shelling.

Lieutenant (jg) Muller ordered Chief Quartermaster George Tappley to tie a white blanket to the after mast as a signal of surrender. The U-boat kept firing because its lookouts could not see the blanket through the thick clouds of smoke that the fires were generating.

Most of the lifeboats swamped when they were launched because the falls had either been shot or burned away, or because the hulls were splintered and water rushed in through the gaps. Madison was placed in a lifeboat which was then lowered away. This was the only lifeboat that did not sink; it bobbed badly on the growing swells.

According to Ringelman, "There was a life raft left on the top of the deck house. We got our wounded men together, lashed them to the life raft, that is those who were able to do this – and shoved the life raft off from the ship. Possibly three or four minutes after that she took the final plunge."

The *Ticonderoga* sank by the stern at 7:45 a.m. Her weather deck was covered with dead and dying men.

Between thirty and forty survivors managed to float for a while in the water. The U-boat fished Muller out of the water and kept him prisoner. The Germans also collected crates of potatoes, but not the wounded and dying men.

The U-boat approached the lifeboat in which Madison lay unconscious. Crewmembers threw water on his face to rouse him. He barely had the strength to peer over the gunwale. A German officer questioned the occupants of the lifeboat. Ensign Gately deliberately provided false information, saying that the skipper was dead.

A German tossed a line to the lifeboat and another German jumped aboard to tie it off. After the German sailor returned to the *U-152*, it attempted to tow the lifeboat to the raft, but the line parted when the U-boat accelerated, and the lifeboat went free. Franz did not go back for it.

The U-boat approached the raft. Again the Germans asked questions, about the transport's ports of departure and destination. Tappley "asked them to give us medical assistance, a number of the men having been seriously wounded, but they ignored our request."

They took First Assistant Engineer Junius Fulcher,

War Cruise of the *U-152*

Lieutenant (jg), off the raft and made him a prisoner. They took two other men, but made them get back on the raft. The wounded men on the raft pleaded for food, water, and medical supplies, all of which was refused. The U-boat departed, leaving the rest of the men to whatever fate awaited them.

In defense of his actions, Franz argued, "I faced perhaps the most difficult decision of my life. After the destruction of *Ticonderoga* the survivors were widely scattered on and in wreckage of the ship, on life-rafts and other floating material. How could we rescue and care for such survivors when there was not even room to stand or lie in a submarine with 77 men of our own crew for whom every nook and corner without exception was required and used? Own personnel lived and slept for weeks on end between the stored ammunition, torpedoes, and mines; even for men in sound health the air in the submarine was almost unbearable in bad weather .... War, it is war .... I therefore quickly formed the decision to limit to the utmost the rescue of survivors. To me as commanding officer, the concern for my own men lay nearest to my heart; the execution of my operation order was my task .... The survivors of *Ticonderoga*, left adrift, did not receive provisions, water, or medical supplies from *U-152* for the following reasons: *U-152* was herself very short of these items; we could assume that the Americans were well supplied therewith; for further rescue work, *U-152* had neither space nor time; *U-152* faced the danger that at any moment the American cruiser would again come in sight; *U-152* was constantly underway, steaming zig-zag courses or in circles, for at all times enemy submarine attacks had to be reckoned with."

The statement above is quoted in full. The groups of periods that look like ellipses were in Franz's original transcript.

With regard to the two men who were taken prisoner, Franz wrote, "Their transfer (from the wreckage) was effected only through the efforts of volunteers of the submarine, who secured by lines jumped into the water fully clothed and swam back to the ship with the two officers, who came willingly and gladly. Immediately thereafter, they lost consciousness and were carefully lowered into the submarine through the forward hatch. One of the two, the first assistant engineer officer of the steamer, Fulcher by name, was wounded in the legs by 3 shell splinters. Our engineer officer, of his own accord, turned over his cabin to the wounded officer who was at once put to bed and operated on by our efficient ship's surgeon with complete success. The other one, the executive officer of the steamer, Muller by name, was likewise undressed, dried, and wrapped in warm woolen blankets. He received a good shot of rum and for a bed the sofa in the officer's messroom was turned over to him; for lack of space this had been the bunk of the mess steward."

The above notwithstanding, the survivors were in dire straits.

Ringelman: "This life boat, the only one afloat, drifted down onto the life raft, and the Captain of the ship who was in the boat, called for myself and several others to get into the boat as there was not a single sailor in that boat to handle her, there being nothing but soldiers in it, and a high sea running called for some-

Lieutenants Muller and Fulcher on board the *U-152*. According to the caption, this picture was taken on October 16, 1918. (Courtesy of the Naval Photographic Center.)

War Cruise of the *U-152*

body to be in that boat to handle it. Well, a few of us got into the boat, which still left a few on the raft – a few unconscious men and some that were not very badly hurt. The sea separated the raft and the boat and we made sail and attempted to get back to the raft in order to tow it, as they had no food on it. The wind and sea grew in violence and after many futile attempts to come close alongside of the raft we had to give up the idea of getting a line to it."

The occupants of the lifeboat spent four hours in their attempts to regain the raft.

"We made sail in the small boat to get away from the submarine in case another ship, or a rescue ship should come along we would be away from the submarine. We sailed day and night for four days and three nights, and on Thursday morning at 8:00 o'clock we sighted a steamer heading west at a distance of five miles. She, however ignored us."

The men on the lifeboat were growing weak from hunger and dehydration. Provisions consisted of two cans of hardtack, one case of apricots, one case of pineapples, and eight gallons of water.

"At 2:00 o'clock in the afternoon we sighted another steamer dead ahead. The steamer bore down on us. When she came alongside she picked us up. The name of the steamer was the *Moorish Prince* – British, bound for New York in command of Captain Birch. We received all the comforts and attention they could give us. They had no medical officer aboard, but the steward, who knew his business very well, attended the men to the best of his ability. While on board the *Moorish Prince* on Sunday October 6th, this steamer, the *Grampian* came alongside, and seven of us were transferred to this ship. There were 22 in the lifeboat all together. We were transferred to this ship because better medical attention and better facilities could be had aboard of her, for the wounded. But two men, the commanding officer and a soldier, who were too severely wounded to be transferred and moved, were kept aboard the *Moorish Prince*, with three other men, soldiers, to attend them."

The life raft was never found. The twenty-two men in the lifeboat, and the two officers who were taken prisoner, were the only survivors.

The death toll was staggering: 215 men were either killed by shellfire or drowned in the aftermath when the *Ticonderoga* slipped beneath the waves. In one action that lasted for two furious hours, the *U-152* was responsible for the demise of more people in the American U-boat war than all the other U-boats combined.

Muller and Fulcher were kept in different compartments on the U-boat. Four days passed before each learned of the other's presence on board. After dressing their wounds, the surgeon attended to them every day. They were treated well.

Galveston's Commander Fewel was brought under charges for "neglect of duty" and for "culpable inefficiency in the performance of duty," because "he did not know that the *Ticonderoga* was missing from the convoy which he was escorting," and because of his failure "to do his utmost to overtake and engage the enemy."

It was true that Fewel did not know that the *Ticonderoga* was missing from the convoy. It was never explained why the *Galveston* did not intercept the transport's wireless messages in which her lagging position was given.

Fewel defended his actions by noting the conditions under which he was forced to make decisions. "On account of the distance, light and the fact that submarine had ceased firing presumably because of our firing, the chance of getting the submarine was zero.

"The merchant vessel got the fire under control in a very short time and was apparently under control as movement of masts when fire was brightest, indicated that she was bringing wind in a favorable direction for fighting fire and she had a chance to escape.

"On account of the number of sick men in the engineers force [due to an outbreak of Spanish influenza], I had to reduce boiler power to four boilers [with a proportionate loss of speed]. The weather was hazy with low visibility. If I left the convoy to protect the unknown ves-

War Cruise of the *U-152*

sel (which so far as I knew at this time was a west-bound empty) I stood a good chance of not being able to rejoin and gave the enemy submarine an excellent opportunity to attack the convoy during my absence."

Three of his lieutenants concurred in Fewel's assessment of the situation, and submitted supporting testimony to that effect.

Fewel was aware of the attack against the *George G. Henry* on the previous day. He took the precaution of changing the course of the convoy in order to avoid the position of the attack.

Fewel's best rebuttal was his remark about leaving the convoy unprotected. In this regard he had been given orders that were quite specific: "If one or more ships in the convoy are torpedoed or mined, the Ocean Escort is to proceed with her convoy; she is not to close the damaged ship."

He followed these instructions precisely. Had he done otherwise, and had one of the vessels that he was escorting been attacked when he was not in a position to fend off the attacker, he would have been guilty of dereliction of duty in not following orders that his superior officers had given to him in writing.

The investigating officer was the vice admiral of the Cruiser and Transport Force. He recommended "that Commander Fewel be immediately detached from command of his vessel, and that he be not given another command afloat during the continuance of the war."

Thus Fewel was made the scapegoat for the *Ticonderoga*'s fatalities. The recommendation for his loss of command did not bring back the lives of 11 naval officers, 102 naval enlisted men, and 100 U.S. Army soldiers. But it exonerated those who were responsible for writing the orders that Fewel was obligated to follow.

The loss of the *Ticonderoga* was the most tragic event of the U-boat war in pursuit of decimating American coastal shipping.

Meanwhile, the *U-152* was still experiencing mechanical difficulties. Its engines needed constant attention and overhaul. The U-boat was unable to reach its design speed of 12 knots. The highest speed that it ever attained was 11 knots. If the seas were favorable, it might be able to cruise on the surface at 10 knots. Even that was a strain. Factor in the contrary Gulf Stream current, and forward progress amounted to 4 knots over ground, or less than 100 nautical miles per 24 hours. Between rough seas and a headwind it could barely maintain steerageway.

Some of the plating was sheered free by wave action. One large sheet of metal was half torn off, and partially covered a bow torpedo tube. Franz had to flood the after tanks in order to raise the bow high enough that the men could remove this metal. "Below the main deck, several larger sheets of metal and angular iron of the boat's superstructure are repeatedly found loose, their rivets having been struck off."

A large oil slick attended the U-boat's wake. "Apparently the bulkheads between fuel tanks and diving tanks on starboard side are not tight." More fuel was lost.

After the action with the *Ticonderoga*, the *U-152* poked along for ten days in a southwesterly direction without sighting a vessel of any kind. This one thousand mile advance placed the U-boat northeast of Bermuda on the latitude of Virginia: more than 1,200 miles from the American coast. This was its closest approach to the eastern seaboard.

On October 11, the *U-152* intercepted a coded wireless transmission from U-boat headquarters: "Leave American waters immediately, conduct merchant warfare off Azores, heed Nauen scrupulously." A follow-up transmission stated, "Sink no ships and vessels which are recognized as Spanish outside and inside of Barrage Area, even if they are cruising in convoy."

Prisoners Muller and Fulcher were told that this was "the first act of our new government." It meant that the Central Powers were negotiating terms for peace.

The *U-152* reversed course to north-northeast and, now going with the Gulf Stream current instead of bucking it, proceeded toward the Azores. The mines that it

War Cruise of the *U-152*

intended to sow in harbor entrances between New Jersey and North Carolina remained in place.

Two days later, Franz violated the neutrality convention by firing shots across the bow of the Norwegian bark *Stifinder*. The vessel was bound from New York to Freemont, Australia with a cargo of case oil, benzene (naphtha), and turpentine. The vessel was unarmed and possessed no wireless equipment.

Captain G. Birkeland, master, hoisted the Norwegian flag in order to claim his neutrality. He drew in the sails and, after the way was off the bark, ordered Chief Mate Tarald Frethe to show the ship's paper to the skipper of the U-boat. Frethe and eight crewmembers sailed a lifeboat to the *U-152*.

A German officer examined the papers. "I see you are going from one enemy country to another, and that your cargo is contraband, so you know what that means."

The *U-152* took the lifeboat in tow and proceeded to the *Stifinder*. They tied the U-boat alongside the bark.

The *Stifinder's* men were given all the time they needed to provision both lifeboats with ample food,

The *U-152* nosing close to the *Stifinder*. (Courtesy of the Naval Photographic Center.)

The end of the *Stifinder*. (Courtesy of the Naval Photographic Center.)

water, and navigational instruments. They had only one chart, so the Germans gave them another one so that there was one for each lifeboat.

Several Germans took pictures.

The men apportioned themselves in the two lifeboats: eleven men including the captain in one, eight men including the chief mate in the other. They were told to steer a course for Newfoundland. It was a thousand miles away but it was the closest point of land.

According to Captain Birkeland, before scuttling the bark, the Germans robbed her of potatoes, onions, canned fish balls, three live hogs, and other miscellaneous victuals.

The deck log of the *U-152* makes no mention of scavenging to take aboard provisions, but: "Prize crew works 2 hours in order to open the extraordinarily tight and thoroughly battened down cargo hatches. I intend if at all possible to take aboard a portion of the valuable turpentine cargo for storage in the tanks that have been emptied of lubricating oil. By dusk cargo hatches are free. Upper cargo consists of cases of gasoline and barrels of petroleum. Prize crew stays aboard during the night in order to reach the turpentine cargo. . . . After discovering that turpentine is stowed under the rest of the cargo and is not to be reached in foreseeable time, prize crew set 3 demolition charges and abandoned sailing ship. Sailing ship heels over to port. Sailing ship sunk."

Meanwhile, both of the *Stifinder's* lifeboats set sails and proceeded on a westerly course. The chief mate's boat was faster than the captain's boat. The chief mate's boat towed the captain's boat throughout the night and all the next day.

Frethe: "During the second night a gale blew up and during the early evening our line parted. We took a reef in our sails as we were moving a little faster than the Captain's boat, hoping to be able to pick them up again. We were able to keep in touch with each other all through that night and until 5:00 A.M., by the use of electric hand flash lights, but about 5:00 A.M. we lost them in a fog and never sighted them again. The next day we saw a steamer eastbound, but she must have been about 15 miles away and it is doubtful if she saw us."

The chief mate's boat sailed steadily and uneventfully for the next week. "About 7 days after we lost the Captain's boat a severe storm blew up, which nearly capsized us. As the Captain's boat was smaller and had quite a lot of provisions on board I doubt very much that he has weathered the storm. We later sighted one eastbound convoy, and one schooner, but they did not answer our signals. The cruiser which was clearly discernible by us, must have been not only 6 or 7 miles away and they should have seen us. We thought our signals had been noticed by the schooner, as she seemed to be making toward us, taking down some of her sails, but when about two miles distant she hoisted her sails and struck off in an opposite direction.

"On Saturday night, October 26th, we passed a camouflaged boat, south bound. On Sunday morning, October 27, in about 39° 18' No. Lat. and 71° West Longitude, we sighted a floating balloon which we came alongside of, and made a half circle around it. It was floating at an angle of about 45°, of sausage shape, and appeared to be practically the same kind as I have seen on the outside of the bay – a regular Naval observation balloon, with the regular U.S. insignia, Red, White and

The *Stifinder's* crewmembers who are shown above survived for fifteen days in the lifeboat that is shown below.

Top row standing: Halmar Iversen, Thomas Johnson, Hlefden Kvikstad, Tarald Frethe (first mate).

Middle row kneeling: Henry Borgensen, John Horme, Erling Erikson.

Bottom row sitting: John Fredrikson, Karl Svere Larsen, Arane Stenby, Alf Mathesan.

Both photographs were taken at Section Base #6 on the day after their rescue. (Courtesy of the National Archives.)

War Cruise of the *U-152*

Blue circles. It was about 3/4 covered by water, but the water was very clear and we could see the submerged part, but could not distinguish any basket. We saw no bodies, dead or alive among the wreckage.

"We sighted Barnegat [New Jersey] about 1:30 P. M. today [October 28], but we headed for Sandy Hook, and later a submarine chaser [*SC-294*] came up to us and took us in tow. I reported to them the sighting of the balloon, and they in turn reported to another boat which went out after it."

These hardy Scandinavian sailors survived for fifteen days in a small open boat, and sailed nearly one thousand miles in the process.

Despite Frethe's dire prediction about the fate of his skipper and the men in his boat, they too survived their terrible ordeal by water. One week later, on November 4, after spending twenty-two days at sea, they landed safely on Turks Island in the Caribbean Sea (one of the Turks and Caicos Islands).

They arrived "in an almost starved condition. The captain said that his small boat made for Halifax, but soon capsized and most of their provisions were lost. They managed to right the craft, and then because of the extremely cold weather they decided to try for Bermuda. "Instead they rowed all the way to Turks Island from a point approximately 1,000 miles east of New York. They suffered intensely, and were in pitiable condition."

Disaster struck the *U-152*: "Upon turning on starboard engine for charging [the battery], starboard V exhaust valve breaks loose, completely destroying the piston head; piston and valve are replaced." The crew spent nearly twelve hours in effecting repairs.

Another problem developed. While conducting a test dive, the U-boat became noticeably heavy by the stern. Inspection established that seawater was leaking into the pressure hull through glands in the exhaust drainage and was accumulating in the engine room bilges. This leakage could not be compensated sufficiently by trimming forward. Furthermore, pumping the bilges left an oil slick on the surface and gave away the U-boat's position under water.

On October 15, the *U-152* chanced to cross paths with the British steamer *Messina*, which was traveling in ballast from Plymouth, England to Baltimore, Maryland. The U-boat opened fire from a distance of four miles. The *Messina* turned away at high speed, transmitted an SOS, made radical course changes, and returned fire. A running gun fight lasted for two hours. Of the estimated sixty shells that the U-boat fired, only one struck the *Messina*; it hit on the port side abaft the bridge, and fractured two hull plates above the waterline.

A cruiser and a destroyer charged over the horizon in response to the *Messina's* call for help. The U-boat crash-dived at an angle of about 45° to a depth of 130 feet. Depth charges rained overhead like confetti in a ticker-tape parade. Nine explosions rocked the U-boat but did no damage.

The next day, the port diesel broke down when the piston linings were stripped. The crew worked feverishly throughout the night to repair the engine.

On October 17, the *U-152* launched a torpedo at the British steamer *Briarleaf*. The torpedo exploded prematurely halfway to its target. The U-boat's log recorded what happened with the second torpedo: "Torpedo does not run. Error in manning. Torpedo gunner's mate had ready bolt in hand and was holding it over the hole in the firing rod under the impression that the order 'ready back' was soon to come. Shortly after 'away,' the bolt slipped from the gunner's hand and fell point-first into the hole so that it was deactivated at time of firing."

The loss of weight of the second torpedo caused the U-boat to rise, and brought the conning tower out of the water. The *Briarleaf* spotted the U-boat and opened fire on the enemy, straddling the hull. The U-boat surfaced and commenced shelling. A running gun battle ensued for two hours, during which time the U-boat expended

War Cruise of the *U-152*

83 rounds of ammunition. Finally the *Briarleaf* outdistanced the U-boat. No hits were scored on either side.

The concussion from the U-boat's firing loosened rivets in the port diving tank, starting leaks which created an oil slick. Sheets of metal were ripped off "the upper deck's fairway."

Engine problems were chronic. It seemed as if the U-boat was rapidly falling apart from hasty or faulty construction.

October 22 brought a message that everyone was anticipating: "Commence return cruise immediately. Due to current negotiations, all manner of merchant warfare forbidden. U-boats already returning attack warships only by day."

Peace negotiations were in full swing.

Repairs continued first on one engine, then on the other; back and forth, day and night, without rest.

Instead of proceeding to its alternative operational area off the Azores, the *U-152* now began the long and laborious northern route around the Faroe Islands and southward through the North Sea. It entered the northern mine barrage at 4 o'clock on the afternoon of November 11. For twelve hours it traveled at full speed on the surface through the center of the minefield, emerging safely at 4 o'clock in the morning.

A wireless message informed the crew: "Armistice concluded. Since it cannot be taken for granted that all hostile naval forces have knowledge of this, continue to count on enemy attacks. Use weapons only for emergency defense. Authorization to cross neutral territorial waters surfaced has been requested of neutral governments."

Germany had capitulated.

On the night of November 12, the *U-152* encountered the *U-53* outside the Skagerrat. The *U-53* was now under the command of Oberleutnant zur See Otto von Schrader. The two U-boats tied off to each other for a couple of hours while their skippers discussed the political situation.

The Kaiser had abdicated. The Imperial government had collapsed. Germany was in chaos. Revolutions swept the country. Shipboard mutinies abounded.

Although all U-boats were ordered to return to Kiel, many opted to be interned in a neutral nation.

The next day, the *U-53* led the *U-152* through the minefield. The *U-53* then continued to Kiel, while the *U-152* anchored off Copenhagen, Denmark. Von Schrader radioed to Franz that all was calm in Kiel, but that nonetheless he and his men decided to proceed to Sweden to be interned.

Franz held a meeting with his officers and men, and explained the situation. The crew took a vote. A few expressed their wishes to go to Sweden, but the overriding majority wanted to return to Kiel. The *U-152* docked at Kiel at 5 p.m. on November 15.

The two prisoners – Lieutenants Muller and Fulcher – were given their freedom. This freedom was somewhat meaningless because they were trapped in Germany without transportation out of the country. For six days they were quartered aboard the *Prinz Heinrich*.

The British took control of the U-boat situation by ordering them to proceed under escort to Harwich, England. Some U-boats defected to neutral nations rather than turn themselves in to the enemy. Others followed the orders of their conqueror.

The wishes of the officers and crew of the *U-152* were divided. Half of them went home, including Franz. The remainder held a meeting during which they voted to turn over command of the U-boat to Oberleutnant zur See Wille. The Germans also agreed to take Muller and Fulcher with them so that they could be repatriated.

The U-boat flotilla departed from Kiel on November 21. The twenty-four U-boats proceeded in two columns. The *U-152* led one column; the *U-155* led the other. The flotilla reached Harwich on November 24, where the U-boats were interned until their ultimate disposition could be decided.

That was how the U-boat war ended – not with a bang but a whimper.

ABORTED WAR CRUISE
OF THE
U-139

The *U-139* departed from Kiel on September 11, 1918, with orders to attack shipping off the American eastern seaboard north of Cape Hatteras, North Carolina. Ostensibly that is reason enough to include the U-boat's war cruise in the present volume. But the *U-139* did not make it across the Atlantic Ocean because the end of the war was in sight before it reached the 40th meridian. If you recall from the first chapter, the U.S. Navy designated 40° west longitude as the arbitrary line of demarcation between the American theater and the European theater. By that criterion, the war cruise of the *U-139* should *not* be included.

Nonetheless, I demur. A great deal of mythology surrounds the final cruise of the *U-139*. Because the *U-139* intended to conduct operations in American waters, I have a bona fide rationale to include its aborted cruise, if only to dispel some misconceptions and embellishments about its cruise. Please bear with me.

The *U-139* was the type class of which three were built (*U-140* and *U-141* being the other two). It measured 311 feet in length. The hull displaced 1,930 tons on the surface, 2,483 tons submerged. Its design speed was 15.8 knots on the surface, 7.6 knots submerged. Its range was more than 12,000 miles. It was armed with four torpedo tubes in the bow, two tubes in the stern, and two 5.9-inch deck guns. It carried no mines.

The *U-139* was under the command of Kapitanleutnant Lothar von Arnauld de la Periere. Von Arnauld was Germany's all-time top ace in U-boat warfare. When he was in command of the *U-35*, he made fourteen war cruises during which he sank nearly two hundred vessels for a total tonnage of close to half a million tons. He made most of these attacks in the Mediterranean Sea. There is enough material there for an entire book – but not this book.

Von Arnauld's measure of success in the *U-139* was less glorious. The records show that on October 1, 1918, he sank the British freighter *Bylands* (3,309 tons) and the Italian steamer *Manin* (2,691 tons) off the coast of Spain. On October 2 he sank the Portuguese lugger *Rio Cavado* (301 tons). On October 14, the *U-139* attacked the Portuguese minesweeper *Augusto De Castilho* (487 tons) while that vessel was escorting the Portuguese steamer *San Miquel*. The minesweeper defended her charge with such bravura that she sacrificed herself in order to let the merchant vessel escape.

Von Arnauld's total tonnage for this cruise was 6,788 tons. Although some secondary sources claim that he sank five vessels (the fifth being unnamed), there is adequate corroboration for the loss of only the four vessels that are named in the previous paragraph.

The *U-139* did not get much farther west than the Azores. Then came the call from U-boat headquarters: "To all U-boats: Commence return from patrol at once. Because of ongoing negotiations any hostile actions against merchant vessels prohibited. Returning U-boats are allowed to attack warships only in daylight. End of message. Admiral."

The *U-139* meandered back along the northern route. It returned to Kiel on November 14, 1918, by which time the Armistice had been signed. The Great War was over, and the first German U-boat campaign in American waters was ended.

In *A History of the Transport Service*, published in 1921, Albert Gleaves wrote that the U.S. troop transport *Henderson* rammed and badly damaged the *U-139* off the coast of New Jersey. Gleaves was in a position to know about the *Henderson* because, after serving as commandant of the Narragansett Bay Naval Station (see pages 42-43), he served as rear admiral in the Cruiser and Transport Force. Here is the story the way he told it:

Aborted War Cruise of the *U-139*

"On August 13, 1918, the *Henderson* was cruising off our Atlantic coast when, soon after midnight, the ship passed through a large oil slick which aroused some suspicion, but it was not until the next day that it was learned that this oil came from the tanker *Frank W. Kellogg*, which had been torpedoed two hours previously by an enemy U-boat. For some reason the *Kellogg* failed to send out an SOS.

"Shortly after the *Henderson* had passed through this oil at about 1:40 A.M., August 14, 1918, Private Roy O. Hicks, Marine Corps, stationed as a lookout in the fore top, sighted a long dark object on the starboard bow about 500 yards distant and coming straight for the ship. This was at once reported to the bridge by Second Lieutenant E. O. Bergert, U.S.M.C., the officer in charge of the watch in the foretop.

"At about the same time, Junior Officer-of-the-Deck Ensign R. McKay Rush also sighted the submarine, and Captain Sayles, who was on the bridge, ordered right rudder, sounded general quarters, and headed for the enemy. The submarine was maneuvering to fire a torpedo, but the ship's prompt maneuver frustrated the attack and the U-boat submerged. The swinging of the ship and the immediate diving of the submarine prevented the gun crews from getting in a shot.

"It was not definitely known at the time whether or not the U-boat succeeded in getting under fast enough to avoid the *Henderson's* ram, but when the ship was next docked, it was found that her starboard bilge keel had been partly bent and broken. As there is no other explanation, it is believed that this damage was caused by striking the conning tower of the submarine as she was in the act of submerging.

"The following excerpts from a subsequent report made by Captain Sayles after the Armistice is an interesting sequel to this attack:

"Captain Sayles' Report

" 'From a statement made during a casual conversation recently held with some French officers in Brest, I learned that when the surrendered submarine *U-139* arrived in Brest there was a former member of her crew on board, a mechanic and an Alsatian by birth, who, at his own request, had been interned with his ship.

" 'This Alsatian had told the French officers with whom I was talking that the *U-139* had encountered an American transport off our Atlantic coast, which had attempted to ram her, and had succeeded in breaking off both periscopes, so that for the remainder of the cruise the submarine was unable to attack while submerged.

" 'This part of the story I verified by personally inspecting the *U-139*. Not only are the periscopes broken but the thin metal weather screen on the forward side of the conning tower was badly bent as the result of the collision.

" 'The following facts are also known: That the *U-139* made but one cruise, which was to the Atlantic Coast in August and September, 1918; that after August 14, 1918, the *U-139* did not make any further underwater attacks, but was strangely occupied in attacking with guns and bombs barges, fishing and sailing vessels off Cape Cod; that on her return to Kiel she was laid up for repairs which had not been commenced up to the date of the Armistice; that the *U-139* was the largest of German submarines and was commanded on her only voyage by Lieutenant Amauld de la Perriere, one of the most successful and enterprising of U-boat Captains, who, upon his return, was given command of another boat in which he had just arrived off the Azores to commence a new cruise when hostilities ceased.'

"There seems to be evidence that the disabling of the *U-139* can be credited to the *Henderson* and perhaps this can be fully established when Perriere can be interrogated and access had to the German records."

Before I conduct a detailed analysis of Gleaves's

Aborted War Cruise of the *U-139*

story, let me correct a few minor and major errors in his account:

1) *Frank W. Kellogg* should be *Frederick R. Kellogg*.

2) The *Frederick R. Kellogg* did not have time to transmit an SOS because she sank in fifteen seconds.

3) The *Frederick R. Kellogg* was torpedoed at 5:00 p.m. on August 13. If the *Henderson* incident occurred at 1:40 a.m. on August 14, that was nine hours and forty minutes later, not two hours.

4) The *U-139* did not leave Germany for its one and only war cruise until nearly a month after the *Henderson* incident.

5) The U-boat that was responsible for sinking barges off Cape Cod was the *U-156* (which Gleaves should have known, as Publication No. 1 was published a year before *A History of the Transport Service*).

6) The shelling of the barges occurred nearly a month before the *Henderson* incident: in July, not August.

7) The fishing vessels were attacked off Maine and Nova Scotia, not off Cape Cod.

8) The *U-139* could not have been laid up for repairs that had not been commenced up to the date of the Armistice because it did not return to port until *after* the Armistice was signed.

9) Amauld de la Perriere should be Lothar von Arnauld de la Periere.

10) Von Arnauld was not given another U-boat command after he returned in the *U-139*, because the war was over and Germany was divested of its U-boats. (The *U-139* was given to France as part of war reparations.)

Gleaves – or perhaps subordinates who actually wrote the book under his byline – clearly did not do his homework.

All this begs two questions, the first of which is this: Is there any basis in fact for the *Henderson* incident?

On August 14 there were three U-boats operating in American waters. The *U-156* was off Nantucket, between two Nova Scotia operations against the fishing fleet. The *U-140* was on its way home from North Carolina, and was hundreds of miles from shore.

The only U-boat in the vicinity at that time was the one that torpedoed the *Frederick R. Kellogg*: the *U-117*. Droscher's log entries are quite clear on that point. According to his chronology, he torpedoed the *Frederick R. Kellogg* at 4:50 p.m. He started laying mines off the Barnegat Light buoy at 8:15 p.m., and was finished by 10 o'clock, after which he proceeded southward along the coast. His subsequent deck log entries read:

"10:50 p.m. – Steamer with steady lights in sight. Avoided same at surface.

"11:15 p.m. – Steamer with steady lights in sight. Avoided same at surface.

"12:30 a.m. (August 14) – A vessel with lights screened sighted in close proximity. A steamer with lights screened follows it. The steamer also follows during further maneuvers. No opportunity for attack. Submerged.

"1:30 a.m. – Sea very phosphorescent. Emerged surface travel.

"7 a.m. – A sailing vessel sighted, distance 6 nautical miles 230° 5 masted schooner. Halted by artillery. Crew leaves ship. At this moment a steamer is sighted. Submerged in order to attack, and if attack not possible to say unseen. Boat is in the vicinity of *Five Fathom Bank* lightship. The latter not yet sighted on account of drizzly weather. Steamer cannot be attacked on account of unfavorable position. As the sailing vessel is made of wood . . . "

The rest of the paragraph is quoted with the account of the *Dorothy B. Barrett*.

According to this verbatim translation, although lookouts on the *Henderson* might have sighted the *U-117*, at no time was it under treat of being rammed. According to Droscher, the close call cited by Gleaves was a distant observation.

The literature of seafaring is replete with sightings that have never been corroborated: mermaids, sea serpents, krakens, and so on.

It is possible that the *Henderson's* lookouts spotted

Aborted War Cruise of the *U-139*

a whale in the process of diving beneath the surface. Whales are not uncommon off the New Jersey coast, and the way they swim is by alternately broaching and diving. Narratives of submarine warfare in World War Two contain numerous accounts of whales being mistaken for U-boats, even to the extent of being rammed, shelled, and depth-charged. Bioluminescence makes appearances and distances deceiving, especially at night.

I do not doubt that the *Henderson's* lookouts saw something that they perceived to be a U-boat at close range. Their minds were attuned to see just that. In all too many instances, a person sees exactly what he expects to see. Perception can be tricked by fear and anticipation.

Furthermore, the deck log of the *Henderson* fails to corroborate Gleaves's assumption. The relevant entry for midnight to 4 a.m. on August 14, 1918 reads, "At 1:35 sighted an object thought to be a submarine bearing 33° to starboard bow, put rudder hard right for about 3 minutes, then hard left for about 3 minutes, sounded general quarters, loaded #1 and 3 5" guns. Object thought to be a submarine sighted at 1:35 disappeared. Position Longitude 74°-00' W Latitude 39°-29' N. At 1:50 sounded retreat from General quarters."

The log does not suggest that the *Henderson* might have rammed anything: no thumps were felt (or recorded), no screeching sounds of metal on metal were heard. The *Henderson* simply maneuvered the way Droscher recorded the incident in his deck log: more like a radical zigzag or avoidance maneuver than an attempt to ram.

Neither vessel's deck log suggests a close call.

Taken as a whole, the account that Gleaves related comes off as a sea story. A sea story is the sailor's version of a tall tale of the Paul Bunyon variety; or, more appropriate in this case, like the fantastic yarns of Baron Munchausen. They are to be taken with a grain of salt, or perhaps a drop of saltwater. Yet there exists confirmation of a sort in another account about the *U-139*.

Perhaps the most famous book about the romance of U-boat operations in World War One is *Raiders of the Deep*, written by Lowell Thomas and published in 1928. Thomas was a war correspondent who traveled extensively and interviewed many important people, some of them behind enemy lines. He continued his travels after the Great War. He was best known at that time for filming and interviewing Thomas Lawrence, the British commando who earned renown as Lawrence of Arabia.

Lowell Thomas turned from journalism to authorship (and later became a radio news commentator, for which he is largely remembered today). After he launched himself to fame with his first book, *With Lawrence in Arabia*, he composed many other oral histories about World War One soldiers and sailors he had met and interviewed.

In *Raiders of the Deep* he lionized the exploits of a number of U-boat commanders with considerable if adolescent verve. Among those commanders was Lothar von Arnauld de la Periere.

In the absence of the deck log of the *U-139*, Thomas's account of the *U-139*'s war cruise is perhaps the only one extant. (It has been alleged that the Germans destroyed the log shortly after the end of the war because of a rumor that the British intended to occupy Sassnitz, where the log was located.) Lacking a first person account from the lips of von Arnauld, Thomas's interpretation of events – putatively based on his personal interview with the Ace of Aces – is the most contemporary source that is available today. As far as I know, von Arnauld did not leave any written record of his own about his final U-boat cruise. Nor did he write an autobiography. He died in 1941 with the rank of admiral.

Although *Raiders of the Deep* reads like a work of historical fiction, spiced with juvenile dialogue that reeks of pulp magazine detective slang, those sections whose references I have compared with primary sources appear to be in keeping with the facts. It seems as if Thomas did not sacrifice accuracy for readability,

Aborted War Cruise of the *U-139* 293

but wrote in an entertaining fashion for an audience that lacked sophistication. His style was anything but textbook standard.

Many modern writers have quoted from or referred to Thomas's account without citing him as the source. This makes it appear that the source was von Arnauld himself, instead of von Arnauld once removed. I think that Thomas should be given credit – or blame, as the case may be – for factuality. Here is how he transcribed his conversations with von Arnauld about the *U-139*, told with schoolboy elan in the first person singular as if von Arnauld were speaking the part:

"On October 1, 1918, the *U-139* lay off Cape Finisterre on the northern coast of Spain. We had just come out from Kiel after one of the stormiest trips I have ever had the misfortune to encounter. For days we had to keep our hatches closed while the tempestuous seas swept over us. Now, though, we were enjoying our first fine day. Everybody was on deck enjoying the fresh air. At ten o'clock smoke was sighted on the horizon and a forest of masts came into view. It was a big convoy. As it came into clear view we counted ten large steamers guarded by two British auxiliary cruisers, one of which led the procession and the other brought up the rear. On each side of the column were fussy little patrol boats. The entire company was zigzagging.

"It is hard to gauge a zigzagging course. We steered to the right and then to the left of the convoy to get into position where we could lie in wait, to allow the convoy to pass in front of us so that we could get a shot. After a lot of manoeuvering [sic] we got a beeline on one of the freighters. Torpedo loosed, we went to the depths to get away from an expected rain of depth bombs. No sound, either of torpedo or of depth bombs. We had missed, and neither torpedo nor our periscope had been noticed. The silence was soon disturbed by a huge rushing and whirring sound, a noise of many propellers. The whole convoy in one of its zigzagging shifts, had passed over our heads.

" 'Blow the tanks!' I called the command into the

speaking tube, and to the surface we rose.

"We had failed with the torpedo; we would have it out with our guns. It was a risky thing, thus to rise so near the convoy and stage a fight with shell fire, but then our submarine cruiser was designed to put up a good skirmish on the surface, and if the going got too hot we could dive out of it.

"We came up gingerly, guiding ourselves by the sound of propellers. We did not want to bump against the bottom of a ship. Now we broke the surface, and in a moment the gun crews were scrambling on deck and forward and aft to the guns. There were all those vessels only a short way off. Pandemonium broke loose. Our guns fired as fast as they could. Every ship that had a gun and was in range popped shells at us. There were explosions all around the U-boat, but the shooting from the ships was confused and bad. We might have sunk several right there by direct gunfire if it hadn't been for one of the auxiliary cruisers. She was too near for comfort in the first place, and now she came at us, her guns blazing away. She was shooting carefully and well. Her shells were bursting in the water a few yards from us.

" 'Below for diving,' I shouted to the men at our guns.

"We were just in time. Just as the water was closing over the conning tower a shell burst up there. The water deadened its explosion, but the shell fragments clanged loudly against our steel plates. This time there was no lack of depth charges. They crashed out a few seconds apart above us, but we had plunged too deep for them.

"Our second attack foiled. "*Donnerwetter*," we said, "this has got to stop." Up to periscope depth and a look around. The convoy was steaming on in the distance. Very well, we have a fast boat – up and after them. We came to the surface and ran at our best speed until we had caught up with the convoy.

"This time luck favored us. The auxiliary cruisers were slow and gave us time to get the range. In good

Aborted War Cruise of the *U-139*

shooting distance, we had a few minutes of precious target practice. We sent our shells as fast as we could at the nearest steamer. She stopped, badly hit. Then we turned on the next one. A few shells, and she was disabled. By this time one of the cruisers was headed for us at full speed, firing and trying to ram us.

"The ocean swallowed us, and in a minute depth bombs came looking for us with their ugly banging voices. When they had their say we returned to periscope depth to see what could be done. The first steamer we had hit was sinking. The cruiser that had attacked us was taking aboard the stricken vessel's crew. The second steamer we had hit was lying well afloat. Patrol boats were standing by, and one of the larger vessels was preparing to take it in tow.

"It was mid-afternoon now, and we still had several hours in which to finish off the disabled ship. Patrol boats had been called to the scene from near-by ports and were swarming around. We had to proceed very carefully, running submerged. It was sundown and dusk was gathering before we had maneuvered into position for a torpedo shot. The damaged steamer was listing. The towline had broken, and the attempt to take the vessel in tow seemed to have been abandoned. The crew was being taken off by patrol boats.

"By now it was so dark through the periscope that the ships above were nothing but shadows. We were about to loose a torpedo when one of the shadows loomed much too close.

" 'Dive!' I called in haste.

"We rested for a little while at twenty metres [sic], listening to the sound of propellers above. I stood in the conning tower. Beside me were my two officers. The helmsman stood behind. down below the men not on duty were eating supper. The noise of propellers died away. Slowly the *U-139* edged up to periscope depth. As I looked in the glass I saw a looming shadow in the twilight, a ship broadside to us and right in line for a torpedo shot. I wasted no time for inspection.

" 'First bow torpedo – fire!'

"The torpedo left the tube, and we dived instantly. After a short wait came the shattering roar of the torpedo explosion. Less than a minute later there was a terrible crash overhead and our boat shook from stem to stern as if it had been cracked open by the giant blow. The lights went out. Water rushed in from above. The boat listed to one side.

"I guessed what had happened. We had been very near the ship we had torpedoed and had drifted under her. And now she had sunk on top of us. She was the vessel we had hit with shell fire and was waterlogged when the torpedo ripped her open. That was why she had plunged so quickly.

"The lights flashed on with that sudden strange startlement that always accompanies lights flashing on.

" 'Man the pumps!' I yelled.

"The water was still pouring down over us from above. The helmsman was trying desperately to close the hatch of the compartment above, from which the drenching shower came. The hatch had been jammed by the shock and would not close. The depth gauge showed that we were sinking at a terrific speed. The sinking ship was carrying us down with her. The sea was three thousand feet deep here in this place. We would soon be crushed like an eggshell by the pressure of the water. Not a word was spoken in the conning tower. Not a sound was heard save the rushing of water and the heavy breathing of the men. Above us sounded the cracking of depth bombs. What a mockery they seemed. There was just one chance.

" 'Air pressure in all tanks.' I could feel my voice go false and strained as I tried to conceal the tone of wild anxiety.

"The boat trembled and lurched as the compressed air blew the water out of the tanks. Could we shake ourselves loose? I could feel the boat sliding. The depth gauge showed that our descent was checked. Then the pointer swung quickly around. The sudden upward drag of the boat had disengaged it from the sinking ship, which had slid off and gone on to the bottom.

Aborted War Cruise of the *U-139*

"The *U-139*, with blown tanks, was rising like a balloon. There was no chance of stopping our ascent until we came to the top, and there the surface craft were waiting. We could hear their depth bombs bursting. Water still poured into the conning tower, but the pumps were able to hold it down. Our upper works had been smashed, and in the conning tower we were blind. Our three periscopes had been carried away. The hand of the depth gauge moved around inexorably. I called to the men to be ready for an order to dive the moment we broke the surface.

"A sound of swishing and splashing, and the shower from above ceased to pour down on us.

" 'Dive!' I shouted.

"Another of those eternities. We were in the midst of the boats that were hunting for us. The sound of depth bombs came from here and there. But the sea was pitch dark and we were not detected. Now we were nosing down, I held the boat just below the surface, where the leakage through the conning tower would be least.

"Expecting to be run down at any moment in that hornets' nest of boats, we limped away a few feet below the surface, and presently the sound of bombs, where they were still gunning for us, was lost in the distance. After an hour we came to the surface. Nothing was near us. Far off to the south we could see searchlights sweeping about the scene of our late adventure.

"Our upper works were hopelessly ruined. The deck was ripped up. Our three periscopes hung by a wire. We were a rather crippled specimen of U-boat. The next day we picked up a small steamer. Our luck still held out. She had a cargo of port wine and cement – just what we needed. With the wine we refreshed our bedraggled spirits and with the cement repaired the conning tower, filling up the breaks so that it was watertight once more. We were still without periscopes, but could put up a surface fight and could navigate the depths again – a blind fish, to be sure, but still a fish.

"We continued our cruise looking for ships to attack with our guns. The wireless told us that our line was being rolled back in France. Yes, Germany was defeated. We were filled with despondency. Off the Azores the *U-139* had its last fight, and a brisk affair it was. We sighted a big steamer escorted by a Portuguese gunboat. We gave chase, but the steamer was too fast. The gunboat attacked us. It was a puny, antiquated thing and had not guns to match ours and had only half as many men aboard as we had. I have never seen a braver fight than that old piece of junk put up. Those Portuguese fought like devils, firing shell after shell from their popguns while we raked them from stem to stern. Fourteen of their forty men lay dead on deck and most of the rest were wounded before the boat surrendered. We took the survivors aboard as prisoners and sank their vessel. Later in the day we sighted a ship, stopped it, put our prisoners aboard, and sent them home. They had fought so gallantly that they deserved all consideration, and, besides, we had scarcely room enough aboard our U-boat to take a score or so of men on board. We thought, of course, the episode was ended there, but there was a sequel. They had a celebration and became fast friends. The Portuguese said that the steamer that escaped us had aboard several American generals who were returning to America from the Western Front.

The *U-139* after its surrender. (Courtesy of the National Archives.)

Aborted War Cruise of the *U-139*

"We were less than half way across when the wireless brought news of the armistice negotiation. U-boat warfare against the United States was suspended, and we were ordered to return to Germany. We got back to Kiel on November 14, 1918. As we steered into the harbour [sic] we saw the red flags of the revolution flying."

Now the reader can see that Gleaves's account is not wholly without foundation. The upperworks of the *U-139* were certainly damaged, and, according to Thomas, in a collision with another vessel – although not in collision with the *Henderson*. Gleaves's version is a miscegenation of incidents that occurred at different times on opposite sides of the Atlantic Ocean, shuffled together like cards in a deck to create a story that lent credence to a legendary episode of the Cruiser and Transport Force: a kernel of truth but clearly not the cob.

Despite the improbability of Thomas's retelling of an underwater collision, I know of at least one similar event that has been authenticated. Let us skip from Germany's first attempt at world domination to its second.

On September 5, 1942, a German U-boat crept around the southern end of Bell Island. The island is located on the "back side" of St. John's, Newfoundland. It has long been a valuable source of iron ore, and sports one of the most productive mines in the world. The onset of hostilities in 1939 dramatically increased the strategic importance of raw iron: for the construction of ships, tanks, and guns that were needed to prosecute the war against the Fuhrer.

A defense garrison was deployed to the island to prevent enemy troops from landing and from sabotaging the entranceways to the mines. The Canadian Air Force patrolled the surrounding waters. When Germany finally focused its aggressive energies against the Bell Island facility, the attack came not from the sea or from the air, but from under water.

Korvettenkapitan Rolf Ruggeberg, skipper of the *U-513*, peered through the sights of his periscope at two

British freighters that floated placidly at their anchorage: the 5,454-ton *Saganaga*, and the 7,335-ton *Lord Strathcona*. Both unsuspecting vessels were laden with iron ore, and were awaiting escort by the Canadian Navy. The skippers were attending a pre-departure briefing ashore.

The water was calm and the air was clear. Bright sunshine illuminated the stationary targets. At 11:45 a.m., the *U-513* fired two torpedoes at the *Saganaga*. Both struck amidships in rapid succession, ripping the hull apart below the waterline. The freighter sank literally like the rock that she was carrying, in less than thirty seconds. There was no time to launch lifeboats or even to abandon ship. Quite the contrary, the *Saganaga* abandoned the crew instead of vice versa.

U-boats were the farthest thought from any British seaman's mind. None was visible in the broad daylight. Witnesses suspected an internal explosion. Crewmembers of the *Lord Strathcona* launched lifeboats at once, and went to the rescue of their companions in the water, half a mile away.

Ruggeberg was more audacious than observant. He charged into the fray like a frenzied fox in a henhouse, but failed to notice the U-boat's proximity to his next intended victim. Cruising at a depth of 55 feet, the U-boat crashed into the bottom of the *Lord Strathcona* – much like a cartoon character running head first into an unseen post. The crushing of the conning tower was clearly heard by the German sailors. To break away from the hull, Ruggeberg ordered the ballast tanks flooded. The U-boat dived out of control, struck the bottom at 150 feet, and stuck there like a bug on a pin. The influx of seawater, leaking into the pressure hull through the direction-finder housing, made rapid release imperative. Positive buoyancy and turning propellers soon freed the U-boat from the suction of the sand.

In his log, Ruggeberg wrote, "Start attack run on the ship which had collided with us." This is hardly a fair description. Blame cannot cast upon the anchored

Aborted War Cruise of the *U-139*

Lord Strathcona any more than a tree can be blamed for jumping in front of a car.

By this time - half an hour after the loss of the *Saganaga* - the *Lord Strathcona* lay completely abandoned. All hands were still in lifeboats, searching for survivors of the *Saganaga*. The *U-513* fired two torpedoes that struck the *Lord Strathcona* as she swung at anchor. Both torpedoes detonated, sinking the abandoned ore carrier in ninety seconds.

As no one was on board the *Lord Strathcona* at the time she sank, no fatalities occurred. But only fourteen men survived the sinking of the *Saganaga*. Twenty-nine others perished in the bold sneak attack. The men were either trapped inside and carried down to Davy Jones's Locker, or they drowned on the surface as they struggled to stay afloat in the frigid water.

The *U-513* made good its escape undetected. Because it was leaking and severely damaged, the U-boat made an immediate and ignominious retreat to Germany for much-needed repairs.

This incident – one war and twenty-four years after von Arnauld's similar incident – lends credibility to the one that Thomas told about the *U-139*.

Perhaps the U-boat war did not end with a whimper after all, but a crash.

Author's note: in case the reader is unfamiliar with "The Hollow Men," a poem written by T. S. Eliot in 1925, the ending couplet explains my allusions:
"This is how the world ends
Not with a bang but a whimper."

VICTORY BOND CRUISE
OF
EX-GERMAN U-BOATS

After Germany capitulated, Great Britain demanded the surrender of the Kaiser's navy. The capital ships were moved to Scapa Flow. Most of the U-boats were moved to Harwich; a few were moved to Plymouth. The German crews were interned; some of them were repatriated in 1919, but some were not repatriated until 1920.

During the winter of 1918-1919, the British government decided on the eventual disposition of approximately 180 surrendered U-boats. The majority was scuttled. A few were taken by Allied nations as part of war reparations.

The United States Navy requested six U-boats for exhibition to the American public in support of the Victory Bond Campaign (also variously called the Victory Bond Drive, the Victory Loan Campaign, the Victory Loan Drive, the Liberty Bond Campaign, the Liberty Bond Drive, the Liberty Loan Campaign, and the Liberty Loan Drive). This campaign or drive was implemented to encourage American citizens to buy war bonds. The government was suffering severe financial deficit due to the cost of the war, and needed to refill its flagging coffers in order to pay off extraordinary debts. The sale of bonds was one way to accomplish this. The government hoped that by the time the bonds matured, the money would be available to repay the original investment plus interest.

These U-boats were to be displayed in American cities the way the *UC-5* had been displayed in 1916.

It was decided that the U.S. Navy would assume ownership of the *U-117*, *U-140*, *U-164*, *UB-88*, *UB-148*, and *UC-97*. The U.S. Navy dispatched half a dozen Navy

Victory Bond Cruise   303

Courtesy of the Library of Congress.

officers and a hundred enlisted men from the Submarine Base at New London, Connecticut. Another thirty or so were gathered from various bases around the British Isles. All the officers had previous submarine experience, and so did about half of the enlisted personnel.

This fleet of Americanized U-boats was pretentiously called the Ex-German Submarine Expeditionary Force.

The first hurdle to overcome for the men who were assigned to this Force, was how to operate a U-boat. Although all submarines are designed along the same basic principles, German submarines differed in layout from American submarines. The difficulties of handling this fleet of unfamiliar submarines were best described by Lieutenant Commander Joseph Nielson, who was assigned to command the *UB-88*:

"The German submarine is, naturally, a distinctive type. True, all submarines are built upon the same general principles, in that they have ballast and trimming tanks, diving rudders, motors, engines, etc. Still the arrangements and installation of all this material may be such as to present to a person who has had experience operating one type, a vessel in which everything will appear entirely different. Our previous experience was to be sure, of great value to us, but on account of the design of the German submarine, it was necessary 'to learn' these boats in every particular. For example: it is a very simple matter to blow tanks on a U.S. Sub-

U-boats at Harwich, England. (Courtesy of the Library of Congress.)

marine – but the problem was, how to blow them on the *UB-88*. First it was necessary to learn the operation of the German type of compressor. Next to learn the air distribution system to the different parts of the ship, then the leads to the air flasks or accumulators, then the leads from the flasks to the manifolds and from the manifolds to the tanks. this would put air into the tanks but it was further necessary to learn the operation of the ballast Kingston and the ballast vents. Then if you had been successful in following out the leads and valves, the problem was solved. This appears, no doubt, simple, and under ordinary conditions it would be, but the German arrangement of piping has not that beautiful symmetry found in our boats and a pipe may wind in and out among its fellows in such a way as to present a veritable Chinese puzzle. Blue prints and drawings were luxuries we did not enjoy, for all these had been very carefully removed.

"The cleaning, repairing where necessary, tracing out fuel oil lines, lubricating oil leads, air lines, water lines, ventilating pipes, battery leads, lighting circuits, took up a great deal of time allotted before the moving parts could be tried. All the name plates, naturally, were in German. We found that the German phraseolo-

Victory Bond Cruise

gy used in engineering was not the same we had learned in school. The amount of work necessary was apparent and the conditions under which we worked can be imagined.

"The *UB-88* was in a filthy condition. Food had been left aboard after she had surrendered. The remnants of the last meals had been thrown in the bilges. The stench from the galley was unbearable. Rust covered all the piping. The engines were one mass of corrosion. The torpedoes had been pulled from the tubes and thrown on the torpedo room deck. The air flasks and after-bodies were coated with rust and badly pitted. The storage battery was almost run down, not having had a charge for over four months. The bilges were full of oil and water. Many parts of the boat had been taken by souvenir hunters while she lay moored in Harwich. The eye-piece on the forward periscope had been broken off and the reflecting prism and lens removed. The stabilizer had been taken from the gyro compass, as had also the azimuth motor. The magnetic compass had disappeared. Out of the dozen cooking utensils on hand, only one would cook, the rest had been smashed or the coils burned out. There were no mess gear, mattresses or blankets. There were no spare parts for the engines. Parts of the radio set had been stolen and the rest smashed in with a hammer. The repeaters for the gyro compass now decorated the homes of the British as souvenirs of the war.

"So many parts of the equipment were out of commission that it was decided to find out first what would work, then go after the parts that would not. This system was followed out. Everything was tested and report made whether or not it was in running order. If not, what was wrong, and what was needed to fix it. In a very short time we had a good estimate of just what we had to do.

"To illustrate our method; The radio set, as stated, had been demolished. The motor generator was there and would work, but sending and receiving sets were almost completely wrecked. By rummaging through about a dozen of the submarines still remaining in the 'Trot' [a nickname for Harwich Harbor], which were going to be sold for junk, we collected enough material to complete a sending set. We were unable to find a detector, however, so that had to be purchased in London, and with parts of a receiving set 'stubbed out' from the U.S.S. *Chester*, the radio outfit was complete, but not efficient. Probably it was the lack of harmony, due to the combination of English, German and American parts. Who knows? It was impossible to improve on the set until the arrival of the U.S.S. *Bushnell*. She had on board six complete outfits. By the addition of a quench gap and an audion bulb to what we already had, the outfit from one of these sets was connected up and tested. Our reward was a set with a hundred miles radius, which was sufficient for our needs.

"I stated before that the magnetic compass had been removed. Search was made through all the German submarines lying in the 'Trot' and none could be found. A U.S. Naval Vessel donated one, but it had been lying idle for so long in one position without any liquid in the bowl that the magnets had lost practically all their directive force. There was not much hope in get-

The control room of the *UB-88*. (Courtesy of the Naval Photographic Center.)

Victory Bond Cruise 307

The forward torpedo room of the *UB-88*. (Courtesy of the Naval Photographic Center.)

ting good results from this compass, but nevertheless it was installed, and after filling the bowl, an attempt was made at compensation on one heading. That night before turning in I looked at the compass and it showed the heading NNW 1/4" W, which was about correct on magnetic North. I looked at the compass the next morning with the ship headed in the opposite direction (having swung with the tide) and it still showed us headed NNW 1/4" W. A call was made on the Senior Submarine Officer at the British Submarine Base, and after a 'search' he supplied us with a compass which had been taken from one of the German submarines. This was installed but on account of the binnacle being placed inside the chariot bridge, its operation was slow and sluggish. A make-shift stand was then installed between the periscopes on the periscope sheer. A block of wood placed directly under the center of the compass and bored with several holes at right angles, served admirably as a compensating rack and in this 'rig' we placed our hopes. True the steering wheel was about ten feet from the compass, but I don't think we worried much about that at the time.

"The German (Anshutz) type of gyro compass was a source of mystery. The stabilizer had been removed as had also the azimuth motor. By again visiting several of the boats up the 'Trot,' an azimuth motor was found and connected up. Also on the same trip we were fortunate in getting three repeaters in good condition. A stabilizer, however, could not be found. There was no one aboard who knew the interior construction of this type of gyro and in consequence no one knew how to operate it. By tracing up the leads from the compass, we found the motor generator and the power leads from the switch boards. That much settled, we went after the compass and by a process of trial and error, it was finally started, and much to the surprise of everyone, it worked satisfactorily. A four degree easterly deviation was removed by balancing the rotors with sealing wax placed in the compass levels to compensate for the loss of alcohol from the levels, which had been broken. The compass is still running perfectly. It has never shown any tendency to 'get off' the Meridian even in the roughest weather.

"The drainage system was of course, a vital problem, although a simple one. Trouble was experienced with the after trimming line pump and it has never been in good condition. The adjusting pump, just abaft the central control room, was working and as it could be connected up to all the bilges through the manifolds, full confidence was placed in this pump. If it had broken down completely the novel situation of bailing out a submarine with buckets or the use of a handy-billy would have resulted. Nothing else could have been done.

"As the safety of the boat on the trip from England to the United States was a paramount factor, it was thought advisable to [dry-]dock the boats at Harwich before sailing. The underwater hull and all tanks were minutely examined. New Kingston gaskets were installed where necessary. The trustworthiness of our

Victory Bond Cruise

late enemies was never mentioned, still I do not doubt that it was in everyone's mind during the period of preparation. However, let credit be given them where it can, for we found no tampering of any kind. The boat was in dock two days, during which time very little opportunity was had for any progressive preparation. After undocking, however, we again turned to.

"The engines were the most important part of the equipment to prepare for operation. I think that everyone who worked on the engines did so with the determination to make them run as well or even better than the Germans had done. It was this or admit that the German crew was the better of the two. Looking at it in that light, the determination to succeed in the preparation of them was to everyone a matter which touched the most delicate spot in the human make-up – Pride.

"In beginning to learn the engines and auxiliaries, we were in the dark, except for our general experience with Diesel engines and the intimate knowledge of a few types which are used in our own service. As all engines

The engine room of the *UB-88*. (Courtesy of the Naval Photographic Center.)

U-boat line-up at Harwich, England. (Courtesy of the National Archives.)

of this type operate upon the same principle it was chiefly necessary to locate the supply, the discharge, if any, and the power of delivery of the circulating water, the air, and the lubricating oil. In the case of the fuel oil, the tanks were first located, then the leads, to the gravity feed tanks, and then the valves and pumps controlling the delivery to the engines. At the same time the fuel compensating system was traced out. The lubricating oil system was followed out and tested in the same way as was also the cooling water. In order not to forget the thousand and one valves with their German names, shipping tags were placed on each valve and gage. On these were written the use of the valve and how to operate it. The explanation of this procedure is brief and to the point and one would judge that we were occupied probably one or two days in this work of tracing out lines and tagging them. But so complicated and intricate was the German system of piping and valve arrangement that the time consumed before we were ready to start the engines was fourteen working days. When everybody had been properly prepared for our first trials of the engines, they were jacked over by hand to insure that everything was clear. The engine clutches were then thrown in and they were turned over slowly with the motors. All looked well. A signal was given to the electrician at the switch board to 'speed her up.' Slowly the lubricating oil built up the required pressure and the discharge pipes into the sight box on the side of the engine showed abundant supply to the piston heads. The circulating water pressure started to climb and was soon up to the required mark on the gage. The

Victory Bond Cruise

spray air pressure was slow in building up, but finally arrived at the proper mark. The oil supply was then opened and the cylinder try-cocks closed, and as the engines had run under the care of the Germans who had built them and studied their operation, so they ran then. There was not a hitch, nor had anything been forgotten. That day we charged batteries for four hours without stopping the engines, in order to be assured there would be enough power in the battery to turn the engines over the next time they were needed.

"After the crew had demonstrated their ability to run the engines, all hands 'turned to' to provide the necessities of life and what few comforts we could gather. The subs up the 'Trot' were ransacked for cooking utensils. We found plenty; terribly dirty and rusty. These we took, and after cleaning them and forgetting the condition in which they were found, the food prepared in them tasted very good. Plates, knives, forks and spoons, and the thousand and one things needed in the preparation and serving of food were purchased in London. Blankets, mattresses, pillows, life belts, sheets, etc., etc., were obtained from the Naval Depot, London. The Red Cross, always on the job when needed, provided us with woolen goods, pajamas, underwear, candy, chocolate, cigarettes, etc.

"Fuel, lubricating oil, provisions and water were taken from the U.S.S. *Bushnell* and the *UB-88* was ready."

Those U-boats that were cannibalized for parts were the ones that were later scuttled.

The date of departure was set for April 3, 1919. All six U-boats were supposed to travel in convoy with the *Bushnell*, but circumstances warranted otherwise. Only four U-boats departed on schedule: *U-117, UB-88, UB-148,* and *UC-97.*

At nearly the last minute, the *UC-97* experienced trouble with one of its engines. The crew set out in the dark to liberate some spare piston heads from a sister ship. They returned successfully from their raid, and commenced to replace the broken pistons, but knew that they could not complete repairs before the 6:30 a.m. departure. They used the electric motors for propulsion. The *UC-97* closed with the *Bushnell*. The tender let a stout hawser off her stern. The towline was secured to the forecastle. The *Bushnell* towed the U-boat until repairs could be completed.

At 8:15 a.m., the *UC-97* suffered another mechanical malfunction: the steering gear jammed. The submarine veered out of control. Quick-thinking men slipped off the towline and turned hard to port in order to avoid ramming the *UB-88*. After the jammed steering gear was repaired, the towline was re-secured (at 9:30 a.m.). Operations proceeded fairly smoothly after this auspicious beginning.

Nielson provided the best description of the Atlantic crossing. The convoy started in hazy atmosphere, mild seas, and gentle ground swells, with the *Bushnell* leading the flotilla at 11 knots. They passed the white cliffs of Dover and the coast of France. For three days they proceeded southward in good weather. They encountered a passing squall on the fourth day. Two U-boats effected minor engine repairs that delayed the flotilla. On the seventh day they reached the Azores, where they spent two days in Ponta Delgada Harbor on the island of San Miguel. The U-boats took on water and provisions, and did more engine repair.

The flotilla departed from Ponta Delgada on April 12. After one day of calm seas the flotilla ran into a storm that was more than a passing squall. Nielson: "The waves built up with the wind and the seas broke over the starboard bow. Spray came continually over the bridge. All the hatches except the one in the conning tower were battened down. The boat rolled and pitched badly. This made it necessary for those men in the boat (except the ones on watch) to turn in their bunks or else be thrown from one side of the boat to the other with the roll and pitch."

Bad air resulted from malfunctioning circulating fans. Everyone suffered. Soon a gale was blowing. The topside watched was constantly inundated by wind-

Victory Bond Cruise

whipped spray. The interior of the hull was "damp and cold." The fierce storm raged for days.

"On the eighth day out the fresh water was found to be contaminated by fuel oil, which rendered it undrinkable. The distilled water, which was intended to be used for watering the batteries, had to be taken for cooking and drinking."

It snowed on the ninth day, with the wind increasing to a heavy gale. Then there was rain and hail, "and the continuance of the howling wind accompanied by the rocking and pitching of the boat."

Some of the submarines got separated. On April 21, the *U-117* was so far ahead that it was out of sight of the *Bushnell*. At the same time, the *UC-97* had engine trouble again, and was proceeding on one engine while repairs were being made to the other one. The *Bushnell* reduced speed so as not to lose sight of the ugly duckling that was in trouble.

On April 25, the deck log of the *UC-97* noted that the *UB-88* and *UB-148* were not in sight.

The *U-117* broke off from the flotilla and proceeded to New York on its own. Then the *UB-88* left the flotilla to continue its cruise solo. The storm finally abated.

"Two destroyers which had come out from New York to meet us appeared on the horizon and were soon alongside. Moving picture machines were turned on us. The officers and crews lined the decks to take a look at the German submarines. They stayed with us for about an hour, then they hauled ahead and slowly disappeared, headed for New York."

The *UB-88* entered the Gulf Stream and milder weather. The men ran out of distilled water and "had to go to the fuel oil. In order to keep the crew from drinking the oily water, black coffee was always ready to be served. This did very well but did not quench the thirst as much as was sometimes desired. It was better, however, than the discomforts of the nausea caused by oily water."

Calm weather enabled them to open the hatches and air out the interior. The crew took frequent strolls

314 **Victory Bond Cruise**

along the deck "holding to the life lines. Everyone took a new lease on life, smiles shone on faces where before there had been looks of anxious waiting. Razors appeared and did their much needed duty."

They sighted the New Jersey coast on April 25. The *UB-88* docked at the Sandy Hook army wharf at 4:30 in the afternoon. Two hours later the *UB-148* showed up. The next morning the *Bushnell* and the *UC-97* put in their appearance. All proceeded to New York and up the North River to the navy yard, which they reached at 8:15 a.m. on April 27.

Nielson did not give the time of arrival of the *U-117*. Other records indicate that it touched land slightly ahead of the other three and proceeded straight to the Brooklyn Navy Yard, where it arrived before nightfall on April 25. Even then it was not the first U-boat to reach the eastern seaboard. Imagine the surprise of the men in the *Bushnell* flotilla when they learned that another U-boat had reached the Brooklyn Navy Yard a full six days before any of the other U-boats.

Back in England, it was found that the *U-164* was

The *U-111* replaced the *U-164*. (Courtesy of the Naval Photographic Center.)

Victory Bond Cruise

in such horrible condition that its deficiencies could not be rectified in time to take part in the Victory Bond Campaign. The *U-111* was selected as a replacement. The newly assigned U.S. Navy crew worked prodigiously to prepare the chosen substitute for the Atlantic crossing, but it was not ready to depart until April 7, by which time the *Bushnell* and her bevy were already on their way.

Lieutenant Commander Freeland Daubin was in command of the *U-111*. Because the *Bushnell* and company had a three-day head start on him, he decided not to follow the others southward to the Azores before turning west, but to cut directly across the Atlantic Ocean by way of the great circle route.

According to Navy records, "Fogs, gales, and heavy seas harassed the U-boat all the way across the ocean. On one occasion, she came near sinking when she began filling with water because of an open sea-cock. However, one of her crewmen crawled under her engines and into the slimy dark water to find and close the offending apparatus. In spite of adversity, *U-111* made her passage successfully and moored in New York on 19 April."

The *U-111* garnered front-page headlines. "The *U-111*, the first of the German submersibles to arrive in the United States steamed into the Brooklyn navy yard at 8 o'clock tonight [April 19] in command of an American crew of four officers and 31 men. As the U-boat passed quarantine on the way up the harbor, she broke out the American flag at her main mast. The imperial German emblem floated below. Harbor craft gave her a salute of three guns."

What happened to the *U-140* has been obscured over time by the paucity of information and differing recollections. Even the Naval Historical Center admits to contradictions in the records: "Accounts vary as to how the *U-140* actually made the voyage to the United States. One source indicates that she made the voyage under her own power with *Bushnell* (Submarine Tender

No. 2) and four of the other five U-boats of the Ex-German Submarine Expeditionary Force. On the other hand, in his account, Vice Admiral Charles A. Lockwood, Jr. – who served in and later commanded *UC-97* – stated that *U-140* preceded *Bushnell* and the four U-boats which sailed with her by several days. He also maintained that she was towed to New York by a collier, but he failed to identify the ship. Be that as it may, *U-140* arrived in New York sometime during May 1919."

If the *U-140* departed before the other U-boats, why did it not arrive until after they did – especially if it had been towed by a collier?

Nielson's published account of the departure appears to add confusion: "Promptly at the hour set, the *UC-97* cast off from alongside and headed down the bay, quickly followed by the *UB-141*, the *UB-88* and the *U-117*. The U.S.S. *Bushnell* brought up the rear."

I think it is fair to say that *UB-141* was a typographical error that should have read *UB-148* – the way it was written later in the article and in the performance report that Nielson wrote for the Navy.

Nielson does not mention that the *U-140* accompanied them, nor does the deck log of the *UC-97* (the only log of the six U-boats that the National Archives possesses). Additionally, the deck log of the *Bushnell* confirms that only the four U-boats noted above were in her escort.

Christie's Auction House added more confusion. In 2006, it put up for auction an item that was described as "Deck Log Book ex-German Submarine *U 140*/Month of march 1919". The description of the item read, "For the dates 31 March 1919 to 14 July 1919 and documenting the names of the American crew, and documenting the delivery of the vessel from Chatham, England to Portsmouth, N.H., USA. This deck log gives a very good account of day to day life in the U.S. Navy after World War I and the work that went into dissecting this ex-German U-boat. Including the arrest of one worker on-board, injuries and illnesses, and the maintenance of the submarine. . . . It is interesting to note

Victory Bond Cruise

that the accounts of how she made her trip from England to the United States vary and that this log book clears up the story that she was towed to the U.S. by the U.S.S. *Saucoma*."

This would seem to put paid to the mystery except for one thing – there has never been a U.S. Navy vessel named *Saucoma*. The solution might rest in the log book itself, but the successful bidder has not seen fit to publish anything about it.

The Naval Historical Center appears to be wrong in other regards: "The submarine was opened for a time to public viewing at New York. No records have been found delineating *U-140's* subsequent service. At the end of the summer, she was laid up at the Philadelphia Navy Yard and remained there, partially dismantled, until the summer of 1921.

Yet elsewhere the historical record shows that the *U-140* was docked at the Portsmouth Navy Yard on May 7, 1920. Archival photographs of the *U-140* are captioned with that place and date. Philadelphia is in Pennsylvania (south of New York), whereas Portsmouth is in New Hampshire (north of New York). Where the U-boat spent the previous thirteen months would thus appear to be another mystery.

I was able to resolve all these inconsistencies and misinformation in nearly one fell swoop. After intensive research, I found an obscure newspaper article in the *Lowell Sun* that mentioned the Navy tug *Sonoma* in connection with the *U-140*. When I delved deeper into the matter, by accessing the *Sonoma's* deck log for the relevant time period, I discovered that she towed the *U-140* from Chatham, England to the Portsmouth Navy Yard by way of the Azores.

Tug and tow departed Chatham on June 10, 1919. They reached Ponta Delgada on June 20. The *Sonoma* took on coal during the night, then departed the following day with the *U-140* in tow. The U-boat never operated under its own power, but was towed all the way across the Atlantic Ocean. Tug and tow entered the Piscataqua River on July 4, and moored that day at the

Victory Bond Cruise

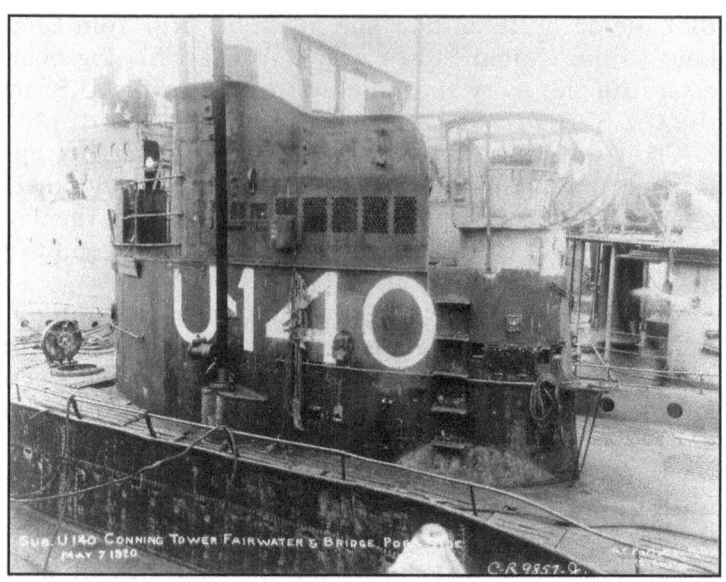

The *U-140* at the Portsmouth Navy Yard. (Courtesy of the National Archives.)

Portsmouth Navy Yard in New Hampshire.

The *U-140* remained there, undergoing extensive examination by naval engineers, until 1921. It took no part in the Victory Bond Campaign.

People swarmed over the decks of the four U-boats at the Brooklyn Navy Yard: reporters, photographers, Red Cross representatives, Salvation Army people, and salespeople for the Fifth Victory Loan, which was about to be launched. Meanwhile, crewmembers were kept busy with maintenance and repairs.

After the initial fanfare, the five participating U-boats were each assigned to visit different ports. They made news and sold bonds wherever they went. Millions of people flocked to see them. A privileged few actually got to go on board: only those who wore a button that signified their purchase of a bond.

The *UB-148* visited Connecticut cities along the north shore of the Long Island Sound: Bridgeport, New Haven, and New London. At the submarine base in New

Victory Bond Cruise

London, the U-boat was "subjected to extensive tests and trials to evaluate" performance capability. Afterward it was laid up at the Philadelphia Navy Yard.

The *U-111* toured New England, with major stops at the Massachusetts port cities of New Bedford and Boston. It traveled as far north as Portland, Maine. By September it was docked at the submarine base at New London to undergo testing along with the *UB-148*. Then it was laid up at the Philadelphia Navy Yard.

The *U-117* visited Baltimore, Maryland before proceeding to the Washington Navy Yard in Washington, DC. May 22 was VIP day. The people who were given a tour of the U-boat included Secretary of the Navy Josephus Daniels, Secretary of War Newton Baker, Army Chief of Staff General Peyton March, and other dignitaries. Daniels went so far as to crank the elevating wheels of the deck gun. The *U-117* remained there for quite a while before shuffling off to the Philadelphia Navy Yard for inactive duty.

At the Philadelphia Navy Yard, the *UB-148*, *U-111*, and *U-117* were partially dismantled, in some cases extensively. The top of the pressure hull above the engine room was removed from the *U-117*. This provided easy access to the engines. Individual parts and assemblies were removed and photographed. The interiors were essentially stripped of their components so that those components could be measured and studied. The deck guns were removed. What remained were hulks that hardly resembled terrible machines of war.

So much machinery and so many components were removed from the U-boats that by the time they were scheduled for scuttling, in 1921, they were not seaworthy enough to be safely towed to sea without a great deal of patching.

Naval and marine engineers had a field day removing "such apparatus from these submarines as will be of value . . . for further service and for test purposes. There will then remain a quantity of material, under the cognizance of the Bureau of Steam Engineering, such as main engines, their auxiliaries, instruments and various other electrical appliances for which the Government has no use. Many commercial concerns interested or engaged in submarine construction are desirous of securing much of this surplus material for study and test for the purpose of improving the design and character of their own product."

All this extra material was given away free of charge. Ultimately, of course, it benefited the U.S. government in future submarine development.

In order to make Americans feel good about the superiority of U.S. submarines, the press waxed long about the inadequacies of German U-boats. This catered to a smug public and may have sold newspapers, but it contradicted the facts. The Navy's initial findings indicated:

"(a) The Diesel engines of these submarines are superior to any other Diesel engines in any other submarine in commission in the world.

"(b) The periscopes are equal, if not superior, to any other periscope.

"(c) The radius of action of these boats, type for type, is greater than that obtained by other nations.

"(d) Their double hull method of construction is probably superior to other types of construction, so far as protection against depth bombs is concerned."

Lieutenant Commander Holbrook Gibson, Commander of the Submarine Repair Division, did not want to file an official report because of the adverse effect this knowledge might have within the Navy bureau. Nonetheless, due to the studies conducted on U-boat diesel engines, the engines of the U.S. submarines *S-10*, *S-11*, *S-12*, and *S-13*, were redesigned using U-boat engines as models.

In his memoirs, Admiral Charles Lockwood noted that U-boats could dive faster than their American counterparts. Also, "Since German optical glass was the best in the world, their periscopes were excellent. Their tops were 'penciled' down to 20 millimeters – slightly less than one inch – which made them extremely difficult for enemy lookouts to spot. Our own

Victory Bond Cruise

periscopes were three inches or more at the top and not infrequently flooded. In the gyroscopic compass, the ingenious Germans had installed a second gyro designed merely to keep the instrument on an even keel; hence no bumbling in a heavy seaway.

"As might have been expected from the inventors of the diesel, the German engines were splendid – and reversible."

The *UB-88* and *UC-97* took different routes in their service to their newly adopted country.

With the Coast Guard cutter *Tuscarora* acting as tender, the *UB-88* departed from the Brooklyn Navy Yard on May 5. Three days later they entered the Savannah River and proceeded upstream to the municipal dock in Savannah, Georgia. Nielson gave a good account of their reception:

"The mayor of the city had been notified several days ahead of our intended visit and had been requested to give all publicity to the event. The result of this publicity was evident. The office forces in the buildings along the waterfront, all left their books and crowded to

Men and women are dressed in their finest Sunday-go-to-meetin' clothes as they throng to visit the *UB-88*. (Courtesy of the North Carolina Division of Archives and History.)

the windows; the dock employees, negroes handling cotton, stevedores unloading ships, ship builders, everyone, quit work and looked at us as we slowly moved up the river. Steamers, dredges and factories all gave the three blast salute. No soon had we moored than thousands flocked to the dock to make a more complete examination of the vessel. Brows were placed for and aft. Police officers were stations at each brow to maintain order and to keep the crowds in line. One member of the crew was placed in each compartment to explain the different parts of the vessel to the visitors and to prevent parts of the vessel being carried away as souvenirs. Visitors were allowed everywhere except in the vicinity of the switch boards. As a matter of safety to them and to the boat, this part of the submarine was roped off. As the people would pass into each compartment the man stationed therein would point out the objects of particular interest and explain their uses. He would also answer any questions which were given him. Then by calling attention to something interesting in the next compartment the crowds were kept moving. The system worked admirably. It was found by actual count that an average of five thousand people a day could be shown through the boat in this way. The visitors after leaving the forward torpedo room were shown into the chief petty officers' quarters, then the officers' room, then to the central operating room, the pump room, the after battery room, the engine room and then through the engine room hatch to the deck where if they so desired, they could climb into the conning tower and look through the periscope."

The next stops were in Florida: Jacksonville, Miami, and Key West. The *Tuscarora* had boiler trouble so she remained at the navy yard in Key West to effect repairs. A minesweeper accompanied the *UB-88* northward in the Gulf of Mexico to Tampa and Pensacola. "In some cases the waiting line was half a mile long, the people sanding two and three abreast. The patience shown in the presence of an almost intolerable heat may be a judge of the popularity of the *UB-88* on this cruise."

Victory Bond Cruise

Then came Mobile, Alabama, where the U-boat stayed for four days. The *Tuscarora* rejoined the U-boat and went with it to New Orleans, Louisiana. After exhibiting the U-boat to record crowds, the *UB-88* proceeded up the Mississippi River to Baton Rouge, Louisiana; thence to Natchez, Mississippi; thence to Vicksburg, Mississippi; thence to Lake Providence, Louisiana; thence to Greenville, Mississippi; thence to Helena, Arkansas; thence to Memphis, Tennessee.

In Memphis the water became so shallow that the U-boat scraped on the bottom. The scheduled visit to St. Louis, Missouri had to be canceled.

The *UB-88* departed from Memphis on June 26. On the return downstream it stopped again at Greenville before continuing to New Orleans, where it arrived on July 1.

Nielson: "On the trip down the river a decided knock developed in the port tail shaft. This was due to the after strut bearings being worn away by the sand and grit of the river. It was so bad by the time the vessel reached New Orleans that [dry-]docking was necessary. As the only dock in New Orleans, the floating dock, at the Navy Yard, was in use, it was necessary to wait two weeks before it became available. The *UB-88* went into dock there on July 14. Upon examination it was found necessary to renew both strut bearings. These jobs were completed on July 22 and the vessel was undocked the same day."

The *Tuscarora* was replaced by the minesweeper *Bittern*, fresh out of the construction yard on her first assignment. She stayed with the U-boat for the rest of its journey.

The next stops were the Texas cities of Galveston and Houston. Pomp and ceremony accompanied the presentation of a miniature bale of cotton that was to become the first cotton bale to be transported through the Panama Canal to Los Angeles, California. The Panama Canal had opened five years earlier.

The *UB-88* departed for the Canal Zone on July 30. Nielson: "Bad weather was experienced during the entire last half of the trip. From the indications of the barometer and the shifting of the wind we were on the outskirts of a West Indian storm. Two hundred miles out of Colon a lubricating pipe to number one cylinder, starboard engine carried away, putting that engine out of commission. It was impossible to repair this at sea. In order to save time a tow line was taken from the U.S.S. *Bittern* and on the following day we entered Colon harbor. The two vessels moored at the Submarine Base, Coco Solo. Repairs were made and stores taken aboard. Saturday and Sunday the boat was open for inspection by the people of Christobal and Colon. On August 12 we sailed through the Panama Canal for Balboa, arriving there the same day. We remained in Balboa for two days to give the canal, army and naval officials and civilian employees an opportunity to visit the submarine. We also had the pleasure of entertaining the ex-president of Peru, the vice-president of Panama and many Panamanian officials."

Heading north along the West Coast, the *UB-88* stopped at Corinto, Nicaragua, then at Acapulco, Mexico.

Once again there was trouble with the starboard engine. Salt water found its way into the lubricating oil and crystallized on the piston heads. To break down the engine, remove the salt, and rebuild the engine would have taken a month. Instead, the ingenious submariners experimented with alternative methods of dissolving the salt: gasoline, kerosene, alcohol, hot water, and steam. Steam worked the best. They connected a steam line to the pump and increased the steam pressure to 100 pounds per square inch. That solved the problem.

The *UB-88* stopped at Mexican cities of Magdalena Bay and Manzanillo, and reached San Diego, California on August 29. From there it went to the California cities of San Pedro, Santa Barbara, Monterey, San Francisco, and the Mare Island Navy Yard; thence to the Oregon cities of Astoria and Portland; thence to the Washington cities of Seattle, Tacoma, the Bremerton Navy Yard,

Victory Bond Cruise   325

and Bellingham.

The return south along the coast took the *UB-88* to San Francisco again, then on to San Pedro, where the U-boat was laid up. The date was November 7.

Nielson estimated that the *UB-88* had traveled more than 15,000 miles since its departure from England, and had been seen by more than 400,000 "enthusiastic visitors." The U-boat never submerged during its entire time in American hands.

The *UB-88* languished in San Pedro for more than a year. It was partially dismantled in 1920: undoubtedly disemboweled like a beached whale, with its parts cut out and distributed among naval engineers for study.

The *UC-97* was still under the command of Lieutenant Commander Holbrook Gibson, who had taken it across the Atlantic. Escorted by the *Bushnell*, the U-boat slipped out of the Brooklyn Navy Yard on May 7. Its destination was the Great Lakes. It had barely poked its nose out of New York Harbor when it paused

The wreath-laying ceremony. (Courtesy of the Naval Photographic Center.)

to conduct an anniversary ceremony. According to a newspaper account:

"On her deck lay a wreath of laurel, woodbine and fern, bound with a broad purple ribbon bearing the words: 'In Memoriam *Lusitania*.' Near the mouth of the Ambrose Channel the submarine's motors stopped, and the boat lay partly awash in the choppy sea. The skipper issued a command and up went the Stars and Stripes, the church flag, and underneath these went the German ensign. Then a bugle sounded 'taps.' With the last note the wreath fell to the surface of the sea. Silent as her sister ship after her murderous deed of May 7, 1915, the *UC-97* stole away."

Lockwood noted, "We who rode in the diminutive minelayer *UC-97* ran into fresh-water problems. The larger, longer-range submarines had ingenious fresh-water distillers operated from the hot gases of the main engine exhausts. We had no such equipment, only a very modest-sized fresh-water tank and no bathing facilities whatever except two washbasins. To complete the sanitary arrangements, there was one toilet for the entire complement of twenty-seven persons."

On May 16, the *Bushnell* and the *UC-97* arrived in Halifax, Nova Scotia. Then occurred a changing of the guard, with the *Bushnell* returning to New York and the U.S. Navy tug *Iroquois* escorting the submarine up the St. Lawrence Seaway and the St. Lawrence River.

According to the Naval Historical Center, "That assignment required her to negotiate the locks of the Canadian-controlled St. Lawrence canal system. *UC-97's* refusal to break with traditional practice on board a man-of-war and fly the Union Jack at the fore caused trouble at each Canadian port of call along the way. However, her commanding officer, Lt. Comdr. Charles A. Lockwood, Jr. – who later rose to fame in World War II as Commander, Submarines, Pacific Fleet – stuck to his guns and was later vindicated by Canadian naval officers who applauded his pertinacious observance of time-honored naval tradition. Once she cleared the last locks and entered the Great Lakes, *UC-97* began a

Victory Bond Cruise

whirlwind series of visits to American ports, large and small, along the littoral of Lakes Ontario, Erie, Huron, and Michigan. Though scheduled to visit Lake Superior ports as well, the U-boat had to cut short its voyage because of wear on the engines."

Wear on the engines was an understatement. Nearly all the piston heads were either cracked or in bad condition. Breakdowns were common. Replacement parts were either unavailable or long delayed in delivery.

June 2 found the two-vessel entourage at Sackett's Harbor, New York, in Lake Ontario. On June 4 they ascended the Oswego River to Oswego, New York. Visitors poured over the submarine for two days.

Gibson left the *UC-97* for an assignment in the District of Columbia, and the command torch was passed to his executive officer, Charles Lockwood.

The next stop was Charlotte, New York. Then came Toronto, Ontario; Burlington, New York, Port Dalhousie, Ontario.

The *Iroquois* was replaced by, appropriately, a pair of submarine chasers: the *SC-411* and the *SC-419*.

The *UC-97* visits Toronto, Canada. (From the author's collection.)

The Union Jack issue continued to plague the *UC-97* whenever it docked at a Canadian City. Lockwood related one instance that had a humorous ending. As the U-boat entered the last of twenty-seven locks that comprised the Welland Canal, a voice rang out through a megaphone, "Why don't you fly the Union Jack? Very rude of you Yanks to use our canal and not fly our flag." Chief Machinist's Mate Schaeffer cupped his hands and called, "Brother, we ain't flown that flag since 1776 – hadn't you heard."

After passing through the Welland Canal and entering Lake Erie, the three American warships reached Buffalo, New York on June 13. The *UC-97* entertained visitors for the next three days.

On June 17, they touched Dunkirk, New York, then departed for Erie, Pennsylvania, which they reached before the end of the day.

Breakdowns were a constant problem. Despite mechanical adversities, the *UC-97* made more than thirty ports of call. Some of them were on the Canadian side of the border. It required all of June, July, and most of August to visit all these cities and exhibit the U-boat to eager crowds. The ultimate destination was Chicago, Illinois, in Lake Michigan, which the U-boat reached on August 19. There it was laid up at the Navy pier and taken out of commission.

During the next year the U-boat was stripped of most of its machinery and brass and copper fittings.

For the *UC-97* – indeed, for all six ex-German U-boats – there was only more port of call that they were destined to make. The submarines sat idle for the next two years, while arrangements were being made for their ultimate disposition.

TARGET CRUISE

In accordance with the terms of the Treaty of Versailles, all captured or surrendered German navy vessels that were in the hands of the Allies had to be scrapped or destroyed by July 1, 1921. They could not be saved as relics. An addendum extended the deadline for capital ships by one month. A vessel could be considered destroyed if it was scuttled irretrievably in water that was too deep to permit its salvage.

On January 3, 1921, the U.S. minesweeper *Pokomoke* towed the *UB-88* out to sea off San Pedro, California. On board was a moving picture crew whose purpose was to record an historic event for posterity. The *Pokomoke* came to a halt about eight miles south-southeast of the Los Angeles breakwater light.

Accompanying the pair was the U.S. destroyer *Wickes*. In command of the *Wickes* was Commander William Halsey, known affectionately as Bull Halsey, who became a famous admiral in World War Two. The *Wickes* had an observation party on board.

At 4:08 in the afternoon, the *Wickes* opened fire with three of its deck guns. For two minutes the guns fired furiously at the *UB-88*. The U-boat sank by the bow four minutes after the *Wickes* ceased fire.

That wrapped up operations for the day. The *Wickes* left the site at 4:20, passed the breakwater light at 4:40, and was back in port by 4:55. It was a short day's work that was done with very little fanfare.

There seems to be a great deal of confusion about the date of the sinking of the *UB-88*. Most secondary sources give the date as March 1, 1921. I suspect that this is because someone at the Naval Historical Center made a mistake during the compilation of the *Dictionary of American Naval Fighting Ships*, in which the entry for the *UB-88* notes, "On 1 March 1921, she took her final plunge when *Wickes* (DD-75) sank her with gunfire." DANF is the main source that is used by casual researchers. DANF is not without errors.

The deck logs of the *Wickes* and *Pokomoke* both agree that the scuttling date was January 3. So how did this error come about? My guess is that one of the compilers wrote the date numerically as 1/3/21, and that someone else transposed the numbers of the month and day, and wrote 3/1/21. The DANF entry is incorrect.

On June 7, 1921, the USS *Hawk* towed the *UC-97* to a point in Lake Michigan some 25 miles outside of Chicago, Illinois. Again there was very little fanfare.

UC-97 and *Hawk*. (From the author's collection.)

Designated to sink the U-boat by gunfire was the USS *Wilmette*. Before its present incarnation, the *Wilmette* was the passenger steamer *Eastland*. The *Eastland* was notoriously known as one of the worst steamship disasters ever to occur in the Great Lakes. Because of inherent instability problems, she rolled over at her dock when she had a full load of passengers on board, resulting in the drowning deaths of more than eight hundred people. The wreck was raised, stripped of the superstructure, then reconstructed in the form of a gunboat.

Target Cruise

UC-97 from the deck of the *Wilmette*. (From the author's collection.)

After taking on a party of observers, the *Wilmette* weighed anchor at 8:17 in the morning. She soon caught up with the *Hawk* and the *UC-97*. All stopped at the predetermined site at 10:20 a.m. They idled for more than an hour, until sub chaser *SC-412* came alongside the *Wilmette* and transferred the Naval District commandant and another party of observers.

At 11:45, the *Wilmette* opened fire with her 4-inch battery. During the course of the next five minutes she fired eighteen rounds at the *UC-97*. The U-boat sank by

The *UC-97* under fire. (From the author's collection.)

the head barely ten minutes after the *Wilmette* ceased fire. The sub chaser parted departed at 12:10 p.m. The job was done.

According to a newspaper account, "At Waukegan, Zion City and other north-shore cities the roar of the naval guns caused considerable excitement. Police headquarters and north-shore newspaper offices were swamped with inquiries about the 'earthquake.'"

As retired U.S. Navy officer James Wise wrote, "This was the first time that a U.S. naval gun had fired an explosive shell on any of the Great Lakes since Commodore Oliver Hazard Perry defeated the British on Lake Erie in September 1813."

The story of the scuttling of the other four ex-German U-boats is deeply intertwined with that of U.S. Army General Billy Mitchell. After the U.S. entered the Great War, Mitchell was sent to France to organize American flying units to fight against Germany. He was a pilot who led his men by example. At war's end, he returned to the U.S. with a firm conviction that the future of warfare lay in aerial combat.

Mitchell became as controversial a figure as the Army ever produced. He saw only reason, and during his entire military career he was forced to combat unthinking conventions. Then, as today, there was plenty of irrationality to fight.

His big bone of contention was the impotence of naval power in light of a technological innovation that had been advanced by the Great War: the airplane. He realized before anyone else that these high-speed gnats in the sky could wreak havoc on ponderous, slow-moving warships that plied the coastal waters.

Although the war had produced a recognizable body of evidence to support his view, the Navy and its career officers, who were steeped in the traditions of the sea, disagreed with him. Mitchell set out to prove to the Navy that capital ships were not invulnerable to attack from the air. The way he decided to do this was by demonstration.

Target Cruise

The vessels that he wanted to sink by aerial bombardment were the German warships that had been taken over by the U.S. government as war reparations. In addition to the six U-boats that comprised the Ex-German Submarine Expeditionary Force, there were three destroyers (*G-102*, *S-132*, and *V-43*), the cruiser *Frankfurt*, and the battleship *Ostfriesland* – eleven vessels in all.

They were all slated for destruction by the terms of the Treaty of Versailles. The Navy completed its performance testing. Except for the *UB-88* and *UC-97*, the rest were laid up in Navy bases along the eastern seaboard.

The nine warships were assembled at Lynnhaven Roads, which lay at the mouth of the Chesapeake Bay. The Navy prepared to scuttle them in deep water off the coast of Virginia – somewhere "beyond the fifty fathom curve." Fifty fathoms equals three hundred feet.

The Navy wanted to use the ex-German warships for gunnery practice. Mitchell wanted to bomb them from the air.

Mitchell had to jump a number of bureaucratic hurdles in order to convince politicians and his military superiors to grant authority for him to proceed with his endeavor. The Navy did everything it could to stymy his plans: it appealed directly to Washington that the general was a madman, that the country needed a stronger Navy and had no allocations for an air force, that planes could have no effect against thickly armored warships.

When the Navy lost the battle to prevent Mitchell from gaining support for his bombing experiments, it tried to have the target ships placed so far offshore that the airplanes would be forced to operate at the extreme limit of their range. The fuel capacity of early biplanes was not great. When Mitchell got wind of this final subversion, he put pressure in the proper places and got the ships moved closer to shore.

Mitchell also had logistical problems to consider. The First Provisional Air Brigade needed planes, practice, and bombs. Mitchell mustered every biplane that the Army possessed. He personally led flights of bombers over the target ship *San Marcos*: the battleship *Texas* under her previous incarnation. The target ship lay off Tangier Island in the Chesapeake Bay. His flyboys made run after run until they scored 94% hits on the target.

The biggest aerial bomb then in existence was a 1,000-pounder: suitable against a submarine, but not large enough to sink a battleship. Mitchell had larger bombs made to his specifications: one hundred fifty 2,000-pounders and seventy-five 4,000-pounders.

The U-boats were in deplorable condition. So much machinery had been removed from them, and so many hull fittings had been tampered with, that they were no longer seaworthy enough to be towed to sea without fear of sinking along the way. They had to be patched for their final cruise. Damaged or missing hull plates were replaced and riveted. Openings had to be blanked where pipes had been removed from the hull. Loose material in the superstructure had to be secured. The barely floating hulks were towed to Lynnhaven Roads and placed on moorings that swung with the changes of the tide.

The *U-111* beat them all to the bottom, although only temporarily. On June 13, 1921, the minesweeper *Quail* towed the U-boat out of the Portsmouth Navy Yard. On June 14, the U-boat appeared to be down by the head by about four feet. It remained in that attitude for the rest of the voyage. Upon their arrival at Lynnhaven Roads, on June 16, the *U-111* was secured to a mooring buoy and an inspection was made. A Navy memorandum stated:

"On opening the hatch of the forward torpedo compartment this compartment was found full of water. The wrecking pump of the tug was able to lower the level of this water until it could be seen that a considerable stream was coming from one of the torpedo tubes. The rear door of this tube had been removed at

Target Cruise

The *U-111* before it was disarmed and stripped. (Courtesy of the National Archives.)

the Navy Yard as had also the hand-wheel for operating the bow door. An inspection of the compartment next astern of the torpedo room showed that there was practically no water in this compartment. No anxiety was felt for the vessel and it was intended to improvise a tube shutter on the morning of 17 June. The *Quail* remained alongside the vessel all night pumping intermittently."

The pump was disconnected in the morning as the *Quail* proceeded to shove off for other duty. The *U-111* began to settle quickly. "An inspection of the compartment next astern showed that some of the wooden plugs in the inner hull of the vessel had come out and that this compartment was also flooding. Two plugs, one of them about six inches in diameter were seen to blow out about this time."

The *Quail* rerigged the towing lines and tried to beach the U-boat. On the way to shore, the *U-111*'s bow grounded in five fathoms. Slowly, the stern sank, until the U-boat rested on the bottom with three feet of water over the conning tower.

No salvage equipment was available in the 5th Naval District. It was therefore suggested that the U.S. salvage tug *Falcon* be assigned to raise the U-boat. At that time the *Falcon* was conducting salvage operations on the U.S. submarine *S-5*, off the coast of Delaware, and could not be spared.

The *U-111* was left on the bottom for more than a year. Obviously it missed the gunnery and bombing tests. It also missed the deadline that was prescribed by treaty, but no one complained.

A gas buoy with a red flashing light was placed on the wreck of the *U-111*. Six mooring buoys were set. The *Falcon* arrived over the U-boat on October 1, 1921. Divers went to work in the pitch-black compartments. After a month and a half of hard work, the *Falcon* was called off for other duty. She wintered in New York, where she underwent a refit. It was not until June 1922 that she returned to the site of the *U-111*.

Divers eventually managed to seal the open torpedo tube, and replace the wooden plugs that had popped out of the inner hull. On July 29, the *Falcon* pumped air into the U-boat's compartments, but succeeded in raising only the stern.

On August 4, the *Falcon* towed two pontoons to the wreck site. After much hard work in securing the pontoons to the sunken hull, the *U-111* was finally raised and towed to dry-dock at the Norfolk Navy Yard, on August 14. There the U-boat was repaired well enough that it could be towed to sea for scuttling.

The *Falcon* departed for the Portsmouth Navy Yard on August 30, with the *U-111* lashed to her starboard side. Aboard the salvage vessel was Mr. H. D. Blaunet, of the Pathe Moving Picture Company. He was assigned the task of recording the scuttling on motion picture film.

Once in the open sea the U-boat was dropped astern of the *Falcon* on a hundred fathoms of wire. The following day, when the *Falcon* reached the prearranged site, a charge was detonated in the forward battery room of the U-boat, blowing a hole in the hull. Another charge was detonated in the aft torpedo compartment.

The *U-111* sank stern first in 266 fathoms.

The U-boat scuttling tests were scheduled for June 22. The hulks were towed off the Virginia capes and

Target Cruise

All the U-boats were in deplorable condition because they had been partially dismantled for study purposes. Shown above is the *U-117* with the hull plates removed from over the engine room in order to permit easy access. (Courtesy of the National Archives.)

anchored. The tests proved hardly a thing.

The destroyer *Dickerson* sank the *U-140* by gunfire, with nineteen hits out of thirty-nine shots fired. It took an hour and twenty-four minutes for the U-boat to sink.

The destroyer *Sicard* sank the *UB-148* by scoring twenty hits out of forty shots. It took eleven minutes to register the first hit, and another twenty-nine minutes for the U-boat to sink.

The only U-boat that Mitchell was allowed to bomb was the *U-117*. He had six flights of planes lined up to make bombing runs. The three planes of the first flight straddled the anchored U-boat with bombs. On the second flight, a direct hit from a single 165-pound bomb that was dropped from a Navy F-5-L seaplane sent the U-boat to the bottom like a rock. The remaining four flights did not have the opportunity to enter the demonstration.

A Navy memorandum stated succinctly, "Valuable

data secured from destruction." If Naval officers had been open-minded, they would have realized that the most valuable datum was that aerial bombardment was more effective than shelling.

This is the end of the story as far as U-boats are concerned: a small bang that was hardly more than a whimper. Yet in order for the reader to fully comprehend events that occurred in 1941, and later in 1992, I need to put the U-boat story in grand historical perspective.

The Navy made the excuse that the *U-117* was a small, unarmored submarine. The effect of bombs on a large capital ship would not be as dramatic.

Exercises were conducted on the decommissioned battleship *Iowa* (renamed *Coast Battleship No. 4*). She became the first radio controlled target ship to be used in fleet exercises. Secretary of the Navy Josephus Daniels outlined the purpose of the "experiments to determine the present value of aircraft operating from shore bases against naval vessels unattended by aircraft."

His memorandum stated, "Actual bombing tests

A direct hit on the *U-117*. Note three observation vessels in the near distance, and three aircraft in the upper left corner. (From the author's collection.)

Target Cruise

from the aircraft to concentrate, using dummy bombs of standard size, form, and weight against the U.S.S. IOWA, steaming at her highest practicable speed and maneuvering under radio control. These tests are for the purpose of determining the accuracy with which bombs can be dropped over the sea." This was carried out on June 29.

Navy flying boats were dispatched first to search for the *Iowa*, then to bomb her. It took them four hours to locate the target. Then, they dropped eighty bombs and scored only two hits. Navy pundits argued that Mitchell could do no better with his army planes on the ex-German warships. But they did not reckon with Mitchell's constant drilling of his men and planes.

The *Iowa* was not sunk at this time, but served in her capacity as a radio controlled target until March 23, 1923, when she was sunk in Panama Bay by a salvo of 14-inch shells.

By July 13, Mitchell was ready to attack the *G-102* with eighteen SE-5 pursuit planes that were armed with machine guns and light bombs, De Havillands that were armed with 100-pound bombs, and Martin bombers that were armed with 600-pounders. The SE-5's raked the decks with pinpoint precision and riddled the hull from bow to stern. Mitchell waved off the De Havillands and brought in the heavy bombers straightaway. Twenty minutes later, the *G-102* lay at the bottom of the ocean. The Navy was still unimpressed, making excuses for the destroyer's quick demise.

Two days later, rather than let Mitchell repeat his successful performance, Navy ships sank the other two German destroyers by gunfire: the *S-132* by the battleship *Delaware* and destroyer *Herbert*, the *V-43* by the battleship *Florida*.

Next on Mitchell's agenda was the *Frankfurt*. The Navy insisted, with good reason for a change, that he work over the cruiser with small bombs first, then work his way up to the larger bombs. Flight after flight of planes dropped 100-pounders all morning, with long intervals between attacks during which observers from the minelayer *Shawmut* boarded the derelict and inspected the damage that the bombs had inflicted. In this instance the Navy was very methodical in studying the results, finding that even 250- and 300-pound bombs were unable to penetrate the upper decks. Goats and other animals, stationed topside to simulate human crews, were found dead and macerated, but the ship itself was intact.

Navy inspectors, smugly inferring that aerial bombs alone could never sink the cruiser, ordered the battleship *North Dakota* to prepare a time bomb. Then came Mitchell's Armageddon with the 600-pounders dropped by heavy Martin bombers. Bombs rained down so fast and furiously that the *Frankfurt* was immediately shrouded in spray. Tons of seawater fell upon the decks. Crews on the observation vessels ran for cover as steel fragments ripped across the water for more than a mile. Before the attack could be called off, so that observers could board the cruiser and make damage assessments, the *Frankfurt* slipped beneath the waves. Photographic planes recorded with a vengeance the events of July 18.

The ultimate test was yet to come. The *Ostfriesland* was protected by twelve inches of armor plate. The hull had four skins for protection against mines and torpedoes. The battleship had so many watertight compartments that naval experts thought that the vessel was impossible to sink. At the Battle of Jutland, the *Ostfriesland* survived a mine explosion and eighteen hits from large shells. It was a floating fortress of arms and armament.

On July 20, the troop transport *Henderson* was packed to the gunwales with more than three hundred distinguished guests. In addition to some fifty reporters, there were eight Senators, twelve Congressmen, three Cabinet members (the Secretaries of War, Navy, and Agriculture), and foreign observers from England, France, Spain, Portugal, Brazil, and Japan.

The battleship *Pennsylvania* was loaded with admirals, generals, and other high-ranking military officers.

Target Cruise

More than a score of other U.S. warships surrounded the *Ostfriesland*.

The day dawned miserably, with thirty-knot winds whipping the sea to froth. Mitchell and his flyboys sat idly at Langley Field, awaiting the call to strike. When nothing was heard by one o'clock in the afternoon, Mitchell jumped into his Osprey and flew out to sea. The Navy wanted to call off the attack because of the weather. Mitchell insisted that the bombing raid be carried out as planned, stating that his planes could fly under those conditions if Navy men could observe under them. He went so far as to order his planes into the air without Navy approval.

The Navy was struck by his impudence, but allowed the attack to proceed. The 250-pound bombs did little damage to the *Ostfriesland's* steel hide. Mitchell's planes landed in a blinding rain storm as reporters were racing for shore aboard the destroyer *Leary*, to report that the German battleship was "absolutely intact and undamaged." Many seasick VIP's also returned to shore, convinced that the planes had lost the day.

Mitchell was not to be dissuaded from his convictions. The next morning found him preparing his planes with blockbuster 2,000-pound bombs. At first he was permitted to drop only the 1,000-pounders. Two scored direct hits, and the Navy called off the rest of the attack so they could send observers on board. They found the *Ostfriesland* so badly torn up that they were unable to go below the third deck. They peered through gaping bomb holes at the water that was flooding into the hull below.

Then came the big bombs. One by one, seven Martin and Handley Page bombers made their drops, aiming for near misses, and timing it so that each tremendous waterspout settled before the next plane came in for its attack. The concussion of exploding bombs was so severe that observation vessels pounded when the shock wave reached them. Planes at an altitude of 3,000 feet rocked violently. Thousands of tons of water descended upon the *Ostfriesland's* decks.

The third bomb scored a direct hit on the forecastle. It tore out a frightful hole in the steel hull, and created a raging fire. Another near miss lifted the battleship visibly out of the water. Bomb number five fell near the stern. The *Ostfriesland* began to settle aft. By the time the sixth bomb struck, the after two turrets were already under water. The battleship's bow nosed upward, the ship rolled over onto its port side, and it disappeared from view. A Handley Page delivered the final stroke by dropping the last bomb on the huge vortex of escaping air.

Although Mitchell was ecstatic, the Navy refused to accept the implications of his success. The Navy Department continued to ridicule the general's allegations that a strong and separate air force would change the tide of future warfare. Mitchell refused to back down from his position. Soon, he was railroaded out of the country on foreign assignments that were intended to lose him in red tape and obscurity. Eventually, as he kept up his verbal attacks against Navy ignorance, using the press as his sounding board, he was brought up on charges of subversion, and was court-martialed.

This censure did not prevent Mitchell's predictions from coming true. As early as 1923, he forecast the buildup of Japanese air power, and outlined in detail how they would attack Pearl Harbor and Clark Field. It happened exactly as he stated in his report – a report that was pigeonholed by military minds that were not prepared to face American vulnerability.

In the event, the Honorable G. Katsuda, member of the House of Peers of Tokyo, was more impressed by the aerial display of might than his American counterparts. He was on board the *Shawmut* as an observer when the *Ostfriesland* was finally bombed into submission. Ironically, when the Japanese bombed Hawaii's battleship row two decades later, the *Shawmut* (renamed *Oglala*) was sunk at her berth during the attack.

Perhaps July 21, 1921 was the real day of infamy.

UNDERWATER CRUISE

As the saying goes, "out of sight, out of mind." So it was for the ex-German U-boats and capital ships that were scuttled beyond reach. By the end of the twentieth century, only a few people in the world remembered them, and fewer cared.

I was one of the few who both remembered and cared.

In the mid-1970's, I started to research what I eventually came to call the Billy Mitchell wrecks: those one-time warships of the German fleet that were scuttled off the Virginia Capes. My original interest was inspired by my quest to discover shipwrecks whose locations were unknown.

At the National Archives in Washington, DC, I examined records that related to the bombing and gunnery tests of 1921. When I saw that the ex-German warships were slated for scuttling "beyond the fifty fathom curve," in order to make them inaccessible to salvors, I quit my research on the Billy Mitchell wrecks because a working scuba dive to those depths was considered impractical, if not impossible.

In 1989, some fifteen years later, I resumed my research on the Billy Mitchell wrecks. My renewed interest came about because I was engaged in a massive project to write a series of books about shipwrecks along the American eastern seaboard: the Popular Dive Guide Series. I reviewed my notes, returned to the National Archives, and accessed the same records again, but this time with the idea of simply obtaining primary documentation to enable me to write an historical account for inclusion in *Shipwrecks of Virginia*.

I spent a week in compiling information. During that week I was scheduled to give a slide presentation to a local dive club called Capitol Divers. At the meeting I met Ken Clayton – a fairly new and overeager diver

I had met several months before while diving on the U.S. cruiser *Wilkes-Barre*, which had been scuttled in 1972 in an underwater demolition test off Key West, Florida. The wreck lay at a depth of 250 feet.

Now comes one of those coincidences which, had it been written in a novel, would have appeared contrived. Clayton showed me a book that contained a picture of the *Ostfriesland*, and asked me if I knew anything about it. I told him that I had been researching the battleship that very day. I gave him the bad news about the depth. He accepted it with equanimity.

The story of my friendship with Clayton, and the ground-breaking dives that we made together over the next seven years, I have already related in exquisite detail in my two-volume history of wreck-diving, *The Lusitania Controversies*. The bulk of that saga lies beyond the scope of the present volume.

Suffice it to say that we embarked on a dedicated program to discover the locations of the Billy Mitchell wrecks. By noting the positions of the numerous observation vessels, and triangulating the bearings and distances of each to the various German warships, we developed a picture of the relationship of each vessel to every other vessel.

Both Ken and I curried the favor of fishing boat skippers who shared with us their "hang" logs. A hang log is a list of coordinates – loran or GPS numbers – on which commercial trawling vessels have "hung" or snagged their nets. In order to avoid losing additional expensive gear, trawler captains maintain records of nasty places to shun. Most hangs are boulders, ledges, or geological outcrops. About one in ten is a shipwreck.

I bought a bathymetric chart of the area. Clayton correlated hang numbers with wreck symbols that were depicted on the chart. There were differences to be sure – in 1921, the observation vessels used sextant, chronometer, and mathematics to calculate their position; in the 1980's they used time delays from transmission stations to an onboard receiving unit: a system called long range navigation, or loran. There was no

Underwater Cruise

satellite global positioning system in those days.

Then we chartered a boat to visit the sites and confirm their existence by means of a depth sounder. All this work enabled us to pinpoint the final resting place of the *Ostfriesland* – our primary goal. It lay at a depth of 380 feet.

Pete Manchee came on board as part of the dive team. In order to consummate a dive on the wreck, we had to invent an entire new order of diving: a quantum leap beyond what was recognized as recreational diving.

Instead of breathing air, which is composed primarily of oxygen and nitrogen, we breathed what is known as mixed gas: either heliox (oxygen and helium) or trimix (oxygen, helium, and nitrogen). This was necessary because, at extreme depth, nitrogen was narcotic and oxygen was toxic. We also had to plan on decompressing for two hours in the open ocean while breathing various blends of nitrox from bottles, and oxygen that was fed to us through hoses from a storage cylinder on the surface support vessel.

The triumvirate made the first *Ostfriesland* dive in 1990. In subsequent years we made more dives on the *Ostfriesland*. We also located and dived on the *G-102* (at a depth of 350 feet) and the *Frankfurt* (at 420 feet).

More relevant to the topic of this book are the three U-boats that were scuttled in the vicinity of the capital ships. We discovered all three. I can still feel the elation of that first find. . . .

At a depth of 200 feet, the cerulean blue water below showed no sign of ending. I raised my eyebrows at my buddy, Ken Clayton. He shrugged. The current was strong and my arms were feeling the strain of the pull down the anchor line. We paused for a moment to rest. It wasn't good to get out of breath at depth, so we paced ourselves accordingly. We didn't know how deep we had to go to touch the wreck that we hoped lay silently on the bottom.

At 210 feet the water continued greenish blue and featureless. At 220 it was the same. At 230 I began to see a dim ghostly outline. At 240 the shadowy shape took on definite form. It was the hull of a sunken ship.

Ambient light visibility was nearly 50 feet, the result of Gulf Stream intrusion which sometimes brushes the offshore waters of Virginia. At 250 feet I could see the hull distinctly. The side facing us rose vertically to an upper edge that curved back to form the deck; the plating was remarkably well preserved. The thinly encrusted metal cast little reflected light, and the overall dull gray was mottled with splotches of lighter shades in a nearly monochromatic design.

What I could see of the wreck so far looked very much like a submarine.

My exhilaration turned to anxiety when I saw that the grapnel had not hooked the hull, but the sand!

The grapnel had dragged over the top of the wreck, fallen to the white sandy bottom on the down-current side, and snagged with a single tine on something that lay completely buried. With a viselike grip on the anchor line in case the grapnel suddenly broke free, I dropped to the sand to examine the stability of the hook.

Although only one tine had caught, it was gripped firmly on the edge of a thick steel plate that lay at a distance of only one foot from where the hull met the sand. No matter how hard I twisted and yanked, I could not move the grapnel – and the boat up above to which it was secured – against the force of the current. I raised my eyebrows at Ken, who hovered above me and oversaw my actions. He nodded.

I let got of the line. Instinctively I felt behind my tanks for my decompression reel, just in case; its presence was reassuring. My depth gauge registered 266 feet. We kicked upward and alighted upon the deck about fifteen feet above the bottom. What looked like the end extended to our left, so we went right.

In just a minute or two we reached an upright structure that was distinctly discernible as a conning tower. And not the conning tower of an American sub, but a German U-boat. And not just any U-boat, but a

Underwater Cruise

U-140: the first World War One U-boat to be discovered and dived in American waters. (Courtesy of the U.S. Navy Library.)

World War *One* U-boat.

Specifically, the *U-140*. The date was June 6, 1992.

On that dive, Clayton and I became the first divers in the world to touch a World War One U-boat that was sunk in American waters.

The next U-boat on our discovery agenda was the *UB-148*. According to our historical documentation, the wreck lay close to the *U-140* in about the same depth. We had promising numbers. On a subsequent trip, we anchored into the *U-140* for the benefit of those who had not dived it before. The rest of us saved our time and breathing gas for the "new" U-boat – hoping, of course, that we could find it.

Chris Stone dived alone. When he returned, Mike Hillier, captain of the *Miss Lindsey*, couldn't get the grapnel out. Stone bounced down and cut the tines free from the net in which they were snagged. Afterward, listening to Stone describe the wreck, Clayton and I had a creepy feeling that either he had been narked the whole time despite breathing mixed gas, or . . .

. . . Hillier accidentally swapped the numbers and took us to the wrong coordinates. Thus Chris Stone made not only the first dive on the *UB-148*, but the first two dives!

With the wreck rehooked, Clayton and I dived separately and alone, although our paths crossed several times on the bottom and on the anchor line: characteristic wreck-diving buddy technique. Thirty feet of ambient light graced the bottom, but I cringed when I saw how tenuous the grapnel was set: it had caught in a twisted knot of netting that was stretched taut to a point some fifteen feet off a break in the hull. The strain of the boat prevented me from budging the grapnel to reset it in metal. When I examined the net closely, I saw with relief that within the mass of rope and twine a thick steel cable lay embedded. I went exploring.

This net was the "hang" that was the origin of the loran numbers.

About twenty feet of the bow had been blown off, exposing two long bronze torpedo tubes, one of which lay almost completely free and appeared to be easily recoverable. The ten-foot gap between the forward compartment and the pressure hull was knitted together by the net in which the grapnel was hooked. The wreck sat upright, and the shell of the conning tower rose about eight above the rusting deck. Twenty feet off the port side of the conning tower, a string of buoys floated a net off the bottom like a thick lace curtain suspended from rods. Abaft the conning tower on top of the hull gaped a hole the size of a double door. I should have been able to peer into the engine room, but the interior was filled with sand and silt to within three feet of the rim.

UB-148. (Courtesy of the National Archives.)

Underwater Cruise

The depth to the bottom was 274 feet. The date was August 17, 1992.

The *U-140* and the *UB-148* were shelled by surface vessels, but the *U-117* was sunk by aerial bombardment from Billy Mitchell's planes. The reason we looked for the *U-117* last, despite its importance to our overall quest to dive on those particular vessels that were sunk by Mitchell's bombers, was a function of progressive depth exploration. Naval records indicated that the *U-117* went down where the water was 300 feet deep. We were working our way down, so to speak.

From historical accounts we chose the most probable location and correlated it with the hang numbers that we had in the area. The following year, after hours of searching with negative result, we resignedly moved off site to check out another set of numbers nearby, but only 230 feet deep. Any unexplored wreck could be interesting.

This time we got lucky and found the numbers right on target. Ken Clayton and Peter Hess went down first. Just as they began their ascent, the grapnel pulled out and the boat went adrift, so the rest of us had to wait out their decompression before entertaining the possibility of a dive. When they finally surfaced, we were as astonished as they were to learn that the wreck was that of a submarine!

I knew of three U.S. submarines that had been scuttled off the Virginia coast, and concluded that we must have stumbled onto one of them. When we rehooked the wreck, the anchor chain fell across the edge of the conning tower, which I studied in detail without observing anything that provided clues to the sub's identity. Dark, dismal conditions prevailed on the bottom, almost like a night dive. I did not stray far.

The date of this discovery was August 12, 1993.

For two years I agonized over which sub it could be. Then we returned on a day in 1995 when visibility exceeded fifty feet ambient. I took a grand tour from end to end. It was immediately obvious how the wreck's location became known: the towing yokes of two trawler rigs – expensive shipwreck locator devices – were firmly implanted in the starboard hull.

Not until I examined the stern carefully, and compared my sketch with historical photos, did I recognize the distinctive slope as the after deck above the mine-laying tubes. It was the *U-117* all along, misplaced by both leagues and fathoms.

Through those tubes once slid the mines that sank the *Chaparra* and the *San Saba* off the New Jersey coast, and the *Saetia* off Maryland. Through one of the tubes in the bow sped the torpedo that sank the *Sommerstad* off Long Island's southern shore, and the *Mirlo* off North Carolina, in that long ago year when war raged over the world.

There is more to behold and explore on these wrecks than I have seen for myself or described. They are three of a kind, if you will, together comprising a rare insight into Germany's first undersea and most effective killing machine, and the precursor of deadly events to come a generation later.

To dive on the Kaiser's U-boats is to touch the heart of history.

The sloping stern was the key that enabled me to identify the *U-117*. (Courtesy of the National Archives.)

APPENDICES

Alphabetization

Lloyd's of London, that time-honored chronicler of ships, has adopted a rather cumbersome method of alphabetization for its Register. Unfortunately, this system has been accepted by museums and other organizations that are involved in modern cataloguing. For example, all ships beginning with initials are found at the beginning of the listing for that letter, instead of at their appropriate place according to customary order. Likewise, double word names stop being alphabetized when the first word reaches its alphabetical location; at that point, all ships with the same first name are listed before a similar name consisting of only one word.

For example, *J.J. Flaherty* is listed before *Jacob M. Haskell*. To complicate matters, *Rob Roy* is listed before *Robert and Richard*, because the space between words is given alphabetical precedence over the "e" after "b" when everyone knows that "e" comes before "r." This system of alphabets within alphabets based upon punctuation and spacing between words is unnecessary and ridiculous.

Therefore, in order to make it easy for the reader who is unfamiliar with such unruly rules, in this book I have arranged all words, places, and names in the simple order of dictionary usage with which everyone is familiar. The only thing to remember is that ships' names are treated contiguously, not in reverse order as people's names. For example, *Sidney B. Atwood* is not listed as *Atwood, Sydney B.*

Abbreviations

SS = steamship
USS = United States Ship
CGC = U.S. Coast Guard Cutter
HMS = His or Her Majesty's Ship

352 Appendices

HMCS = His or Her Majesty's Canadian Ship
GRT = Gross registered tonnage (except for navy vessels, which calculate displacement tonnage)
fisher = fishing vessel (sail or motorized)
B.d.U. = Befehlshaber der Unterseeboote (translates as Commander in Chief of U-boats)
KTB = Kriegstagebuch (translates as deck log)

Nat. = Nationality (country of registration)

Bel = Belgian	Dut = Dutch
Br = British	Fr = French
Bra = Brazilian	Ital = Italian
Can = Canadian	Jap = Japanese
Chi = Chilean	Nor = Norwegian
Cu = Cuban	Por = Portuguese
Dan = Danish	Swe = Swedish

US = United States

Method of Attack

T = Torpedoed
S = Shelled
M = Mined
B = Bombed (with scuttling charges)
F = Set afire
C = Collision

not sunk = vessel was damaged but escaped
salvaged = vessel was partially sunk but later raised
Location = Attack position referenced to nearest State or Province; "offshore" means so far at sea that land reference is not meaningful

Survivors

NG = Not Given - used when the records did not tabulate the number of people aboard a vessel, or the number of survivors.
A = Approximate - used when the number of survivors is approximated or can be inferred from the records.
NOTE: Extant historical records do not always provide all information. Some information is contradictory.

APPENDIX 1
ATTACK CHRONOLOGY

Not every vessel attack is included in this list: only attacks that resulted in damage, loss, or injury. A vessel at which a U-boat fired shells is not included unless the vessel was actually struck.

Date	Vessel Name	U-boat	Result
10/8/16	*Strathdene*	*U-53*	sunk
10/8/16	*Chr. Knudsen*	*U-53*	sunk
10/8/16	*West Point*	*U-53*	sunk
10/8/16	*Blommersdijk*	*U-53*	sunk
10/8/16	*Stephano*	*U-53*	sunk
11/17/16	*T. A. Scott, Jr.*	*Deutschland*	sunk
5/25/18	*Hattie Dunn*	*U-151*	sunk
5/25/18	*Hauppauge*	*U-151*	salvaged
5/25/18	*Edna*	*U-151*	salvaged
6/2/18	*Winneconne*	*U-151*	sunk
6/2/18	*Isabel B. Wiley*	*U-151*	sunk
6/2/18	*Jacob M. Haskell*	*U-151*	sunk
6/2/18	*Edward H. Cole*	*U-151*	sunk
6/2/18	*Texel*	*U-151*	sunk
6/2/18	*Carolina*	*U-151*	sunk
6/3/18	*Herbert L. Pratt*	*U-151*	salvaged
6/3/18	*Samuel C. Mengel*	*U-151*	sunk
6/4/18	*Edward R. Baird, Jr.*	*U-151*	salvaged
6/5/18	*Eidsvold*	*U-151*	sunk
6/5/18	*Harpathian*	*U-151*	sunk
6/5/18	*Vinland*	*U-151*	sunk
6/8/18	*Pinar del Rio*	*U-151*	sunk
6/10/18	*Vindeggen*	*U-151*	sunk
6/14/18	*Henrik Lund*	*U-151*	sunk
6/14/18	*Samoa*	*U-151*	sunk
6/14/18	*Kringsjaa*	*U-151*	sunk
6/15/18	*Tortuguero*	*U-156*	sunk

Appendix 1 - Attack Chronology

Date	Vessel Name	U-boat	Result
6/18/18	Dwinsk	U-156	sunk
6/22/18	Chilier	U-151	sunk
6/23/18	Augvald	U-151	sunk
7/7/18	Marosa	U-156	sunk
7/8/18	Manx King	U-156	sunk
7/19/18	San Diego	U-156	sunk
7/21/18	Perth Amboy	U-156	salvaged
7/21/18	Lansford	U-156	sunk
7/21/18	No. 703	U-156	sunk
7/21/18	No. 766	U-156	sunk
7/21/18	No. 740	U-156	sunk
7/22/18	Robert and Richard	U-156	sunk
7/27/18	Porto	U-140	sunk
8/1/18	Tokuyama Maru	U-140	sunk
8/2/18	Dornfontein	U-156	salvaged
8/3/18	Muriel	U-156	sunk
8/3/18	Sydney B. Atwood	U-156	sunk
8/3/18	Annie Perry	U-156	sunk
8/3/18	Rob Roy	U-156	sunk
8/3/18	Nelson A.	U-156	sunk
8/4/18	O. B. Jennings	U-140	sunk
8/5/18	Stanley M. Seaman	U-140	sunk
8/5/18	Agnes G. Holland	U-156	sunk
8/5/18	Gladys H. Hollett	U-156	salvaged
8/5/18	Luz Blanca	U-156	sunk
8/6/18	Merak	U-140	sunk
8/6/18	Diamond Shoals	U-140	sunk
8/8/18	Sydland	U-156	sunk
8/10/18	Aleda May	U-117	sunk
8/10/18	Progress	U-117	sunk
8/10/18	Reliance	U-117	sunk
8/10/18	William H. Starbuck	U-117	sunk
8/10/18	Old Time		not attacked
8/10/18	Cruiser	U-117	sunk
8/10/18	Earl and Nettie	U-117	sunk
8/10/18	Mary E. Sennett	U-117	sunk
8/10/18	Katie L. Palmer	U-117	sunk
8/11/18	Penistone	U-156	sunk

Appendix 1 - Attack Chronology

Date	Vessel Name	U-boat	Result
8/12/18	*Sommerstad*	*U-117*	sunk
8/13/18	*Frederick R. Kellogg*	*U-117*	salvaged
8/14/18	*Dorothy B. Barrett*	*U-117*	sunk
8/15/18	*Madrugada*	*U-117*	sunk
8/16/18	*Mirlo*	*U-117*	sunk
8/17/18	*Nordhav*	*U-117*	sunk
8/17/18	*San Jose*	*U-156*	sunk
8/20/18	*Ansaldo*	*U-117*	not sunk
8/20/18	*Lucille M. Schnare*	*U-156*	sunk
8/20/18	*Francis J. O'Harra, Jr.*	*U-156*	sunk
8/20/18	*A. Piatt Andrew*	*U-156*	sunk
8/20/18	*Pasadena*	*U-156*	sunk
8/20/18	*Uda A. Saunders*	*U-156*	sunk
8/21/18	*Diomed*	*U-140*	sunk
8/21/18	*Sylvania*	*U-156*	sunk
8/22/18	*Notre Dame de la Garde*	*U-156*	sunk
8/23/18?	*Triumph*	*U-156*	sunk
8/24/18	*Bianca*	*U-117*	salvaged
8/25/18	*Erik*	*U-156*	sunk
8/25/18	*E. B. Walters*	*U-156*	sunk
8/25/18	*C. M. Walters*	*U-156*	sunk
8/25/18	*Varna D. Adams*	*U-156*	sunk
8/25/18	*J. J. Flaherty*	*U-156*	sunk
8/26/18	*Gloaming*	*U-156*	sunk
8/26/18	*Rush*	*U-117*	sunk
8/27/18	*Bergsdalen*	*U-117*	sunk
8/30/18	*Elsie Porter*	*U-117*	sunk
8/30/18	*Potentate*	*U-117*	sunk
8/31/18	*Gamo*	*U-155*	sunk
9/2/18	*Stortind*	*U-155*	sunk
9/7/18	*Sophia*	*U-155*	sunk
9/11/18	*Constance*	*U-152*	salvaged
9/13/18	*Leixoes*	*U-155*	sunk
9/13/18	*Newby Hall*	*U-155*	not sunk
9/20/18	*Kingfisher*	*U-155*	sunk
9/29/18	*George G. Henry*	*U-152*	not sunk
9/29/18	*Minnesota*	*U-117*	not sunk
9/30/18	*Ticonderoga*	*U-152*	sunk

Appendix 1 - Attack Chronology

Date	Vessel Name	U-boat	Result
10/1/18	*Bylands*	*U-139*	sunk
10/1/18	*Manin*	*U-139*	sunk
10/2/18	*Rio Cavado*	*U-139*	sunk
10/3/18	*Alberto Treves*	*U-155*	sunk
10/4/18	*Industrial*	*U-155*	sunk
10/4/18	*San Saba*	*U-117*	sunk
10/12/18	*Amphion*	*U-155*	not sunk
10/13/18	*Stifinder*	*U-152*	sunk
10/14/18	*Augusto De Castillo*	*U-139*	sunk
10/15/18	*Messina*	*U-152*	not sunk
10/17/18	*Lucia*	*U-155*	sunk
10/27/18	*Chaparra*	*U-117*	sunk
11/9/18	*Saetia*	*U-117*	sunk

The after battery compartment of the *U-140*. (Courtesy of the National Archives.)

APPENDIX 2 - U-BOAT ATTACKS (BY SUBMARINE)

Not every vessel attack is included in this list: only attacks that resulted in damage, loss, or injury. A vessel at which a U-boat fired shells is not included unless the vessel was actually struck.

M = Method of attack   S = Number of survivors   F = Number of fatalities

Appendix 2 - Attacks (by Submarine)

Date	Vessel name	GRT	Type	Nat.	M	Result	S	F	Location
			U-53						
10/8/16	*Strathdene*	4,321	freighter	Br	TS	sunk	30	0	Nantucket
10/8/16	*Chr. Knudsen*	3,878	tanker	Nor	TS	sunk	32	0	Nantucket
10/8/16	*West Point*	3,847	freighter	Br	S	sunk	38	0	Nantucket
10/8/16	*Blommersdijk*	4,850	freighter	Dut	T	sunk	43	0	Nantucket
10/8/16	*Stephano*	3,449	liner	Br	BST	sunk	163	0	Nantucket
	Total tonnage sunk:	20,345			Total sunk:	5	306	0	
			Deutschland						
11/17/16	*T. A. Scott, Jr.*	62	tug	US	C	sunk	1	5	Connecticut

Appendix 2 - Attacks (by Submarine)

U-151

Date	Vessel name	GRT	Type	Nat.	M	Result	S	F	Location
5/25/18	Hattie Dunn	435	schooner	US	B	sunk	6	0	Virginia
5/25/18	Hauppauge	1,446	schooner	US	SB	salvaged	11	0	Virginia
5/25/18	Edna	325	schooner	US	B	salvaged	6	0	Virginia
6/2/18	Winneconne	1,869	freighter	US	B	sunk	26	0	New Jersey
6/2/18	Isabel B. Wiley	776	schooner	US	B	sunk	8	0	New Jersey
6/2/18	Jacob M. Haskell	1,778	schooner	US	BS	sunk	11	0	New Jersey
6/2/18	Edward H. Cole	1,791	schooner	US	B	sunk	11	0	New Jersey
6/2/18	Texel	3,210	freighter	US	SB	sunk	36	0	New Jersey
6/2/18	Carolina	5,093	liner	US	S	sunk	320	13	New Jersey
6/3/18	Herbert L. Pratt	7,145	tanker	US	M	salvaged	39	0	Delaware
6/3/18	Samuel C. Mengel	915	schooner	US	B	sunk	11	0	Maryland
6/4/18	Edward R. Baird, Jr.	279	schooner	US	SB	salvaged	6	0	Virginia
6/5/18	Eidsvold	1,570	freighter	Nor	S	sunk	25	0	Virginia
6/5/18	Harpathian	4,588	freighter	Br	T	sunk	41	0	N. Carolina
6/5/18	Vinland	1,143	freighter	Nor	B	sunk	19	0	N. Carolina

Appendix 2 - Attacks (by Submarine)

6/8/18	*Pinar del Rio*	2,504	freighter	US	S	sunk	33	0	N. Carolina
6/10/18	*Vindeggen*	3,179	freighter	Nor	B	sunk	34	1	N. Carolina
6/10/18	*Henrik Lund*	4,322	freighter	Nor	B	sunk	34	0	N. Carolina
6/14/18	*Samoa*	1,138	bark	Nor	S	sunk	15	0	offshore
6/14/18	*Kringsjaa*	1,750	bark	Nor	S	sunk	20	0	offshore
6/18/18	*Dwinsk*	8,173	liner	Br	TS	sunk	125	28	offshore
6/22/18	*Chilier*	2,966	freighter	Bel	BS	sunk	25	6	offshore
6/23/18	*Augvald*	3,406	freighter	Nor	S	sunk	11	17	offshore
Total tonnage sunk:		50,606			Total sunk:	19	873	65	

Appendix 2 - Attacks (by Submarine)

U-156

Date	Vessel name	GRT	Type	Nat.	M	Result	S	F	Location
6/15/18	Tortuguero	4,175	freighter	Br	T	sunk	NG	12	offshore
7/7/18	Marosa	1,987	bark	Nor	B	sunk	22	0	offshore
7/8/18	Manx King	1,729	ship	Nor	B	sunk	19	0	offshore
7/19/18	San Diego	13,680	cruiser	US	M	sunk	1,117	6	New York
7/21/18	Perth Amboy	830	tug	US	S	salvaged A-17	A-17	0	Mass.
7/21/18	Lansford	732	barge	US	S	sunk	A-6	0	Mass.
7/21/18	No. 703	934	barge	US	S	sunk	A-6	0	Mass.
7/21/18	No. 766	527	barge	US	S	sunk	A-6	0	Mass.
7/21/18	No. 740	680	barge	US	S	sunk	A-6	0	Mass.
7/22/18	Robert and Richard	140	fisher	US	B	sunk	23	0	Maine
8/2/18	Dornfontein	766	schooner	Can	F	salvaged	10	0	Maine
8/3/18	Muriel	120	fisher	US	B	sunk	22	0	Nova Scotia
8/3/18	Sydney B. Atwood	100	fisher	US	B	sunk	NG	0	Nova Scotia
8/3/18	Annie Perry	116	fisher	US	B	sunk	19	0	Nova Scotia
8/3/18	Rob Roy	112	fisher	US	B	sunk	11	0	Nova Scotia

Appendix 2 - Attacks (by Submarine) 361

8/4/18	Nelson A.	72	fisher	Can	B	sunk	18	0	Nova Scotia
8/5/18	Agnes G. Holland	100	fisher	Can	B	sunk	NG	0	Nova Scotia
8/5/18	Gladys H. Hollett	203	fisher	Can	B	salvaged	NG	0	Nova Scotia
8/5/18	Luz Blanca	4,868	tanker	Can	TS	sunk	32	0	Nova Scotia
8/8/18	Sydland	3,031	freighter	Swe	B	sunk	30	0	Nova Scotia
8/11/18	Penistone	4,139	freighter	Br	TB	sunk	39	1	Nantucket
8/17/18	San Jose	1,586	freighter	Nor	B	sunk	25	0	Nantucket
8/20/18	Lucille M. Schnare	121	fisher	Can	B	sunk	NG	0	Nova Scotia
8/20/18	Francis J. O'Hara, Jr.	117	fisher	US	B	sunk	17	0	Nova Scotia
8/20/18	A. Piatt Andrew	141	fisher	US	B	sunk	24	0	Nova Scotia
8/20/18	Pasadena	119	fisher	Can	B	sunk	17	0	Nova Scotia
8/20/18	Uda A. Saunders	124	fisher	Can	B	sunk	NG	0	Nova Scotia
8/21/18	Sylvania	136	fisher	US	B	sunk	23	0	Nova Scotia
8/22/18	Notre Dame de la Garde	145	fisher	Fr	B	sunk	27	0	Nova Scotia
8/23/18?	Triumph	239	fisher	Can	B?	sunk	NG	0	Nova Scotia?
8/25/18	Erik	583	freighter	Br	SB	sunk	18	0	St. Pierre
8/25/18	E. B. Walters	126	fisher	Can	B	sunk	24	0	St. Pierre
8/25/18	C. M. Walters	107	fisher	Can	B	sunk	26	0	St. Pierre

Appendix 2 - Attacks (by Submarine)

U-156 (Continued)

Date	Vessel name	GRT	Type	Nat.	M	Result	S	F	Location
8/25/18	*Varna D. Adams*	132	fisher	Can	B	sunk	NG	0	St. Pierre
8/25/18	*J. J. Flaherty*	162	fisher	US	B	sunk	25	0	St. Pierre
8/26/18	*Gloaming*	136	fisher	Can	B	sunk	25	0	St. Pierre
	Total tonnage sunk:	41,216				33	1,654+	19	

NOTE: *San Diego* tonnage is displacement tonnage, which is approximately double gross tonnage

Adjusted tonnage: 34,376

Appendix 2 - Attacks (by Submarine)

U-140

Date	Vessel name	GRT	Type	Nat.	M	Result	S	F	Location
7/27/18	Porto	1,079	bark	Por	BS	sunk	18	0	offshore
8/1/18	Tokuyama Maru	7,029	freighter	Jap	TS	sunk	A-86	0	offshore
8/4/18	O. B. Jennings	10,289	tanker	US	S	sunk	49	1	Virginia
8/5/18	Stanley M. Seaman	1,060	schooner	US	B	sunk	9	0	N. Carolina
8/6/18	Merak	3,024	freighter	US	T	sunk	43	0	N. Carolina
8/6/18	Diamond Shoals	590	lightship	US	S	sunk	12	0	N. Carolina
8/21/18	Diomed	7,523	freighter	Br	S	sunk	104	2	offshore
Total tonnage sunk:		30,594				7	A-321	3	

Appendix 2 - Attacks (by Submarine)

U-117

Date	Vessel name	GRT	Type	Nat.	M	Result	S	F	Location
8/10/18	Aleda May	31	fisher	US	SB	sunk	7	0	Georges B.
8/10/18	Progress	34	fisher	US	SB	sunk	7	0	Georges B.
8/10/18	Reliance	19	fisher	US	SB	sunk	6	0	Georges B.
8/10/18	William H. Starbuck	53	fisher	US	B	sunk	8	0	Georges B.
8/10/18	Old Time	18	fisher	US		not attacked		0	Georges B.
8/10/18	Cruiser	28	fisher	US	S	sunk	5	0	Georges B.
8/10/18	Earl and Nettie	24	fisher	US	S	sunk	5	0	Georges B.
8/10/18	Mary E. Sennett	27	fisher	US	S	sunk	7	0	Georges B.
8/10/18	Katie L. Palmer	31	fisher	US	B	sunk	7	0	Georges B.
8/12/18	Sommerstad	3,875	freighter	Nor	T	sunk	31	0	New York
8/13/18	Frederick R. Kellogg	7,127	freighter	US	T	salvaged	34	7	New Jersey
8/14/18	Dorothy B. Barrett	2,088	schooner	US	S	sunk	11	0	New Jersey
8/15/18	Madrugada	1,613	schooner	US	S	sunk	22	0	Virginia
8/16/18	Mirlo	6,978	tanker	US	T	sunk	42	10	N. Carolina
8/17/18	Nordhav	2,846	bark	Nor	B	sunk	26	0	N. Carolina

Appendix 2 - Attacks (by Submarine)

Date	Name	Tonnage	Type	Flag	S	Fate			Location
8/20/18	*Ansaldo*		steamer	Ital	S	not sunk		0	offshore
8/24/18	*Bianca*	408	schooner	Can	B	salvaged	NG	0	Nova Scotia
8/26/18	*Rush*	162	schooner	US	B	sunk	21	0	Nova Scotia
8/27/18	*Bergsdalen*	2,550	freighter	Nor	T	sunk	NG	1	Nova Scotia
8/30/18	*Elsie Porter*	136	schooner	Can	B	sunk	20	0	Nova Scotia
8/30/18	*Potentate*	136	schooner	Can	B	sunk	NG	0	Nova Scotia
9/29/18	*Minnesota*		battleship	US	M	not sunk		0	Maryland
10/4/18	*San Saba*	2,458	freighter	US	M	sunk	7	30	New Jersey
10/27/18	*Chaparra*	1,505	freighter	Cu	M	sunk	23	6	New Jersey
11/9/18	*Saetia*	<u>2,873</u>	freighter	US	M	<u>sunk</u>	<u>85</u>	<u>0</u>	Maryland
	Total tonnage sunk:	27,467				20	374+	54	

Appendix 2 - Attacks (by Submarine)

Date	Vessel name	GRT	Type	Nat.	M	Result	S	F	Location
			U-155						
8/31/18	*Gamo*	315	fisher	Por	B	sunk	NG	NG	offshore
9/2/18	*Stortind*	2,560	freighter	Nor	S	sunk	NG	NG	offshore
9/7/18	*Sophia*	162	fisher	Por	B	sunk	NG	NG	offshore
9/13/18	*Leixoes*	3,345	freighter	Por	T	sunk	52A	3 or 12	offshore
9/13/18	*Newby Hall*		freighter	Br	S	not sunk		0	offshore
9/20/18	*Kingfisher*	353	trawler	US	B	sunk	26	0	Nova Scotia
10/3/18	*Alberto Treves*	3,838	steamer	Ital	TS	sunk	13	21	offshore
10/4/18	*Industrial*	330	fisher	Br	B	sunk	NG	0	offshore
10/12/18	*Amphion*		freighter	Br	S	not sunk		1	offshore
10/17/18	*Lucia*	6,744	freighter	US	T	sunk	86	4	offshore
Total tonnage sunk:		17,647				8	177+	29 or 38	

Appendix 2 - Attacks (by Submarine)

Date	Vessel name	GRT	Type	Nat.	M	Result	S	F	Location
			U-152						
9/11/18	*Constance*	199	schooner	Dan	B	salvaged	0	0	offshore
9/29/18	*George G. Henry*	6,936	tanker	US	S	not sunk	NG	0	offshore
9/30/18	*Ticonderoga*	5,130	transport	US	S	sunk	24	213	offshore
10/13/18	*Stifinder*	1,746	bark	Nor	B	sunk	19	0	offshore
10/15/18	*Messina*	4,271	freighter	Br	S	not sunk	NG	0	offshore
	Total tonnage sunk:	7,075				2	43	213	
	Grand totals:	188,172	(adjusted *San Diego*)			95	3,744+	388 or 397	
			U-139 (Not in American Waters)						
10/1/18	*Bylands*	3,309	freighter	Br	S	sunk	NG	NG	offshore
10/1/18	*Manin*	2,691	steamer	Ital	ST	sunk	NG	NG	offshore
10/2/18	*Rio Cavado*	301	lugger	Por	S	sunk	NG	NG	offshore
10/14/18	*Augusto De Castilho*	487	sweeper	Por	S	sunk	26	14	offshore
	Total tonnage sunk	6,788				4	26+	14	

APPENDIX 3

German / American Comparative Ranks

German Navy	U.S. Navy
Offiziere mit Patent	**Commissioned Officers**
Grossadmiral	Commander in Chief, Admiral of the Fleet
Generaladmiral	Admiral, Commander of a Fleet
Admiral	Admiral
Vizeadmiral	Vice Admiral
Kapitan zur See	Captain
Kommodore	Commodore, Courtesy Title (senior captain
Fregattenkapitan	Commander (junior captain)
Korvettenkapitan	Lieutenant Commander
Kapitanleutnant	Lieutenant (senior grade)
Oberleutnant zur See	Lieutenant (junior grade)
Oberleutnant (Ing.)	Lieutenant (j.g.) (engineer)
Leutnant zur See	Ensign
Offiziersnachwuchs	**Officer Candidates**
Oberfahnrich zur See	Senior Midshipman
Fahnrich zur See	Midshipman
Fahnrich (Ing.)	Ensign (engineering duties only)
Seekadett	Naval Cadet
Seeoffiziersanwarter (Matrose)	Seaman (officer's apprentice)
Offiziere ohne Patent	**Noncommissioned Officers**
Obersteuermann	Quartermaster of Warrant rank
Obermaschinist	Warrant machinist
Oberbootsmann	Chief Petty Officer
	Chief Boatswain's Mate
Bootsmann	Petty Officer, first class
	Boatswain's Mate, first class
Mechaniker	Artificer's Mate, first class
	Torpedoman's Mate, first class
Oberbootsmannsmaat	Artificer's Mate, second class
	Torpedoman's Mate, second class
Oberfunkmaat	Radioman, second class

Appendix 3 - Comparative Ranks

German Navy	U.S. Navy
Offiziere ohne Patent	**Noncommissioned Officers**
Bootsmannsmaat	Petty Officer, third class
	Coxswain
Maschinistenmaat	Fireman, first class
Mechanikersmaat	Artificer's Mate, third class
	Torpedoman's Mate, third class
Funkmaat	Radioman, third class
Mannschaften	**Enlisted Personnel**
Stabsmatrose	Seaman, first class
Matrosenobergefreiter	
Mechanikerobergefreiter	
Funkobergefreiter	
Maschinenobergefreiter	Fireman, second class
Obermatrose	Seaman, second class
Matrosengefreiter	
Mechanikergefreiter	
Funkgefreiter	
Maschinengefreiter	Fireman, third class
Matrose	Seaman, Recruit (apprentice)

The complexity of a U-boat is amply shown by this photograph of the *U-111*. The interior is crammed with machinery, tubing, hydraulic lines, electrical cables, hand wheels, and gauges. Every available space is occupied. Note the small size of the hatchway that leads to the adjacent compartment. (Courtesy of the National Archives.)

LIST OF ILLUSTRATIONS

Front cover (top): A lifeboat from the *Dwinsk*.

Front cover (middle): The *Dorothy B. Barrett* after being shelled and set afire.

Front cover (bottom): A World War One U-boat.

Page 25: A German mine that washed ashore on Fire Island, New York. The horns that trigger the explosive charge are to the left.

Page 33: This postcard picture shows the tublike shape of the *Deutschland* and its tiny conning tower. The tug is the *Thomas J. Timmins*.

Page 35: The bow of the *Deutschland* protrudes beyond the hull of a lighter. The *Neckar* is in the background. The warehouse is on the pier. Note the onlookers in the foreground, and the log barricade in the water.

Page 43: A postcard picture of U.S. Navy officers visiting the *U-53* at Newport, Rhode Island.

Page 45: The conning tower of the *U-53*.

Page 65: A postcard picture of the *UC-5* in captivity.

Page 67: Cutaway diagram of the *UC-5*.

Page 69: The minelayer *UC-5* was exhibited in New York as an object-lesson in piracy and as a stimulus to subscriptions to the Liberty Loan. These official photographs show the submarine being drawn through New York, and (right) being unloaded at 132nd Street.

Page 70: The *UC-5* in Central Park. Note the staircases between the disjointed sections.

Page 76: The gun of the *U-151* is aimed at the *Hattie Dunn*.

Page 80: The salvage of the *Edna*.

Page 101: Survivors of the steamship *Carolina* coming ashore on the beach at Atlantic City, New Jersey.

Page 104: The *Herbert L. Pratt* prior to salvage.

List of Illustrations

Page 108: The *Edward R. Baird, Jr.* is lashed to the side of the *Harvey H. Brown*.
Page 112: The *Vinland* is settling by the stern.
Page 114: The *U-151* as seen from the *Pinar del Rio*.
Page 119: The *Samoa's* end.
Page 126: The *Chilier* settling by the stern.
Page 127: The *Chilier* taking the final plunge.
Page 134: The *San Diego* was the largest U.S. Navy warship that was lost during World War One.
Page 148: Some of the shell damage to the *Perth Amboy*.
Page 150: The still-smoking hull of the *Dornfontein*. Note the boat tied to the bow, and men standing on the bowsprit and amidships.
Page 156: Oberleutnant zur See J. Knoeckel signed this receipt for the *Sydland* before giving it to Captain Alexandre Larson.
Page 168: This picture of the *U-140* was taken after the war. The view is facing forward at the aft end of the conning tower.
Page 178: The *U-140* at the Portsmouth Navy Yard, in New Hampshire, after the war. Boat stowage is behind the vertical plates under the raised deck.
Page 193: Starboard torpedo tubes of the *U-117*.
Page 194: The passageway of a mine laying tube of the *U-117*.
Page 212: The *Frederick R. Kellogg* resting on the bottom.
Page 213: The *Frederick R. Kellogg* resting on the bottom.
Page 216: The *Dorothy B. Barrett* afire.
Page 227: Examining papers on board the *U-117*.
Page 237: This picture of the deck gun on the *U-117* was taken after the war.
Page 256: The *Lucia* low in the water.
Page 261: The *U-155* in England after the war.
Page 272: Lieutenants Muller and Fulcher on board the *U-152*. According to the caption, this picture was taken on October 16, 1918.
Page 277: The *U-152* nosing close to the *Stifinder*.

List of Illustrations

Page 278: The end of the *Stifinder*.

Page 280: The *Stifinders* crewmembers who are shown above survived for fifteen days in the lifeboat that is shown below. Top row standing: Halmar Iversen, Thomas Johnson, Hiefden Kvikstad, Tarald Frethe (first mate). Middle row kneeling: Henry Borgensen, John Horme, Erling Erikson. Bottom row sitting: John Fredrikson, Karl Svere Larsen, Arane Stenby, Alf Mathesan. Both photographs were taken at Section Base #6 on the day after their rescue.

Page 298: The *U-139* after its surrender.

Page 303: Poster: Victory bonds will help stop this: kultur vs. humanity

Page 304: U-boats at Harwich, England.

Page 306: The control room of the *UB-88*.

Page 307: The forward torpedo room of the *UB-88*.

Page 309: The engine room of the *UB-88*.

Page 310: U-boat line-up at Harwich, England.

Page 314: The *U-111* replaced the *U-164*.

Page 318: The *U-140* at the Portsmouth Navy Yard.

Page 321: Men and women are dressed in their finest Sunday-go-to-meetin' clothes as they throng to visit the *UB-88*.

Page 325: The wreath-laying ceremony.

Page 327: The *UC-97* visits Toronto, Ontario.

Page 330: *UC-97* and *Hawk*.

Page 331 (top): *UC-97* from the deck of the *Wilmette*.

Page 331 (bottom): The *UC-97* under fire.

Page 335: The *U-111* before it was disarmed and stripped.

Page 337: All the U-boats were in deplorable condition because they had been partially dismantled for study purposes. Shown above is the *U-117* with the hull plates removed from over the engine room in order to permit easy access.

Page 338: A direct hit on the *U-117*. Note the three observation vessels in the near distance,

List of Illustrations

and the three aircraft in the upper left corner.

Page 347: *U-140*: the first World War One U-boat to be discovered and dived in American waters.

Page 348: *UB-148*.

Page 350: The sloping stern was the key that enabled me to identify the *U-117*.

Page 356: The after battery compartment of the *U-140*.

Page 369: The complexity of a U-boat is amply shown by this photograph of the *U-111*. The interior is crammed with machinery, tubing, hydraulic lines, electrical cables, hand wheels, and gauges. Every available space is occupied. Note the small size of the hatchway that leads to the adjacent compartment.

Page 373: The torpedo room of the *U-140* was little more than a cubicle. Note that the tube doors have been removed and replaced with blanks.

The torpedo room of the *U-140* was little more than a cubicle. Note that the tube doors have been removed and replaced with blanks. (Courtesy of the National Archives.)

VESSEL INDEX

Acushla: 200
Agnes G. Holland: 152-153
Alban: 266
Alberto Treves: 249-251, 253
Albert W. Black: 198
Aleda May: 197, 199, 201-202, 205
Algeria: 227-228
Alleign: 230
A. M. Nicholson: 111-112
Amphion: 254
Anchisis: 132
Androscoggin: 53
Anglia: 64
Annie Parker: 165
Annie Perry: 152
Ansaldo: 226
A. Piatt Andrew: 160
Appleby: 96
Arabian: 80
Aramis: 209
Athlete: 165
Augusto De Castilho: 286
Augvald: 128-129
Aungban: 190
Balch: 52
Baron Napier: 195
Bell: 148
Bencleuch: 185
Benham: 51
Bergsdalen: 229-230
Beskytteren: 264
Bianca: 228
Bifrost: 49

Birmingham: 42, 48
Bittern: 323-324
Bjornstjerne Bjornson: 264
Blommersdijk: 49-55
Bremen: 41, 61, 73
Briarleaf: 282
Bridgeport: 120
Briefond: 234
Bristol: 92-93
British Major: 170-171
Bushnell: 306, 311-316, 325-326
Bussum: 141
Bylands: 286
Carolina: 89-103
Cassie: 61
Catherine Burke: 161
Chaparra: 235, 350
Chester: 306
Chilier: 126-128
Chr. Knudsen: 47, 49, 50, 52
City of Savannah: 128
C. M. Walters: 163
Coast Battleship No. 4: 338
Columbia: 157
Constance: 262-264
Corinthian: 200
Crenella: 75
Cretan: 185
Cruiser: 198, 200, 203, 204, 205
Delaware: 187, 339
Derbyshire: 159

Vessel Index

Deutschland: 26-40, 41-42, 56-63, 73, 130, 169, 193, 238, 261
Diamond Shoals: 182-186, 189
Dickerson: 337
Diomed: 189-190
Dornfontein: 150-151
Dorothy B. Barrett: 2, 213-216, 290
Drayton: 50
Dwinsk: 2, 121-126
Earl and Nettie: 198, 200, 201, 204, 205
Eastland: 330
E. B. Walters: 163
Edgar F. Luckenbach: 124
Edna: 79-81, 83, 95, 118
Edorea: 103
Edward H. Cole: 85-86, 92
Edward R. Baird, Jr.: 106-109
Edwin F. Luckenbach: 124
Eidsvold: 109-111
Elizabeth von Belgie: 155
Ellen: 5
Ellen Benja: 264
Elsie Porter: 230
Ericsson: 52
Erik: 162-163, 166
Eva B. Douglas: 95-97
Evelyn: 23
Fairfax: 256
Falcon: 335-336
Firedrake: 65-66
Fish Hawk: 246
Five Fathom Bank: 74, 215, 290
Florida: 339
F. P. Jones: 141
F. Q. Barstow: 154
Francis J. O'Hara: 160
Frankfurt: 333, 339-340, 340, 345
Frank H. Buck: 191
Frank W. Kellogg: 287, 289
Frederick R. Kellogg: 210-213, 289-290
Freehold: 234
Fulton: 120
G-102: 333, 339, 345
Galveston: 267, 269, 273-275
Gamo: 239, 243
George G. Henry: 266, 274
George M. Marshall: 124
George W. Truitt, Jr.: 119
Georgia: 103
Gesto: 49
Gladys H. Hollett: 152-153
Gleaner: 198
Gloaming: 165
Goodspeed: 200
Grampian: 273
Guaratuba: 157
Gulflight: 23
Hanover: 232
Harpathian: 111
Harrisburg: 143-144
Harry Luckenbach: 46
Harvey H. Brown: 108
Hattie Dunn: 76-79, 83, 95, 118
Hauppauge: 77-81, 83,

118
Haverford: 129
Hawaiian: 254, 255
Hawk: 330-331
Helen E. Murley: 199
Henderson: 286-291, 299, 340
Henrik Lund: 116-117
Herbert: 339
Herbert L. Pratt: 103-105
Hopkins: 218
Hull: 107, 109, 176
Huntington: 256-257
Huntress: 75
Huron: 211
Ina: 146
Industrial: 253
Iowa: 338-339
Iroquois: 326-327
Isabel B. Wiley: 82-84, 89, 92
Israel: 233
Jackbow: 171
Jacob M. Haskell: 84-85, 93, 95
James M. Marshall: 124
J. Henry Edmonds: 121
J. J. Flaherty: 163-165
John J. Fallon: 229
Jonancy: 75
Joseph Cudahy: 170
Judge Boyce: 174
Kansan: 45, 46
Kaspana: 49
Katie L. Palmer: 198-200, 204, 205, 229
Kearsarge: 225-226
Keemun: 118
Kennebec: 237
Kermanshah: 172-173

Kingfisher (minesweeper): 214
Kingfisher (trawler): 244-249
Kringsjaa: 121
Kronprinzessim Cecile: 38
Lackawanna: 158-159
Lake Bridge: 130-131, 166
Lake Felicity: 234
Lansford: 144, 145
Leary: 341
Legonia: 222
Lehigh: 149
Leixoes: 240-241
Llanstephan Castle: 118
Lord Strathcona: 300-301
Lucia: 254-257
Lucille M. Schnare: 160
Lusitania: 20, 23, 54, 326, 344
Lutetia: 251
Luz Blanca: 153-155
Madrugada: 216-218
Maindy Court: 182
Malden: 141
Manin: 286
Manx King: 132-133
Mariners Harbor: 185
Marosa: 131-132, 132
Mary E. Sennett: 198, 200, 203, 204, 205, 229
Mary Olsen: 114
Maui: 141
McDougal: 51
Melitia: 170-171
Melville: 48
Merak: 182-186, 189
Messina: 281-282

Vessel Index

Mexico: 89
Minnesota: 232-233
Miramar: 103
Mirlo: 219-223, 350
Miss Lindsey: 347
Mohawk: 80
Montoso: 239
Moorish Prince: 273
Morrell: 234
Muriel: 151
N-2: 148
N-7: 215
Nantucket: 45-49, 173
Narada: 174
Nelson A.: 152
Newby Hall: 241-242
No. 703: 144, 146
No. 740: 144, 146
No. 766: 144, 146-147
Nordhav: 224-226
North Dakota: 340
Notre Dame de la Garde: 161-162, 166
Neckar: 35, 62
O. B. Jennings: 174-180
Oglala: 342
Old Time: 198, 202-205, 229
Olaf Maersk: 170
Orizaba: 251-253
Osterley: 171, 173
Ostfriesland: 333, 340-342, 344-345
Overfalls: 103
Oxfordshire: 257
Pasadena: 160
Pastores: 188, 254
Patterson: 121
Paul Jones: 120
Penistone: 157-158, 159

Pennsylvania: 340
Perkins: 140, 141, 143
Perth Amboy: 144-149
Philadelphia: 96
Pinar del Rio: 113-115, 218
Pleiades: 190-191
P.L.M. No. 4: 48-49
Pokomoke: 329-330
Porto: 171
Potentate: 230
Potomac: 111
Preble: 140, 142
Prinz Eitel Friedrich: 23
Prinz Heinrich: 261, 284
Progress: 197, 200, 205, 229
Pro Patria: 163
Proteus: 110
Quail: 334-335
Radioleine: 107
Reginolite: 249
Relay: 81
Reliance: 197-200, 205
Relief: 212
Resolute: 211
Restless: 160
Rijndijk: 200, 203
Rio Cavado: 286
Robert and Richard: 149-150
Rob Roy: 152
Rondo: 125, 239
Rush (gunboat): 218
Rush (schooner): 205, 228-229
Rutt: 261
S-5: 335
S-10: 320
S-11: 320

S-12: 320
S-13: 320
S-132: 333, 339
Saetia: 235-237, 350
Saganaga: 300-301
Samuel C. Mengel: 105-106
Samoa: 118-121
San Diego: 133-143
San Jose: 159, 228
San Marcos: 334
San Miquel: 286
San Saba: 95, 233-234, 350
Saucoma: 317
SC-55: 140, 142
SC-56: 140
SC-59: 140
SC-166: 200
SC-223: 200
SC-411: 327
SC-412: 331
SC-419: 327
SC-2840: 158
Schleswig: 27
Shawmut: 340, 342
Shubrick: 141-142, 211
Siboney: 123, 251-252
Sicard: 337
Smith: 5-6
Snug Harbor: 150
Solberg: 230
Sommerstad: 205-210, 350
Sonoma: 317-318
Sophia: 240
Sorkness: 131
S.P. 251: 140
S.P. 371: 237
S.P. 427: 143

S.P. 507: 97
S.P. 740: 140
S.P. 966: 140
S.P. 2840: 200
Standard II: 150
Stanley M. Seaman: 180-182
Stephano: 51-52
Stifinder: 276-281
Stortind: 239-240
St. Pierre: 163
Strathdene: 45-46, 48-49
Stringham: 186-187
Surge: 200
Svarsard: 238-239
Sydland: 155-156, 167
Sydney B. Atwood: 151-152
Sylvania: 160-161
Talbot: 251-253
T. A. Scott, Jr.: 61-63
Taunton: 114, 218
Taylor: 223
Teal: 223, 234, 237
Terranova: 163
Texas: 334
Texel: 86-88, 93, 96, 99, 102
Thespis: 226-227
Thomas J. Timmins: 32-33, 39
Ticonderoga: 239, 266-275, 276
T. M. Werner: 106
Tokuyama Maru: 173-174
Tortuguero: 130
Triumph: 160- 161, 166, 245
Tungus: 239

Vessel Index

Tuscarora: 321-323
U-1: 15
U-35: 285
U-38: 249
U-53: 41-55, 169, 259, 283
U-111: 314-315, 319, 334-336
U-117: 167, 191, 193-237, 290, 302, 311, 313, 316, 319, 337-338, 349-350
U-139: 260-261, 285-301
U-140: 168-192, 193-194, 214, 231, 285, 289, 302, 315-318, 337, 347, 349
U-141: 285
U-151: 73-129, 130, 233, 260-261
U-152: 73, 262-284
U-153: 73, 260-261
U-154: 73
U-155: 73, 189, 238-261, 284
U-156: 73, 130-168, 189, 228, 245, 289
U-157: 73
U-164: 302, 314
U-513: 299-301
UB-64: 259
UB-88: 302-314, 316, 321-325, 329-330, 333
UB-141: 316
UB-148: 302, 311, 313-314, 316, 318-319, 337, 347-349
Uberaba: 186
UC-5: 64-72, 301
UC-97: 302, 311-314, 316, 321, 325-328, 330-332, 333
Uda A. Saunders: 160
Umbria: 176
Uppland: 170
V-43: 333, 339
Verna D. Adams: 163
Victor and Ethan: 46, 48
Vindeggen: 113-115, 117
Vinland: 112-113
Von Steuben: 122-123
Walke: 90, 112
War Jackdaw: 171
War Ranee: 230-231
War Rifle: 130
West Durfee: 254
West Haven: 165
West Point: 47-48
Wickes: 148, 329-330
Wilkes-Barre: 344
Willehad: 57, 60
William Green: 215
William H. Starbuck: 198, 200, 205
William P. Frye: 23
Willie G.: 162-163
Wilmette: 330-331
Winneconne: 82-83, 88, 93, 95
Winslow: 48
Winter Quarter: 76, 218
Yankton: 249
Zahringen: 238

The Popular Dive Guide Series

Shipwrecks of Massachusetts: North
Shipwrecks of Massachusetts: South
Shipwrecks of Rhode Island and Connecticut
Shipwrecks of New York
Shipwrecks of New Jersey (1988)
Shipwrecks of New Jersey: North
Shipwrecks of New Jersey: Central
Shipwrecks of New Jersey: South
Shipwrecks of Delaware and Maryland (1990 Edition)
Shipwrecks of Delaware and Maryland (2002 Edition)
Shipwrecks of Virginia
Shipwrecks of North Carolina: from the Diamond Shoals North
Shipwrecks of North Carolina: from Hatteras Inlet South
Shipwrecks of South Carolina and Georgia

Shipwreck and Nautical History

Andrea Doria: Dive to an Era
Deep, Dark, and Dangerous: Adventures and Reflections on the Andrea Doria
The Fuhrer's U-boats in American Waters
Great Lakes Shipwrecks: a Photographic Odyssey
Ironclad Legacy: Battles of the USS Monitor
The Kaiser's U-boats in American Waters
The Lusitania Controversies: Atrocity of War and a Wreck-Diving History (Book One)
The Lusitania Controversies: Dangerous Descents into Shipwrecks and Law (Book Two)
The Nautical Cyclopedia
Shadow Divers Exposed: the Real Saga of the U-869
Shipwreck Heresies
The Shipwreck Research Handbook
Shipwreck Sagas
Stolen Heritage: the Grand Theft of the Hamilton and Scourge
Track of the Gray Wolf
USS San Diego: the Last Armored Cruiser
Wreck Diving Adventures

Books by the Author

Dive Training
Advanced Wreck Diving Guide
The Advanced Wreck Diving Handbook
Primary Wreck Diving Guide
Ultimate Wreck Diving Guide
The Technical Diving Handbook

Nonfiction
Wilderness Canoeing

Science Fiction
A Different Universe
A Different Dimension
A Different Continuum
Entropy
A Journey to the Center of the Earth
The Mold
Return to Mars
Silent Autumn
The Time Dragons Trilogy
    A Time for Dragons
    Dragons Past
    No Future for Dragons

Action/Adventure Novels
Memory Lane
Mind Set
The Peking Papers

Supernatural Horror Novel
The Lurking

Vietnam Novel
Lonely Conflict

Videotape (NTSC/VHS) and DVD
The Battle for the USS Monitor

Visit the GGP website for availability of titles:
http://www.ggentile.com